CW01521576

# Mystery Babylon

## Prophecy Revealed from the Book of Revelation

By

**Jeanne Trovato**

© 2003 by Jeanne Trovato. All rights reserved.

No part of this book may be reproduced, stored in a retrieval system, or transmitted by any means, electronic, mechanical, photocopying, recording, or otherwise, without written permission from the author.

ISBN: 1-4107-0699-0 (e-book)
ISBN: 1-4107-0700-8 (Paperback)
ISBN: 1-4208-4420-2 (Hard Cover)

This book is printed on acid free paper.

1stBooks - rev. 06/27/06

# Acknowledgement

## My thanks to:
## Pat Marvenko Smith

for her permission in using her inspired artistry which
I have chosen to use as the front cover for my book.

For a complete brochure of Pat's
Revelation art and videos

### Contact
Revelation Productions
1740 Ridgeview Dr.
North Huntington, PA 15642

**Visit Pat's web Site at: www.RevelationProductions.com**

# Contents

## Continuing Medieval Period

## Sectarian Period

## Continuing Sectarian Period

**Restoration Period**

# PREFACE

Someone may be asking... Who is this book written for? This book has been written for ALL God's people in particular. Also included are those who desire to hear what the Word and the Spirit of God has to say to them in particular. I would perhaps call them, "seekers of truth." I pray that my answer will prompt all who begin this book to pursue this vital "End Time" prophetic message to the end.

What is this book about? It is about the historical trace of true Christianity from God's prospective. He revealed these prophetic messages to His servant John. These messages are recorded in the very last book of the Bible called, *The Revelation of Jesus Christ."* The voluptuous looking woman seated on the scarlet beast pictured on the cover of this book, is the primary focus of this prophecy.

According to the scriptures, her full tittle is...

### *"MYSTERY, BABYLON THE GREAT,*
### *THE MOTHER OF HARLOTS*
### *AND THE ABOMINATIONS OF THE EARTH."*

This graphic description comes directly from God, the Author who inspired the writings of the Bible. The events that are related in my book have all been revealed through the book of Revelation. God has intrusted me with the solemn responsibility of presenting these prophetic truths in a simplified way, for those who would be interested in hearing what this vital prophecy proclaims.

The Revelation message is based upon the visions that the Lord Jesus Christ gave to His servant John over two thousand years ago. The apostle John had been condemned for his faith in Christ and had been exiled to the Island called Patmos. It was there that John received these various visions as God flashed them into the ethereal heavens. He then wrote these prophetic messages down which comprise the last book within the Bible which we call, *"The Revelation of Jesus Christ."* These prophetic visions that were given to John are more relevant today than when they were shown to John over two thousand years ago! We shall prove this statement true as we pursue this God inspired prophecy. This is why it is written: *"Blessed is he that readeth, and they that hear the words of this prophecy, and keep those things which are written therein: for the time is at hand." {Revelation 1:3}*

## This is God's message for the hour!

If we would know the fullness of truth about, *"Mystery Babylon,"* we must first hear the beginning to understand the ending. However, I can promise you that this message will hold your interest and perhaps reveal answers to other questions that you may have had concerning this, *"More sure Word of prophecy."* I ask the reader to refrain from passing any preliminary judgement until the entire book has been read. Please read this book with an open mind and heart with confidence in the Word of God, for these things were written for our eternal good and His glory.

It is evident that the majority of denominations have excluded this Revelation prophecy from their curriculum. The remaining few who do consider this prophecy, propagate what is termed, "Dispensationalism." There is a great deal of controversy of thought even among those who claim this Dispensational theory! This should cause some doubt as to its validity. Some of these denominations believe in a Pre-Tribulation period, some in a Post-Tribulation period and others in Mid-Tribulation period. All Dispensationalists teach that there will be another age to come, called the "Millennial Age." This theory has no Biblical foundation, as we shall prove through this present book of prophecy. Multitudes of people have been influenced by a variety of movie thrillers based of fiction and fantasy, with a trace of scripture mixed in portraying an ill-conceived horrifying so-called Tribulation period. Popular films such as Left Behind; 666; Omega Code # 2; Megiddo and others, have filled the minds of the curious and have lead many people into great error. Great attention has been directed to a devious beast/man called the *"Anti-Christ"* who will supposedly rule over the world in this illusion of another age to come. Much speculation and fantasies are connected with the Dispensational view. I would make this statement unequivocally! The origin of Dispensationalism is not found in the Bible!

I share this information from H. C. Heffren's writings, which should be ample proof for the sincere Bible student to discern truth from error. This man of God was a gifted minister of the prophetic word, who spent his life writing many books on these important prophetic issues. H.C. Heffren also had a "Bible Correspondence School" in Canada, which has ministered to countless thousands of people throughout his lifetime and beyond.

## The Origin of Dispensationalism
## By: H.C. Heffren

"Dispensationalism originated in England about the year 1840. Several prominent names such as Irving, Maitland, and J.N. Darby were among the first to preach and publish articles and books on the subject. In America, it engaged such outstanding men as Dr. C.I. Scofield, James M. Gray and Harry Ironside. All of these men were connected with the Moody Bible Institute. These men contributed tremendous influence to its' propagation. A natural question at this point is, "Where did J.N. Darby and his group discover this doctrine? Dispensationalists would have us believe that it came from discovering new truth from the Bible itself, but the facts lead us elsewhere. The real source of the doctrine came from a book that was written much earlier by two Jesuit Priests by the names of Ribera and Alcaser. These men were commissioned by the Pope to publish a teaching that would counteract the prevalent Protestant belief that proclaimed that the Pope was the Anti- Christ. Eventually this book fell into the hands of Irving and from its interpretation, Bible Dispensationalism was born. History makes it clear that the very heart of the reformation preaching attacked the Papal claims of supremacy and as a result of this onslaught they rocked Catholicism to its foundation. Luther and Calvin, as well as countless other reformation preachers fearlessly proclaimed that the Pope was the ANTI-CHRIST of prophecy, and the beast that overcame the saints mentioned in the Revelation. As a result, the stranglehold of Papal authority was gradually weakened and the Papal power began to crumble as multitudes embraced this liberating truth.

What a task that confronted Ribera and Alcaser. However, they cunningly conceived a plot to rival the interpretation of the Protestants. They sought to prove that Luther was wrong concerning the Pope. To accomplish this, they speculated a FUTURE ANTI-CHRIST who would oppose Christ with all infernal powers under his control. Dispensationalism adopted the future theory with its future Anti-Christ and a future millennium. It should be pointed out here, that there is nothing in Dispensationalism that in any way identifies Catholicism with its rightful place in prophecy. Yet, history labels their long night of tyranny over man as the Dark Ages. The Bible says, "They made war on the saints." The Reformation was born with the proclamation that the Pope was the Anti-

Christ. Dispensationalists have relegated all the scriptures relating to the Anti-Christ to a mysterious creature of horror in some unknown future. When a substantial segment of the Protestant faith accepted this interpretation, the Jesuits had finally accomplished their purpose beyond their fondest hopes. The Bible says there are only two dispensations, namely the Old Testament and the New Testament. The teachings of seven dispensations came from these two Jesuit priests. Their purpose was to blunt the attack of the Reformers on the Papacy and to direct it to some future mysterious Anti-Christ. In this subtle manner, Satan accomplished his objective by infiltrating the ranks of Protestantism with the doctrine that offers a glorious earthly millennium filled with carnal delights and the possibility of getting saved under more favorable conditions, leaving a purgatory as an escape from hell for the Catholics." End quote

According to the false theory of Dispensationalism, during this supposed great tribulation period, it is said that all people will be required to "worship" this so-called Beast/Man. Many mystical illusions have been associated with the number 666. The consensus is that everyone is supposed to receive this mark of 666 in their forehead or in their hand in order to *"buy or sell"* during this so-called Millennial Age. In the proper context of this prophecy, we will present the full understanding of this mark of the Beast. Great emphasis has also been placed upon a theory of the reestablishment of the Jewish nation and a rebuilding of the Temple in Jerusalem. According to the Dispesationalist view, these events will determine the time of Christ's return. As this message of truth from the Revelation unfolds, the Word of God will correct these false concepts!

## A Proper Understanding of Christian Dispensational Guidance

Those who are familiar with the A-Millennial stance and have accepted the Revelation message as symbolic, recognize that this prophecy has been given as a Dispensational guidance for the Christian era. Many scriptures throughout the Old and the New Testament prove this. God has never left His people without prophetic guidance. The Revelation prophecy is in fact the historical trace of Christianity. This era began in the first century when Christianity was birthed into the world. It will continue until Christ splits the Eastern sky at His final return. This will then be the culmination of all things.

There are seven sealed scrolls, which convey the Revelation prophecy. As Christ opened these scrolls, the specific messages were given in chronological order. Each scroll reveals a separate message concerning the events and circumstances that effected Christians down through the ages. Remember that John was instructed to... *"Write the things which thou has seen, and the things which are, and the things which shall be hereafter."* {Rev.1: 19} Christ gave John one vision after another, which described the events, conflicts and struggles of Christianity from its birth.

I will be writing about what John saw, revealing those same events, conflicts and struggles, which he described. Ultimately we will arrive with the fullness of understanding concerning, "Mystery Babylon." This woman seated on the scarlet colored beast is called the *"Mother of harlots."* This infers that she also has illegitimate "daughters." These daughters are revealed as the prophecy unfolds. God calls this voluptuous woman the *"Abomination of the earth,"* In John's continuing description, we see that the woman was drunk with the blood of the saints and with the martyrs of Jesus. It is also written that all nations have been made drunken with her fornication and have committed fornication with her. In our final messages, we will be giving a full detailed understanding of what this symbolic picture represents. What an indictment has come from God against…

## *"MYSTERY, BABYLON THE GREAT, THE MOTHER OF HARLOTS AND THE ABOMINATIONS OF THE EARTH."*

Who is She? Where is Her place in the scheme of prophetic things? These questions will be answered from God's *"more sure word of prophecy"* through the messages in this book. I believe that this is my calling from God and the reason for this present writing about, *"Mystery Babylon."* I humbly say before my God, "I believe that I have been born into Your Kingdom for such a time as this." Amen…

**As the angel spoke these words to John saying…**
*"Come hither; I will shew unto thee the judgement of the great whore that sitteth upon many waters"*

**So I will also do the same through the prophetic messages within this book.**

**This is my earnest intent and prayer of faith to the God and the Father of our Lord Jesus Christ**

# INTRODUCTION

It is a well recognized fact that Satan has always used a philosophy of...some other time than now or some other way than God's plan in which to deceive mankind. God's word proclaims that *"Now is the day of salvation."* We are NOW living in the day of God's grace. He does not promise another time for anyone's salvation. Dispensationalism presents another time than now and some other way than God's plan.

The term "Millennium" comes from the Latin words mille meaning thousand and ennium meaning years...hence a thousand years. This time period is mentioned six times in Revelation and nowhere else in the Bible. Many expositors take these scriptures and try to prove that Christ will return to the earth and rule over it for 1,000 years. Some contend that He will rule amidst great blessings and righteousness for all mankind. Others proclaim that He will establish the Jew's as His chosen people and reign with them.

Others proclaim a pre-tribulation, yet others argue there will be a post-tribulation period. God is not the Author of confusion! The truths that are written in this present book will clear up the error of these speculated theories that have been propagated down through the ages. A minority of believers in the mainstream of Christianity {of which I am a part of} still hold steadfastly to the A-Millennial Biblical stance.

## A-Millennialists believe in what is called,

## "Scriptural Millennialism."

The word millennial referring to an indefinite period of time identifying the Gospel Age from the day of Pentecost until Christ's return. This stance is scripturally supported in Peter's writings. *"But beloved, be not ignorant of this one things, that one day is with the Lord a thousand years, and a thousand years as a day."*
{2 Peter 3:3-8}

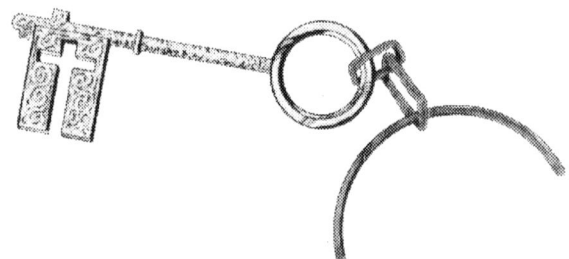

**This key to understanding prophecy
is based on analogy.**

The A-Millennial belief is founded upon the understanding given in the book of Revelation through using God's key of symbolism. In His infinite wisdom, God has chosen this method for one essential reason. Mankind's languages are arbitrary or changeable. Meanings may vary from one generation to another. Meanings may even change from one dialect to another. However...symbols that are analogous to another object never change. For instance: Things of nature never change. The sun will always be the brightest and hottest heavenly body. The moon will always be the lesser light of the heavens. In the animal kingdom, a lion will always have a ferocious nature. A lamb will always be docile. Following these basic guidelines will assist the reader with that understanding.

## The prophesies fall into two major divisions:

**1<sup>st</sup> Ecclesiastical...**This would imply to religious circumstances, events and situations specifically involving God's people in this Christian dispensation.

**2<sup>nd</sup> Civil and Political...**This involves the influence of civil powers, as they would have a direct effect on the Divine purpose and will of God for His people.

## Symbolic understanding:

{A} If symbols are drawn from an inferior department, such as animal life, or an inanimate form of nature, they will consistently represent civil or political powers.

{B} If symbols are drawn from human life or angelic beings, they will represent the spiritual happenings of humanity whether good or evil.

{C} Symbolism transfer may be used only if the objects were exalted through consecration, thus loosing their original characteristics and becoming red objects. These objects would be examples: Temple; Altar; Incense; Candlesticks; Holy City etc.

### The book of Revelation is not written as one uninterrupted narrative

**There are seven parallel themes** presented in the book of Revelation. Each theme when connected in proper chronological order reveals a detailed historical account of the events of the Christian era or dispensation. These events represent the persecutions, struggles, conflicts and victories of God's people throughout the ages.

**Seven sealed scrolls** arc opened as an index of things to come. It is said of the "book" that Christ held in His right hand that things were written within and on the backside, were sealed with seven seals. This was not a bound book as we make them today. These were seven parchments, each one rolled upon the other and sealed separately.

**Seven trumpets are sounded** to call our attention to seven significant historical events, which involve God's people throughout the past ages.

**The word "angel"** is also used to **symbolize human** agents that were sent from God to deliver the messages of the seven judgement vials.

## The scriptural definition of "prophecy"

The prophetic truths of the events that will be shared within the pages of this book have been proven by their fulfillment. The events that we will be writing come to pass! This stance is scripturally based upon fulfilled prophecy. God's word affirms this truth in...*Deuteronomy 18: 20-22. "But the prophet, which shall presume to speak a word in my name, which I have not commanded him to speak, or that shall speak in the name of other gods, even that prophet shall die. And if thou shalt say in thine heart, How shall we know the word which the Lord hath not spoken? (Then he gives us the answer) When a prophet speaketh in the name of the Lord, if the thing follow not, nor come to pass, that is the thing which the Lord hath not spoken, but the prophet hath spoken presumptuously..."*

We state unequivocally that the book of Revelation is the fulfillment of prophecy...if...God's key of interpretation is used. The Dispensational believers have devised their whole theory on a future age to come, which of course has not come to pass! It cannot be proven! According to the Lord, they all speak presumptuously! As we have just read from the scriptures, the Lord tells us how we can know a true prophet from a false one. The speculations and fantasies of another supposed age to come cannot be termed *"prophecy"* by God's definition.

The message that I am sharing in this book *"Mystery Babylon"* will prove conclusively that the things that John wrote about have already come to pass. The Revelation prophecy is truly and in fact the historical trace of Christianity. It is God's plan and desire that all of His people be made aware of the truth concerning, *"Mystery Babylon."* Mankind is NOW living in the time of her last greatest deception! The messages of the 7 sealed scrolls have been opened progressively from the book of Revelation. We are now living in the 7th Sealed Scroll Age! I would invite and admonish the reader to order a copy of my previous book..."The 7 Sealed Scrolls" in order to gain an in-depth understanding of God's prophetic truth. God has forewarned us that even the very elect can be deceived, if possible. The if possible, is our responsibility. We need to search the scriptures to be knowledgeable of Mystery Babylon's great deception! May each believer and seeker of truth be challenged to, *"prove all things,"* by the reading of this prophetic message.

God has called the Revelation prophecy *"The more sure word of prophecy."* It does appear rather strange, that multitudes of those who claim to be of the Christian faith have excluded it from their curriculum. It is important to remember that the last book of the Bible is called, *"The Revelation of Jesus Christ."* If it is called the *"Revelation"* then we should expect to understand what is being revealed. This scripture bears repeating...God has pronounced this blessing to all...*"Blessed is he that readeth, and they that hear the words of this prophecy, and keep those things that are written therein: for the time is at hand." (Relation. 1:3}*

If this pronounced blessing fails to stir up our interest in what is written in this final book, then God has given us a much more profound admonition in the final chapter of this most neglected and misrepresented book of prophecy. Hear and heed! *"For I testify to every man that heareth the words of the prophecy of this book, If any man shall add unto these things, God shall add unto him the plagues that are written in this book. And if any man shall take away from the words of this prophecy, God shall take away his part out of the book of life, and out of the holy city, and from the things that are written in this book."* (Rev. 22:18-19

To *"add to"* would include the many private interpretations of Pre and Post-Millennialism, along with other private interpretations based on the Jewish Talmud. The addition of an expected literal kingdom to come by Dispensationalists is an addition. Christ refuted this erroneous concept audibly when He walked among men over two thousand years ago. Hear his answer... *"My kingdom is not of this world: if my kingdom were of this world, then would my servants fight, that I should not be delivered unto the Jews: but now is my kingdom not from hence."* (John 18:16)

## Christ never changed His plan!

He never will! Those who seek to make Jesus an earthly King with a literal kingdom to come make void the reality of His present Spiritual Kingdom. They have missed the purpose of Christ's mission completely! Jesus speaks emphatically and often in all the gospels of His *SPIRITUAL* Kingdom. It is a *SPIRITUAL* kingdom into which men can only enter into by being born again. Listen to the clear teaching of Jesus as He spoke to the Pharisees... *"And when he was demanded of the Pharisees, when the kingdom of God should come,* he *answered them and said, The kingdom of God cometh not with observation: Neither shall they say, Lo here! Or, lo there! For behold, the Kingdom of God is within you."* {Luke 17:20-21}

Jesus cried out on the cross of sacrifice *"It is finished."* If Christ pronounced God's plan of perfect salvation finished, let us accept that *IT IS FINISHED!* Those who teach of another earthly literal kingdom to come have missed the transition that God made from the Old Covenant to the New Covenant. Then...To neglect the study of this Revelation prophecy is to take away from the word of God! We dare not add to or take away! I would speak pleadingly to the Body of Christ and to all other earnest seekers...Do not neglect the study of this very last message from God! God has revealed His Divine purpose and plan within this Revelation prophecy for ALL mankind…IF…it will be accepted in the symbolism based on analogy that He has intended. It is God's ultimate plan to restore the pristine glory and power of the first century Apostolic Church! It is His promise to again restore the Unity of the Body of Christ, as it was in the Apostolic Period! As true believers and true seekers of truth, we are called to BE the answer to Christ's priestly prayer in John's gospel. *"That they all may be one; as thou, Father, art in me, and I in thee, that they also may be one in us: that the world may believe that thou hast sent me." {John 17:21}*

I only share this key verse, but I admonish the reader to review Christ's entire prayer as it is written in this chapter. God awaits the cooperation of His redeemed people that He may accomplish His purpose. God's people must of necessity hear this prophetic message to know and follow His plan. God is a God of faith! How can we believe unless we hear what the Spirit and the Word saith unto the church about the church! How shall we hear without a preacher? I am a prophetic preacher and am heralding this *"More sure word of prophecy"* in the Love of Christ. This book has been written with that express purpose from my heart.

This prophetic message concerning *"Mystery Babylon"* is not a condemning message! However! It is a message of reproof, correction and instruction in righteousness wherever needed! It is a message of enlightenment, blessing and power. It is God's prophecy for the hour! It does command every true believer's consideration and attention! This message will ultimately require a personal decision to be made by every one that hears it. It is my earnest and fervent prayer that God will open the hearts and minds of all to receive this glorious prophetic truth which I am sharing with *"whosoever"* will hear.

*"Let us be glad and rejoice, and give honour to him: for the marriage of the Lamb is come, and his wife hath made herself ready." {Rev.19: 7}*

# Mystery Babylon
## By: Jeanne Trovato

*"And there came one of the seven angels which had the seven vials, and talked with me, saying, come hither, I will shew unto thee the judgement of the great whore that sitteth upon many waters: With whom the kings of the earth have committed fornication, and the inhabitants of the earth have been made drunk with the wine of her fornication. So he carried me away in the spirit into the wilderness: and I saw a woman sit upon a scarlet coloured beast, full of names of blasphemy, having seven heads and ten horns. And the woman was arrayed in purple and scarlet colour. And decked with gold and precious stones and pearls, having a golden cup in her hand full of abominations and filthiness of her fornication: And upon her forehead was a name written, MYSTERY, BABYLON THE GREAT, THE MOTHER OF HARLOTS AND THE ABOMINATIONS OF THE EARTH. And I saw the woman drunken with the blood of the saints, and with the blood of the martyrs of Jesus: And when I saw her, I wondered with great admiration. And the angel said unto me, Wherefore didst thou marvel? I will tell thee the mystery of the woman, and the beast that carried her, which hath the seven heads and ten horns." {Rev. 17:1-7}*

God does keep His word! If He says He will tell us what the mystery of this woman is and of the beast that carried her, then we can expect Him to do it! Amen? All of the events that preceded this seventeenth chapter of Revelation have laid the foundation for the answer that John will be given concerning…

### *"MYSTERY, BABYLON THE GREAT, THE MOTHER OF HARLOTS AND THE ABOMINATIONS OF THE EARTH."*

The woman that John describes is seated upon a scarlet colored beast, full of names of blasphemy. What is blasphemy? Blasphemy is usurping the authority of God. We want to keep this definition in mind as we pursue our investigation of this voluptuous woman. She has the look of an ecstatic harlot and is decked with gold and precious stones and pearls. She holds a golden cup in her hand, which is filled with abominations and filthiness of her fornication. As we progress, we shall learn what all this symbolic language is revealing concerning this Great Harlot and the Beast that carried her.

We will come to understand that God has given a graphic symbolic description here of the Apostate Church. This Apostate Church developed after the falling away of pure Christianity in the latter part of the second century. It will be necessary for us to journey back through history, if we are to comprehend the magnitude and influence that this mysterious woman has had upon humanity. I have trusted the great Intelligent Author of His Book to give me a format that would convey this prophetic truth in a simplistic manner to others.

## The following chart will lead us through our historic journey...

# The 4 Historical Periods of Prophecy

| Apostolic 33 -270 AD | Medieval 1, 260 Years | Sectarian 1530 AD | Restoration 1880...... |
|---|---|---|---|
| White Horse and Rider Rev. 6 : 1 - 2 | Black Horse and Rider with balances in his hand Rev. 6 : 5 - 6 | Pale Horse and Rider of death Rev. 6 : 7 - 8 | Revival of Two Witnesses Rev. 11 : 11 - 13 |
| Star Crowned Woman Rev. 12 : 1 - 2 | Star Crowned Woman in the wilderness 1,260 years Rev.12 : 6 & 14 | Two Horned Beast Rev. 13 : 11 - 18 | Great Babylon is fallen Rev. 18 |
| Red Horse and Rider Rev. 6 : 3 - 4 | Measuring the Temple of God The Holy City trodden down The Two witnesses clothed in sackcloth Rev. 11:1 - 6 | Two Witnesses slain Rev. 11 : 7 - 11 | 144,000 on Mt. Zion Rev. 14 : 1 - 8 |
| Great Red Dragon Rev. 12 : 3 - 11 | The Diverse Leopard Beast Rev. 13 : 1 - 4 | Battle of Armageddon Rev. 16 : 12 - 16 | Great Harlot is judged Rev. 17 |
| Kingdom of God Established Dan. 2: 28 - 45 | The reign of the "Little Horn" with the eyes of a man Dan. 7 : 8 also 20 - 25 | Two Suppers Rev. 19 : 17 - 18 Rev. 19 : 7 - 9 | White Horse and Rider re-appears Rev. 19: 11 - 16 |

## "BABYLON THE GREAT, THE MOTHER OF HARLOTS AND ABOMINATIONS OF THE EARTH."

In chapter eighteen John writes…*"And after these things I saw another angel come down from heaven, having great power, and the earth was lighted with his glory. And he cried mightily with a strong voice, saying, Babylon the great is fallen, is fallen, and is become the habitation of devils, and the hold of every foul spirit, and the cage of every unclean bird. For all nations have drunk of the wine of her fornication, and the kings of the earth have committed fornication with her, and the merchants of the earth are waxes rich through the abundance of her delicacies. And I heard another voice from heaven, saying, Come out of her, my people, that ye be not partakers of her sins, and that ye receive not her plagues. For her sins have reached heaven and God hath remembered her iniquities. Reward her even as she rewarded you, and double unto her double according to her works: in the cup which she hath filled fill to her double.*
*(Revelation 18:1-6)*

Since *"MYSTERY BABYLON THE GREAT"* is the main focus of this prophetic message, we are introducing our subject matter first. We are actually beginning with the ending as we direct our attention upon these two chapters of Revelation, for we will be journeying back through history. We will return again to these opening scriptures, giving full details in the final summation. John had accomplished the time consuming endeavor of writing down all the previous visions that were shown to him. Now, he begins this particular discourse with, *"And after these things."* We will follow his charted course…

## After what things?

*After…*The White Horse and Rider came forth conquering and to conquer.

*After…*The Star Crowned Woman gave birth to the man child; then fled into the wilderness.

*After*...The Red Horse and Rider that took peace from the earth had completed his dastardly deeds.

*After*...The Great Red Dragon appeared to devour the man child that the woman gave birth to.

*After*...the Kingdom of God was established in the earth.

*After*...The Black Horse and Rider with balances came forth.

*After*...The Star Crowned Woman fled into the wilderness.

*After*...Measuring the Temple of God; The Holy City trodden down; and the Two Witnesses prophesied in sackcloth for 1,260 years.

*After*...The Diverse Leopard came forth out of the sea.

*After*...The reign of the "Little Horn" with the eyes of a man took his place in the development of the Apostate Church.

*After*...The Pale Horse whose Rider brought death and hell appeared.

*After*...The Two Horned Beast came forth from the earth.

*After*...The Two Witnesses were slain and lay dead in the street of that Great City of religion.

*After*...The Battle of Armageddon.

*After*...The Two Suppers.
{Supper of the Great God and the Supper of the Lamb}

*After*...The Revival of the Two Witnesses

*After*...The 144,000 appear on Mt. Zion.

*After...*Babylon the Great is fallen.

*After...*The Great Harlot is judged.

**After...**The White Horse and Faithful Rider re-appears to gather His army together.


## *After...*

We investigate all these things that came to pass,
we shall also come to understand,
*"the mystery of the woman and the beast that carried her."*

Let us now enter into these prophecies that reveal the events of the four historical periods of the Christian dispensation...

# The Apostolic Period
## *"The Four Horsemen"*

A note of explanation: The term *"Apostolic"* refers to that first century church which was begun under the Divine direction of Christ and the writings of His chosen Apostles. Therefore, we will be charting our course from the birth of Christianity, which began A. D. 33. All the events listed on the chart within this Apostolic period coincide with each other. We will be presented with literal events that actually took place historically, as they have been described through the symbolic visions in the book of Revelation.

**Four horses and their riders appear singularly on the apostolic stage but in succession.**

Each rider and horse is described with very different and distinctive symbols. The events that are spoken of as each sealed scroll is opened will portray the events that will come to pass. Each event will follow in chronological order. Each horse and rider has various symbolic distinctions, which will identify their characteristics and their activities.

Using our symbolic key of understanding, we recognize them to be associated with religious and civil affairs. The horses being in the animal realm, are symbols of a civil authority. The riders being human agents will represent religious affairs.

# *"The White Horse and Rider"*

*"And I saw when the Lamb opened one of the seals, and I heard, as it were the noise of thunder, one of the four creatures saying, Come and see. And I saw, and behold a white horse: and he that sat on him had a bow; and a crown was given to him: and he went forth conquering, and to conquer." {Rev. 6:1-2}*

This message was given to John as the first sealed scroll was opened. The first verse of this chapter relates that John had seen the Lamb {meaning Christ} as He opened one of the seven sealed scrolls. Upon these seven sealed scrolls were written seven different messages in chronological order pertaining to the events that would come to pass throughout this gospel dispensation. Within the book of Revelation, we find that each index scroll is followed by a parallel theme. Each parallel theme relates the further details of the events that will take place.

The *"noise of great thunder"* drew John's attention to this symbolic scene of the first of four horsemen that will appear in the apocalypse. This demonstration of thunder is analogous to that which took place when Mosses received the Ten Commandments. The Lord had sent an unusual display of lightening and thunder on Mt. Sinai, when He gave Mosses these commandments written by the His own hand on tablets of stone. The Lord is letting us know through this analogy that the opening of the seven sealed scrolls will prove to be of even greater importance than the Ten Commandments!

The *"noise of great thunder"* is symbolizing the New Covenant, which is written on the fleshly tablets of men's hearts. This everlasting covenant came through Christ's sacrifice on Calvary and His glorious resurrection! This was the New Covenant that God had promised, for He said…*"I will put my laws in into their mind, and write them in their hearts: and I will be to them a God, and they shall be to me a people: And they shall not teach every man his neighbour, and every man his brother, saying, Know the Lord: for all shall know me, from the least to the greatest." {Hebrew 8:10b}*

## The support of the *"White Horse"*

Using our key of understanding through symbols, we know that each of these four horses symbolize the support of some form of government. This White Horse represents the powerful support of the Kingdom of God with it's Divine government. Isaiah wrote: *"For unto us a child is born, unto us a son is given: and the government shall be upon his shoulder: and his name shall be called Wonderful, Counselor, The Mighty God, the everlasting Father, The Prince of Peace. Of the increase of his government and peace there shall be no end, and upon the throne of David and upon his kingdom, to order it, and to establish it with judgement and with justice from henceforth forever. The Zeal of the Lord of hosts shall perform this."*

*{Isaiah 9:6-7}*

Perform this He did! This is a fulfillment of what the Lord God accomplished when He sent His Son into the world over two thousand years ago. Christ came as the promised Messiah! Though the Jews rejected Him, He still accomplished His purpose! He established His Kingdom! His Kingdom was never intended to be an "earthly" Kingdom. By His own words He said, *"My kingdom is not of this world."* Jesus Christ's Kingdom is in the hearts of believers! His is a "Spiritual" Kingdom. He is the Savior, Redeemer and King of "whosoever" will believe and receive Him NOW! This is not a speculated future Kingdom with a civil government in a supposed millennial reign to come! No! Jesus Christ is reigning NOW! He sits on His meditorial throne at the right hand of the Divine Majesty on High. He is NOW the King of Kings and Lord of Lords! He has a Kingdom and He is reigning over His people NOW! I can say with assurance that I am NOW under His reign, His rule, and His government. I have been born again into His kingdom. *"Thy kingdom come, thy will be done,"* is born into the heart of every true believer. NOW...In this life! In this last dispensation! It is written: *"NOW is the accepted time, NOW is the day of salvation."* There will be no future age! The Gospel Age is called the last age throughout all the Holy Writ!

## The purity of the *"White Horse"*

As we have reviewed this symbolic scene thus far, we understand that this *"White Horse"* represents the supporting governing power of God for His true church. The color of this horse being *"white"* symbolizes the "purity" of Christ's church. All who are born again into God's church are made pure in heart by the Blood of the Lamb. Their "life-style" becomes "HOLY." Biblical Christianity is pure, just as God is pure. Biblical Christianity is Holy because God is Holy. That which He births must be Holy also. The Bible calls this purity by various words…Righteousness, sinlessness, sanctification, and holiness. Most all of these expressions can be incorporated into the one word which would be, "Godliness." Pure Christianity is Godly because it comes from God. Christians are Godly because they are born of God. It is written that, *"only the pure in heart shall see God."*

Let us do some extensive research through the scriptures and we shall know what is meant by the purity of Christianity. *Our instruction comes through the epistle of Titus…"For the grace of God that bringeth salvation hath appeared unto all men, Teaching us that, denying ungodliness and worldly lusts, we should live soberly, righteously, and godly, in this present world; Looking for that blessed hope and the glorious appearing of the great God and our Saviour Jesus Christ; Who gave himself for us, that he might redeem us from all iniquity, and purify unto himself a peculiar people, zealous of good works. These things speak, and rebuke with all authority. Let no man despise thee." {Titus 2:11-15}*

Primitive Christianity was pure! That meant that Christians were pure! The scriptures give witness to the reality of people who had experienced salvation through the grace of God. Thousands of Pagan people who had previously worshipped idols turned to Christ through the witness and the miracles of those who were His followers. Their lives were changed immediately! They were translated from the kingdom of darkness into the kingdom of God's dear Son. The book of Acts {meaning the acts of God through the early church} is the record of true Christianity's conquering power. It is the record of God's Kingdom being established in the earth. The government shall be upon His shoulders was applied to every true believer. It was a Kingdom governed by love and power through Christ's doctrines. Jesus said, *"Because ye love me, you will keep my commandments."*

As the apostle Paul traveled throughout the various countries preaching the gospel of the Kingdom of God, thousands were brought to this experience of purity and holiness. They repented, turned from sin, believed in the resurrected Christ, and He changed their lives! It is written that those who believed in Christ brought their curious arts, idols and books before the apostles and burned them. The scriptures were fulfilled in their lives. *"Therefore if any man be in Christ, he is a new creature: old things are passed away; behold, all things are become new."* *{2 Corinthians 5:17}*

It was the grace of God that taught these believers to deny ungodliness and worldly lusts. They lived soberly, righteously, and Godly in this present world. The living Christ had redeemed these believers from ALL iniquity and purified unto Himself a peculiar people. Their faith in what He had promised that He would do changed their lives forever!

**This was the reality of their heart and in their lives!**
*"So mightily grew the word of God and prevailed."*

It may appear that I am laboring long on this particular issue of Godliness, holiness, sinlessness, righteousness, and the purity of Biblical Christianity. However! It is an essential part of our understanding, if we are to comprehend the full meaning of *"Mystery Babylon."* It is imperative that we view God's redeemed, saved, Spirit filled children through the scriptures as living a victorious sinless life in Christ. It is an absolute promise from God that Christians have the power to reign over sin, the flesh and the Devil in this present world! The entire sixth chapter of the book of Romans affirms the believer's freedom from sin. Read it! Believe it! Receive it! Act upon it! And rejoice in it!

## The Rider

We keep in mind our key of understanding that symbols taken from human life refer to religious agencies. We therefore affirm that this Rider introduces a mighty religious force coming on the earth. In this symbolic scene John sees is a conquering warrior. This imagery is an illusion to the mighty conquering warriors of that ancient era. Rome paid great tribute to their conquering warriors as they returned from their battles. They honored them by placing golden crowns upon their heads as they held their bow in hand symbolizing their great triumph! In like manner Christ's triumphant church came forth in this Apostolic age as symbolized by the White Horse and Rider going forth to conquer. The vast difference between the Roman warriors and Christ's church was that believers went forth to conquer men's hearts!

This was done as the glorious gospel of Christ was preached through the triumphant power of the Word of God. The power of this Rider, which represents Christ's Body, changed the whole course of history from that time to the present day. God's Kingdom had come! This White Horse and Rider symbolize the fulfillment of God's promise to the world! This is that great transition that took place from the Old Testament law into the New Testament of Grace!

Listen to Peter's sermon which he preached on the day of Pentecost... *"And it shall come to pass, saith God, I will pour out my Spirit upon all flesh: and your sons and your daughters shall prophesy, and your young men see visions, and your old men shall dream dreams: And on my handmaidens I will pour out in those days of my Spirit; and they shall prophesy: And I will shew wonders in heaven above, and signs in the earth beneath; blood, and fire, and vapour of smoke: the sun shall be turned into darkness, and the moon into blood, before that great and notable day of the Lord shall come. And it shall come to pass that whosoever shall call on the name of the Lord shall be saved."* {Acts 2:17-21}

Many commentators literalize this display of unnatural phenomena and place these events at the appearance of Christ's Second Coming. This could not be so! When Christ appears, there will be *NO* time for people to, *"call on the name of the Lord and be saved."* The very second of His appearing, time shall be no more! It is thus written...*"Now is the day of salvation, now is the accepted time."*

These unnatural celestial and earthly phenomenons concerning the signs and wonders in the heaven above and in the earth below are written in figurative language. This is similar to symbolic language and used as an analogy. What does this analogy represent? It portrays the catastrophic Spiritual change that has now taken place in the Jewish polity of the Old Testament! How can we be sure of this? Because Peter is quoting a prophecy from Joel 2:28-32.

# Joel's Prophecy fulfilled

Let us compare these scriptures. You will find them identical with one acceptation. Verse 32b is not quoted in the book of Acts as it is in Joel's prophecy. We will examine verse 32 as it is written in the book of Joel. *"And it shall come to pass, that whosoever shall call on the name of the Lord shall be delivered: for in mount Zion and in Jerusalem shall be deliverance, as the Lord hath said, and in the remnant whom the Lord shall call."* This *"remnant"* is speaking of the few Jewish people who did accept Jesus as the promised Messiah. In Joel's writings, the word *"delivered"* is used rather than *"saved."* Does this have any significance? Yes, as a matter of fact it does. Jesus Christ came into the world to save sinners.... *ALL* sinners! He came to deliver *"whosoever"* will. He was breaking tradition! What tradition? Jewish tradition. Yes, Christ came to establish a *NEW* Covenant with the house of Israel. He came to establish a *"Spiritual nation"* a "Holy nation" which the New Testament writers call Spiritual Israel. Listen to what Paul writes concerning this transitional change... *"For in Christ Jesus neither circumcision availeth anything, nor uncircumcision, but a new creature. And as many as walk according to this rule, peace be on them, and mercy, and upon the Israel of God."* Paul tells us here that those who are new creatures in Christ are the Israel of God. Joel said, that in mount Zion and in Jerusalem would be deliverance.

Dispensationalists teach that Christ will return to establish a literal Jewish nation. These scriptures and many others deny this false concept. What does mount Zion and Jerusalem symbolize? Let us examine closely this transition from literal Israel to the Spiritual Israel of God. We receive the greater light through these scriptures in the book of Hebrews...*"But ye are come unto mount Sion, and unto the city of the living God, the heavenly Jerusalem, and to an innumerable company of angels. To the general assembly of the firstborn, which are written in heaven, and to God the Judge of all, and to the spirits of just men made perfect. And to Jesus the mediator of the new covenant, and to the blood of sprinkling, that speaketh better things than Abel."* {Hebrews 12:22-24}

This *"mount Sion"* is the anti-type of the literal Mt. Zion of Old Testament times. This mount Sion is the fulfillment of the Spiritual pattern of the city of the living God, the heavenly Jerusalem or the

New Testament church. All nations flow into it now that Christ has come! *ALL* people can be a part of His Kingdom! *ALL* people can be a part of His Holy Nation according to Peter's writings. *"But ye are a chosen generation, a royal priesthood, and holy nation, a peculiar people; that ye should shew forth the praises of him who hath called you out of the darkness into his marvelous light." {1 Peter 2:9}*

God's nation is NOW comprised of ALL who have been called out of the darkness of the old life of sin, into His marvelous Light! Praise God! God no longer has a "chosen Jewish nation." God has NO future plan of establishing one. God has no recognized Jewish temple in Jerusalem today and He has no intention of becoming a part of ever building one there! As Christian believers, WE have become His temples. These previous scriptures from the Hebrew letter concerning Mt. Zion as the city of the Living God and the heavenly Jerusalem all identify the church of the living God...the NEW ISRAEL of God. The general assembly of the first born are those who have been born again of the Spirit of God; those who have had their names written in heaven or the Lamb's book of life. These have come through and to Jesus who is the mediator of the New Covenant or the New Testament. We marvel at the way in which God has given these scriptures for our understanding...if...we will take the time to glean out these precious promises. Throughout the New Testament writings of the apostles, it is plain to see that this transition had taken place. Yes! God has predestined *ALL* mankind to be delivered from Satan's bondage and translated into the Kingdom of His dear Son. Christ's mission to this earth brought deliverance from the law and provided freedom to live in the grace of God. We affirm then that Joel's prophecy is relating to the catastrophic change that ended the Jewish ceremonial temple worship. This came to pass in the transition from the Old Covenant to the New Covenant of Christ.

## The entire book of Hebrews is dedicated to the explanation of this transition.

This transition from Jewish polity was so traumatic that God chose to use this catastrophic display in the heavenly and earthly realm to symbolize this change. Blood, and fire, and pillars of smoke; the sun turned into darkness; the moon into blood; before the great and terrible day of the Lord. When God poured out His Spirit upon *ALL* flesh, He was confirming that the great and terrible day of the Lord had come! This was the "Day of Jubilee," the day of a new beginning again! Jesus was the Lord who had come from glory; He was despised and rejected of His own; He was crucified, dead and buried, resurrected and ascended! He had finished His mission upon this earth. Again I reiterate...How could we deny His final words that He spoke on the cross? He cried out! *"It is finished."*

If every believer and seeker of truth will take the time to read and study Peter's dynamic sermon as it is recorded in Acts 2: 22-36, this transition will be crystal clear. Let me relate to you that concluding scripture from this passage... *"Therefore let all the house of Israel know assuredly, that God hath made that same Jesus, whom ye crucified, both Lord and Christ."* God has fulfilled His promise, for Christ is now seated on David's throne. It is a meditorial throne of Grace for all people for all time. The Abrahamic covenant has been fulfilled! We reiterate...that great and terrible and notable day of the Lord was when God sent His only begotten Son into this world to be our Saviour, our Deliverer, and our Messiah. God had chosen Abraham and created Israel as a nation to represent Him as the One true and Living God throughout the Old Testament times. He had proven Himself to be the true and living God by the great wonders and care that was bestowed upon Israel as a nation.

The Jewish people were the chosen ones to recognize and accept the Messiah through all the prophecies and yet these sad words are written in the gospel. *"He came unto His own and His own received him not."* This rejection changed nothing as far as God's plan was concerned! He did not "postpone" His plan for Christ's mission and Kingdom for a future time! For this is the hope of the New Covenant...*"But as many as received him, to them gave he the power to become the sons of God, even to them that believe on his name."* *{John 1:11-12}*

Christ had given these instructions to His disciples...*"Tarry ye and wait for the promise of the Spirit."* After He ascended into Heaven, He sent His Holy Spirit to dwell within *EVERY* man. This was that great transition! It is Christ within the hope of glory! This is what Joel's prophecy was speaking of!

# No more a nation of Israel
# The Jews are no longer God's chosen people

If all the Old Testament prophesies are examined carefully and in proper context, you will find that every one of them was fulfilled concerning the Jewish nation. God deals with every man now through faith in His Son Jesus, the Christ. Paul also affirms the truth pertaining to this transition in his letter to the Galatian church... *"There is neither Jew nor Greek, there is neither bond nor free, there is neither male nor female: for ye are all one in Christ Jesus." {Gal. 3:28}*

This should be a settled position for all who seek God's truth. I trust that these foundational scriptures have been relevant to the understanding of the reader as we have shared the message concerning the... *White Horse and Rider*

# *"The Star Crowned Woman"*

*"And there appeared a great wonder in heaven; a woman clothed with the sun, and the moon under her feet, and upon her head a crown of twelve stars. And she being with child cried, travailing in birth, and pained to be delivered." {Revelation 12:1-2}*

Through our Divine key of understanding, the word "heaven" symbolizes the church realm on the earth. The apostle Paul writes these words verifying this experience…*"But God, who is rich in mercy, for his great love wherewith he loved us, Even when we were dead in sins, hath quickened us together with Christ, (by grace are ye saved;) And hath raised us up together, and made us sit together in heavenly places in Christ Jesus." {Ephesians 2:4-6}*

As believers, we are now sitting in heavenly places in Christ Jesus. The symbolic scene in Revelation, presents an analogy representing the birth of believer's into the church here on this earth. What a "wonder" this event was! An event that was in the mind of God before the foundation of the world! God was in Christ reconciling the world unto Himself! *"Of which salvation the prophets have inquired and searched diligently, who prophesied of the grace that should come unto you." {1 Peter 1:10}*

To think that God came to dwell within mankind! To think that this was the mystery that was hid from the foundation of the world, and now is manifested to all who would but believe in Christ! *"Whosoever will"* may come to God and be born-again into His church, and become a part of His Kingdom. In this vision John saw a woman clothed with the sun, and the moon was under her feet. If we rightly divide this word of truth through symbolic language, we have been given this analogy. The Woman representing the church is clothed with the sun. The sun being the greater celestial light symbolizes the greater Light of the glorious gospel through the New Testament or New Covenant that was established by Christ. This Woman is seen with the moon under her feet. The moon being the lesser luminary is symbolizing the lesser light of the Old Testament or Old Covenant of the Lord through the law and the prophets.

The Hebrew writer speaks of this wonder…*"God, who at sundry times and in divers manners spake in time past unto the fathers by the prophets, Hath in these last days spoken unto us by his Son, whom he that appointed heir of all things, by whom also he made the worlds; who being the brightness of his glory, and the express image of his person, and upholding all things by the word of his power, when he had by himself purged our sins, sat down on the right hand of the Majesty on high." {Hebrews 1:1-3}*

The "crown" the Woman wears with twelve stars symbolizes the twelve apostles, which Christ choose for His ministry while He walked here upon the earth. Again, we see this symbolic truth substantiated as Paul wrote concerning the church... *"And are built on the foundation of the apostles and prophets, Jesus Christ himself being the chief corner stone." {Ephesians. 2:20}*

## The Man Child

*Revelation 12: 2* ...tells us that this Woman was also with child travailing in birth to be delivered. The *"man child"* here in this scripture and also described in Revelation 12:5 symbolizes the first converts or believers in Christ during this Apostolic period. We will always find verification of the symbolic truths within the writings of the apostles. In his letter to the Ephesian church the apostle Paul writes... *"Having abolished in his flesh the enmity, even the law of commandments contained in ordinances; for to make in himself of twain one new man, so making peace." {Ephesians 2:15}*

The allegory, which Paul wrote about in the Galatian letter, also speaks about these two covenants. His conclusion lends support to this prophetic event mentioned here in the Revelation prophecy. He speaks of the Spiritual Jerusalem as being the New Testament church, which is free and is the Mother of all believers. {Galatians 4:24-28} We affirm that the Woman pictured in Revelation is symbolizing the church of Living God, who is the Mother of all believers. We affirm that this *"one new man"* represented God's New Covenant with *"whosoever"* would believe. He is not the God of the Jews anymore! He is the God of *ALL* who become true believers in Christ. Christ is the single heir of Abraham. *"Now to Abraham and his seed were the promises made. He saith not, And to seeds, as of many; but as of one, And to thy seed, which is Christ,"* {Galatians 3:16} ONLY believers are joint heirs with Christ. This *"man-child"* represents the continuing birth of believers into the church.

The prophetic event of the birth of this man child is the fulfillment of Isaiah's prophecy...*"Before she travailed, she brought forth; before her pain came, she was delivered of a man child. Who hath heard such a thing? Who hath seen such things? Shall the earth be made to bring forth in a day? Or shall a nation be born at once? For as soon as Zion {church} travailed, she brought forth her children."* *{Isaiah 66:7-8}* The fulfillment of these scriptures has been verified in this Revelation prophecy.

There are also other important factors associated with the man-child to be considered. John writes in Revelation 12:5...*"And she brought forth a man child, who was to rule all nations with a rod of iron: and her child was caught up unto God, and to his throne."* John wrote that this man-child was to, *"rule with a rod of iron."* What is this rod of iron? David wrote in the psalms... *"Thy rod and thy staff they comfort me."* The Word of God is spoken of as the rod of correction and reproof in many scriptures. The first century church ruled with the Word of Christ through the scriptures. As believers, we gladly accept the comforting guidance and correction of God's rod or Word to govern our lives. As believers, we willingly come under the authority of our great King when we are born again into His Kingdom of righteousness.

It is also written that this man child, *"was caught up unto God, and to his throne."* Under the opening of 5th. sealed scroll message we view this man child again. *"And when he had opened the fifth seal, I saw under the altar the souls of them that were slain for the word of God, and for the testimony which they held: and they cried with a loud voice, How long, O Lord, holy and true, dost thou not judge and avenge our blood on them that dwell on the earth? And white robes were given unto them; and it was said unto them that they should rest for a little season, until their fellowservants also and their brethren, that should be killed as they were, should be fulfilled."* *{Rev. 6:9-11}*

This symbolic scene is now focused on the *"man child"* who represents all the Christian martyrs that have been slain for their faith in Christ. The figurative or symbolic term *"for a little season"* is used which represents an indefinite period of time known only to the Lord. These departed saints are still in the presence of the Lord awaiting His judgement on those who had slain them.

This same assembly of God's children are pictured again in *Revelation 20:4... "And I saw thrones, and they that sat upon them, and judgement was given unto them: and I saw the souls of them that were beheaded for the witness of Jesus, and for the word of God, and which had not worshipped the beast, neither his image, neither had received his mark upon their foreheads, or in their hands; and they lived and reigned with Christ a thousand years.*

John has related a more detailed description in these scriptures about the man-child that was caught up to the throne of God. Notice carefully that this gathering of people were not reigning on the earth with Christ. This group is identified as the *"souls"* of those who had been *"beheaded"* for the witness of Christ. They were the martyrs that were now living and reigning in the Heaven of Heavens where God dwells. They were living souls in their heavenly bodies. They were alive and reigning with Christ in Paradise. Is it not written... *"To be absent from the body is to be present with the Lord."* Let us elaborate on this symbolic term used here of *"a thousand years."* Peter confirms this analogous terminology of a thousand years in his writings..."*But beloved, be not ignorant of this one thing, that one day is with the Lord as a thousand years, and a thousand years as one day. {2 Peter 3:8}*

We adopt this analogous term in keeping with the symbolic language used throughout the book of Revelation. If we are to arrive at God's truth, we must always stay within the realm of using the key to symbolic language based upon analogy. We reiterate...this symbolic term of *"a thousand years"* is used to convey an indefinite period of time. The symbolic term of a *"little season"* known unto God alone is referring to this same indefinite period of time and to the same group of people. {Revelation 6:11b} At the appropriate chronological time later in these messages, we will elaborate on these scriptures concerning the worshipping of the beast and his mark.

## Speaking of this "manchild"

John wrote..."*Blessed and holy is he that hath part in the first resurrection: on such the second death hath no power, but they shall be priests of God and of Christ, and shall reign with him a thousand years." {Revelation 20:6}*

According to these scriptures, this man-child which included the martyrs, had taken part in the first resurrection. What was that first resurrection and when did it take place? Let the scriptures give us the answer. It is written that believers are *"resurrected in newness of life"* when they hear the call of God, repent of their sin, and believe on the Lord Jesus Christ as Saviour and Lord.

# The
# "First Resurrection."

Believers experience the first resurrection because they have been born again of the Spirit of God while on their earth's journey. It is in this life that..."*Christ hath made us kings and priests unto God and his Father."* *{Revelation 1:6}* The Word of God identifies all mankind as being, *"dead in their trespasses and sins."* Paul affirms this truth as he wrote..."*And you hath he quickened, {made alive} who were dead in trespasses and sins."* *{Ephesians 2:1-5}*

We know that Adam's transgression brought Spiritual death to the human race when he committed high treason against God. This Adamic sin is called the first death, because all are born in sin and separated from God. All mankind is born in Adam's image, not the image of God! {Genesis 5:3} However, we know that God has made the Way of restoring us to His image through Christ. God has created man as a free moral agent. We all have a choice to make in this life that determines where we will spend eternity. If we choose to be born again, we are reconciled to God by the death of His Son. We receive the Spirit of Christ, which gives us eternal Life. This is the promise of Jesus when He said, *"I am the resurrection, and the life: he that believeth in me, though he were dead, yet shall he live: And whosoever believeth in me shall never die, Believest thou this?"* *{John 11:25-26}*

Therefore, the *"second death"* could have no power over the one who has been resurrected in newness of life, for he shall NEVER die. He has been given eternal Life, even the Life of Christ within. The *"second death"* must be applied to all who fail to respond to God's mercy, love and forgiveness in their present life on earth. These unbelievers will experience the *"second death."* This is that final separation {death} from His presence for the ceaseless ages of eternity! They have made their choice for eternity in the place

21

prepared for the Devil and his angels called Hell. God "sends" no one into Hell. They arrive there by there own choosing, because they have rejected God's mercy, love and grace through Christ in this life! Our sojourn on this earth is a probationary period.

# The
# "Second Resurrection"

The second resurrection is spoken of in Paul's letter to the Thessalonian church. *"But I would not have you to be ignorant, brethren, concerning them which are asleep {have died} that ye sorrow not, even as others which have no hope. For if we believe that Jesus died and rose again, even so them which also sleep in Jesus will God bring with him. For this we say unto you by the word of the Lord, that we which are alive and remain unto the coming of the Lord shall not prevent them {precede them} which are asleep. For the Lord himself shall descend from heaven with a shout, with the voice of the arch angel, and with the trump of God: and the dead in Christ shall rise first: Then we which are alive and remain shall be caught up together with them in the clouds, to meet the Lord in the air: and so shall we ever be with the Lord." {1 Thessalonians 4:13-17}*

I believe that we have covered the key points in identifying this *"great heavenly wonder"* as the Star Crowned Woman.

This is truly the Church of the Living God that has blest humanity throughout the endless ages.

# *"The Red Horse and Rider"*

*"And when he had opened the second seal, I heard the second creature say, Come and see. And there went out another horse that was red: and power was given unto him that sat thereon to take peace from the earth, and that they should kill one another: and there was given unto him a great sword." {Revelation 6:3-4}*

We keep in mind that the seven sealed scrolls are actually used as an index to let us know in brief what events will follow. The connecting themes throughout the chapters of the book of Revelation then relate the extended details of those events. We have previously identified the conquering White Horse and Rider as representing Christ's church. The next Horse to come forth in this Apostolic Period is described as "red" in color. As the "white" horse was symbolic of the purity of Christianity, this color "red" also has a significant symbolic meaning. Throughout the ages, the color of "red" has always represented Paganism, meaning a godless philosophy or Idolatry. Even in our present day, the color red is still associated with godlessness. Communist Russia is known to be the great RED Bear. The central part of their city is called RED Square. Communist China is also referred to as RED China.

This Red Horse, being in the animal realm, symbolizes the supporting civil power of the Pagan Roman Empire in the first century. As a horse in the natural realm supports its rider so, Rome supported their Pagan religions of that day. The Rider then being a human agent, symbolizes the Pagan Priesthood that directed or controlled that society. There is a drastic contrast seen in the mission and actions of this Rider and his steed from the previous White Horse and Rider. The former went forth conquering for the good of humanity. This Rider was to, *"take peace form the earth, and kill with the sword."* His mission was destructive! Take peace from the earth he did! This Rider represents the civil authority of Rome, as it took up the sword to kill this new sect they called, "Christians." The civil authorities of Rome even backed up the unbelieving Jewish High Priests.

The book of Acts records the severe persecutions of the early church...Paul and Silas were beaten and thrown into prison with their feet in stocks. At midnight they were heard praying and singing praises unto God. He sent an earthquake and the foundations of the prison were shaken! Paul and Silas were freed and the keeper of the prison and his family believed on the Lord because of this miracle!

Stephen preached a stirring message in the presence of the High Priests telling them about their own history leading up to the Messiah. {Acts 7} In his ending discourse, he accused them of murdering the Prince of glory. They stoned him to death! However, as he was dying, he looked up into the heavens and saw the glory of God, and Jesus standing on the right hand of God. He knelt down and cried with a loud voice to the Lord... *"Lay not this sin to their charge."* The Bible tells us that Saul was watching and consented to his death! This experience surely was used mightily of the Lord to convict Saul who was later converted and became the great Apostle Paul.

## The Persecution of Christians

Yes! The Bible relates to us... *"And at that time there was a great persecution against the church which was at Jerusalem: and they were scattered abroad throughout the regions of Judaea and Samaria, except the apostles." {Acts 8:1}* Again it is written; *"Now about that time Herod the king stretched forth his hand to vex certain of the church. And he killed James the brother of John with the sword. And because he saw it pleased the Jews, he proceeded further to take Peter also."{Acts 12:1-11}* {This is that same Herod that an angel of the Lord smote who was eaten up by worms} Peter was cast into prison and bound with chains, however prayer was made without ceasing by the church and God sent an angel and delivered Peter! {Acts 12:20-23} Yet! Even through all this persecution against the Christians it is written: *"But the word of God grew and multiplied,"{Acts 12:24}*

Many other historical accounts verify these severe persecutions against Christianity, thus confirming the *"more sure word of prophecy."* Foxes Book of Martyrs records the beginning of these persecutions under Nero in A.D. 67. I would share but a few... Nero blamed the burning of Rome on the Christians, which he himself caused. For their punishment, he had Christians sewed into the skins of wild beasts, and then worried by dogs until they expired; others were dressed in shirts made of stiff candle wax, fixed to axletees, and set on fire to light his gardens.

Fox inermerates the continuing persecutions under Domitian A.D. 81 who crucified thousands of Christians. He writes that a variety of lies were told against Christians during the reign of Domitian in order to persecute them. The Pagans blamed Christians for the famines, pestilences and earthquakes that came upon the Roman provinces. Christians were made a sporting event for the Coliseums. They were placed in the arena with starving ferocious lions that tore them to death! Fox records ten severe persecutions under various rulers who continued to persecute all who professed faith in Christ. Yes! Christians were tortured, beheaded, crucified, and ravished in heinous manners during this Apostolic Period of history.

The emperor Diocletian waged the tenth and last persecution upon Christians in A.D. 303. His reign was a bloody one for Christians! This severe persecution lasted for ten full years! It was Diocletian's intent to exterminate ALL Christians from the face of the earth. He methodically began with confiscating all the sacred writings, which the Christians had and burned them. An edict was given to destroy all the buildings where Christians gathered. Multitudes of houses were set on fire and the people perished in the fires. Entire cities where Christians abode were burned! Hundreds of people were sent out in boats that had been riddled with holes and drowned at sea.

## Fox writes...

"Racks, scourges, swords, daggers, crosses, poison and famine, were made use of in various parts to dispatch the Christians; and invention was exhausted to devise tortures against such as had no crime, but thinking differently from the voltaries of superstition." It has been said that the lives of the early Christians consisted of "persecution above the ground and prayer below the ground." Their lives are expressed by the Coliseum and the catacombs. Beneath Rome are excavations, which we call catacombs, which were at once temples and tombs. The early church of Rome might well be called the Church of the Catacombs. There are some sixty catacombs near Rome, in which some six hundred miles of galleries have been traced, and these are not all. These galleries are about eight feet high and from three to five feet wide, containing on either side several rows of long, low, horizontal recesses, one above another like births in a ship. In these the dead bodies were placed and the front closed, either by a single marble slab or several great tiles laid in mortar. On these slabs or tiles, epitaphs or symbols are engraved or painted. When the Christian graves have been opened, the skeletons tell their own terrible tale. Heads are found severed from the body, ribs and shoulder blades are broken, bones are often calcined from fire. But despite the awful story of persecution that we may read here, the inscriptions breathe forth peace and joy and triumph. Here are a few: Here lies Marcia, put to rest in a dream of peace." "Lawrence to his sweet son, borne away with angels." Victorious in peace and in Christ." "Being called away he went in peace." Remember when reading these inscriptions the story of the skeletons tell of the persecution, of torture, and of fire. Both Pagans and Christians buried their dead in these catacombs. The full force of these epitaphs is seen when we contrast them with the Pagan epitaphs, such as: "Live for the present hour, since we are sure of nothing else." "I lift my hands against the gods who took me away at the age of twenty though I had done no harm." "Once I was not. Now I am not. I know nothing about it and it concerns me not." "Traveler, curse me not as you pass, for I am in darkness and cannot answer." The most frequent Christian symbols on the walls of the catacombs, are the good shepherd with the lamb on his shoulder, a ship under full sail, harps, anchors, crowns, vines and above all the fish." End quote

What a tremendous price these first Christians paid for their faith! We should not forget! We are surely indebted to them. The course of history verifies that which the Revelation has prophesied...*And there went out another horse that was red: and power was given unto him: that sat thereon to take peace from the earth, and that they should kill one another: and there was given unto him a great sword."* *Revelation 6:4*

# *"The Great Red Dragon"*

*"And there appeared another wonder in heaven; and behold a great red dragon, having seven heads and ten horns, and seven crowns upon his heads. And his tail drew the third part of the stars of heaven, and did cast them to the earth: and the dragon stood before the woman which was ready to be delivered, for to devour her child as soon as it was born." {Rev.12: 3-4}*

This is the connecting parallel theme to the sixth sealed scroll which will give further details of this first great conflict that Christians were faced with against this Great Red Dragon. Another *"wonder in heaven"* is seen which again is symbolizing those events that are happening in the heavenly realm, meaning the church on earth. We will be following these events progressively through this twelfth chapter, as they come to pass. We have previously identified the Woman as the church of the Living God who continued to give birth to new converts. In this present theme, the events that took place through the power that came forth to oppose the Woman will be seen. As the scriptures tell us, this opposing power came through the one that is called, *"The Great Red Dragon."* This Dragon can be identified symbolically and historically as Imperial Rome. How can we be certain of this? Because it is placed in the proper time frame and the continuing description of the seven heads confirm these symbols. Remember that we are not considering a "literal" monstrosity of a seven-headed beast! We remain in the Divine key of understanding symbolic language based upon analogy.

**The 7 heads on the Dragon...** symbolize the 7 consecutive forms of government that ruled Rome.

**1.Regal 2.Consular 3.Decemvirate
4.Military Tribunes 5. Triumvirate
6. Imperial 7. Patrition.
The ten horns on the heads of this Dragon symbolize
the ten lesser provinces that developed
in the later years of Rome.**

It is written that this Great Red Dragon, which we have identified as Rome's Pagan society, stood before the woman to devour her child. Yes! An immediate conflict took place in the Pagan society as the church of God was birthed! We have considered this conflict briefly as we opened the index scroll of the Red Horse and Rider. We are now given more details concerning the persecuting power of Pagan Rome in this scene. The Emperors of Rome united with the Pagan priests in severe persecutions to stamp out {devour} this new Christian sect. It is written that, *"The dragon's tail drew a third part of the stars of heaven and cast them to the earth."* Revelation 1:20 tells us that the, *"stars are the angels of the seven churches."* The word *"angel"* means one sent.

These *"stars"* are symbolizing the ministry or leadership of the church. These *"stars"* that were cast down then are representing the stalwart apostles who were slain for fearlessly preaching the gospel of Christ. As we have previously mentioned in the great persecutions that took place in the early church, the first Christian martyr was Stephen who was stoned to death for his faith in Christ! {Acts 7:59-60} James was beheaded, and history records that Peter was crucified upside-down.

Yes! All the apostles met certain death at the hands this Great Red Dragon which symbolizes Paganism! We can identify this prophetic scene as the continuing spiritual conflict, which took place between Paganism and Christianity during the first century. This symbolic scene under consideration in Revelation 12: 3-4 is describing a *SPIRITUAL* war or conflict, NOT a literal war! These facts are evident by the *"more sure word of prophecy."*

## A War in Heaven

This same *SPIRITUAL* conflict is also symbolized by a, *"war in heaven."* John sees another vision in which he writes…"*And there was war in heaven: Michael and his angels fought against the dragon and the dragon fought against his angels, And prevailed not; neither was their place found any more in heaven. And the great dragon was cast out, that old serpent, called the Devil, and Satan, which deceiveth the whole world: he was cast out into the earth, and his angels were cast out with him."* {Revelation 12:7-9}

Does this mean there was an actual literal war being waged in the Heaven of Heavens where God dwells? How could this be? If Christ forbade Peter to, *"take up the sword,"* how could He charge His chosen archangel Michael to lead a whole company of angels into a literal battle in the Holy place where God dwells? No! These scriptures are not referring to a literal battle in the Heaven of Heavens where God dwells. We are viewing a more detailed description of that which is happening in the church realm here on earth. Remember! God has given us the key of understanding this prophecy through symbolic language, which is based on analogy. If we violate this key of symbolism, we will loose God's true message that He has given through this prophecy!

What is the analogy that these symbols are describing? As we have related in part, these symbols are describing the *SPIRITUAL* conflict that took place in the heavenly places in Christ Jesus or within the church on earth. We are viewing in more detail the Spiritual conflict that is taking place between Christianity and Paganism during the Apostolic period. It is written that Michael and his angels fought against the Dragon and his angels. Michael, being the archangel or protector of ancient Israel symbolizes the stalwart apostles of the New Testament Israel. His angels fighting with him symbolize the believers in Christ. The Dragon symbolizes the civil powers of the Emperors of Rome. The angels that fought with the Dragon are representing the Pagan priesthood, with their angels or millions of Pagan believers. The word "angel" means one sent in the scriptures.

The "angels" mentioned here in these scriptures symbolize human messengers. We recognize that Satan must have human messengers or agents to serve him just as God has human messengers or agents to serve Him. Verse eight of our present chapter tells us that the, *"dragon prevailed not; nether was their place found anymore in heaven."* What does this scripture convey? It is relating the actual events that took place historically in this Apostolic period. Paganism could no longer prevail against Christianity. Christians became the conquerors! Christianity cast down the Great Red Dragon of Paganism in that first century! Paganism lost its place as the accepted religion of the world! Even as it is written... *"Neither was "their place" found any more in heaven, "* meaning the realm of religion.

The written record of Paul's ministry verifies this progressive downfall of Pagan idolatry. *"And many that believed came, and confessed, and shewed their deeds. Many of them also which used curious arts brought their books together, and burned them before all*

29

*men: and they counted the price of them, and found fifty thousand pieces of silver. So mightily grew the word of God and prevailed."*
*{Acts 19:18-20}*

## Was Satan ever an angel in Heaven?

Revelation 12:9 needs some final clarification..."*And the great dragon was cast out, that old serpent called the Devil, and Satan, which deceiveth the whole world: he was cast out into the earth, and his angels were cast out with him."* Many people mistakenly think that this symbolic imagery is referring to the evil one himself and his angels being cast out of the Heaven of Heavens where God dwells. These scriptures are not dealing with the fate of the personal Devil at all, but with the human agents he was using to work through. I have highlighted the word "called" in this scripture to draw our attention to the fact that this scripture is not referring to the fate of Satan at all. It is referring to the fate of the Great Red Dragon. It was the Dragon that was called the Devil. This scripture is referring to the human agency that Satan was working through. Satan was working through the Great Red Dragon {Paganism}| to deceive the world! Who did the Great Red Dragon represent? It represented Rome with all its idolatrous worship of many gods and goddesses.

Please take particular notice of just how the first Christians in the Apostolic period overcame Satan's deception of Paganism..."*And I heard a loud voice saying in heaven,* {heaven is the analogy of the church on earth} *Now is come salvation, and strength, and the kingdom of our God, and the power of his Christ: for the accuser of the brethren is cast down, which accused them before our God day and night. And they overcame him by the blood of the Lamb, and by the word of their testimony; and they loved not their lives unto death."* *{Revelation 12:10-11}*

How do we know that this announcement refers to what was happening in the church realm on the earth? We know this because there is no need for salvation in Heaven. Salvation can only be received during our earth born sojourn. Secondly and most importantly, there will be no Devil in the Holy Heaven where God dwells to "cast out." The Devil has never dwelt there! He never will be there! There is ample proof of this within the Bible...IF...the Word is rightly divided. I can state unequivocally and prove scripturally that God did not create an evil being called Satan. This truth needs to be understood, because it effects so many other relevant connected Biblical truths. This is surely an important part of this Revelation prophecy!

## Satan has never dwelt in the "Holy Heaven" where God dwells!

Let me pose these questions...Where did Satan come from? Where did God come from? We all know that the Bible assumes the existence of an eternal Supreme Almighty invisible Spiritual Being by the name of "God." Our finite minds find it difficult to comprehend anything or anyone that did not have a beginning! We cannot give an answer...Yet! We accept by faith alone that God exists. The Bible only tells us, *"In the beginning God."* We assume His existence. God is presented as intrinsically or inherently "good." This means that He cannot be anything else! He cannot conduct Himself in any other way but GOOD! The BIG question...Would a Holy God then create and evil being? The scriptures declare that God pronounced everything that He created good.

Now...Let us consider the eternal evil being the Bible calls "Satan." We also find that the Bible assumes Satan's eternal being. He is placed in the same plain of faith. No where in the Holy writ will you find that Satan was a created being by the One called God! Satan is presented as the exact opposite of God. He is intrinsically or inherently evil! This means he cannot be anything else!

## The Bible then affirms the existence of two spiritual beings.

**1. The Holy One called God,** who was able and did create the world, the reaches of space and the ages of time and all that our eyes do behold! He has made of one blood all nations. He is the One who can call into existence those things that be not as though they were!

**2.The evil one called Satan,** who comes to steal, kill and to destroy. He has NO power to create! He has been the enemy of God, His Goodness, His Mercy and Righteousness from the beginning.

When was this beginning? It is written... *"In the BEGINNING God."* It is also written that, Satan or the Devil was a murderer from

31

the beginning! Listen to the words of Jesus Himself as He spoke of the Devil...

*"Ye are of your father the devil, and the lusts of your father ye will do. He was a murderer from the BEGINNING, and abode not in the truth, because there is no truth in him. When he speaketh a lie, he speaketh of his own: for he is a liar, and the father of it." {John 8:44}*

If Satan was a liar from the beginning and no truth was ever in him, he surely could not have been in God's Holy Heaven! Everything in God's Holy Heaven is intrinsically good. Are there liars in Heaven? Are there murderers in Heaven? Angels could not have made a decision to oppose God if they have no will. According to Hebrews 1:14, angels have no will of their own for they were created to do God's will. God created man as a free moral agent to have a will to choose, not angels. This eliminates the myth of Satan rebelling against God in Heaven and becoming a "fallen angel."

Strange as it may seem, this "mythology" has been accepted by multitudes of Christians as a Biblical concept. Where did this "myth" originate? Lets find out...It originated from the mythology and poetry of John Milton during the Renascence period of the 16th century. This man wrote ten volumes of poetic mythology which he called, "Paradise Lost." In these volumes, he invents the myth of Satan's rebellion. He writes that the story of Satan's rebellion is being "narrated" to Adam by the Archangel Raphael. In the first part of Paradise Lost Satan is found immediately after his fall; he and his fellow angels then plot the downfall of God's new creation, humanity. As Satan leaves to somehow thwart humanity, God sends Raphael down to earth to warn Adam of the impending danger. In this way, according to God, humans will have no excuse if the temptation succeeds. To warn of the danger, Raphael explains the entire history of the fall of angels, the battle in heaven between good and bad angels, and the subsequent creation of Adam and Eve. ALL mythology!

What a lie! What a distortion of Biblical truth! Yet! Seemingly the whole Christian community has swallowed this myth for several centuries! Theologians and commentators have wrested many scriptures trying to prove this myth! The scripture most usually taken out of context is found in the fourteenth chapter of Isaiah. I will use a brief summary in order to show how ridiculous this concept is...Verse

4 says, *"Thou shalt take up this proverb against the KING OF BABYLON." NOT SATAN!*

**The SUBJECT** matter in this proverb was a MAN. King Nebuchadnezzar. NOT a fallen angel which the myth calls Lucifer.

**The LOCATION** where the prophecy was given was in a CITY called Babylon. NOT in the place the Bible calls Heaven.

**The MESSAGE** is a proverb of reproof from the Lord concerning King Nebuchadnezzar's arrogance, power and pride. It is not a message addressed to Satan.

## Satan is not "Lucifer"

A departure from the proper subject matter comes in verse 11... *"How art thou fallen from heaven, O Lucifer, son of the morning! How art thou cut down to the ground which did weaken the nations!"*

A whole scenario is built upon this scripture which is lifted out of its' proper context by those who connect it with the Satan myth. "Lucifer" is not Satan! Lucifer is still referring to King Nebuchadnezzar. If the entire chapter is read and studied in its proper context, this myth about Satan would be dissolved once and for all! Symbolic or figurative language is used concerning the King. Yes! The King had fallen from his "heavenly state" because of his pride and arrogance. Yes! God called the King, *"Lucifer, son of the morning"* because the King had been blest as a light of God to bring this great kingdom of Babylon into existence.

The same false scenario is used in Ezekiel chapter twenty eight to support the error of this myth. It is thus written: *"The word of the Lord came again unto me saying, Son of man, say unto the PRINCE OF TYRUS, {NOT SATAN} Thus saith the Lord God; Because thine heart is lifted up, and thou hast said, I am God I sit in the seat of God, in the midst of the seas; yet THOU ART A MAN, and not a God, though thou set thine heart as the heart of God."* {Ezekiel 28:1-2} Read both chapters carefully and you will see that these proverbs are reproofs to MEN not Satan!

The fallacy has been taught that these men {prince of Tyrus and Nebuchadnezzar} are supposed to be a "type" or "anti-type" of Satan. God's Word does not make types or anti-types unless there is a scriptural analogy to back it up! Men's traditions have no foundation to base this false assumption on. Satan would like to have everyone think that he is that great-exalted angel that had the audacity to oppose the very God of Heaven in His own domain! As Jesus said, Satan is a liar and the father of it. When he speaketh, he speaketh a lie! I hope that this clears up ALL misunderstandings, myths and errors concerning Satan's whereabouts!

Returning to what John wrote…He said that the accuser {meaning Satan} of the brethren was *"cast down."* Satan is a spiritual being not a fleshly being. He cannot be physically cast down or out of any place. He can however be cast down in the Spiritual realm! This means a loss of his power! Exercising our faith in what God has promised can defeat Satan! It is the sword of the Word of God that has the power to defeat Satan. Listen to this clarification from the scriptures…Jesus had sent out seventy of His disciples to heal the sick and minister to the people. They came back rejoicing and excited about the mighty power that they had experienced. Jesus answered them…*"I beheld Satan as lightening fall from heaven."* *{Luke 10:17}* Did Jesus mean that He actually saw Satan in the flesh falling out of the Heaven of Heavens where God dwells? I think not! Christ is simply relating that He saw Satan's power fall or defeated in the Spiritual realm! In other words, Satan's fall from power was diminished as quickly as a bolt of lightening! Christ is using symbolic language in this expression as He did in many other places. Jesus called Herod an old fox. Did he mean Herod was actually a fox? No! He meant that Herod was sly like a fox. Jesus said to Peter… *"Get thee behind me Satan."* Did Jesus mean that Peter had become Satan? No! He just meant that Peter was being used as a human agent of the Devil to hinder Him. Jesus said of Satan, *"the prince of this world is judged."* {John 16:11} He meant that Satan's power over mankind had been judge by His salvation and deliverance had come through His Atonement. Now…Every Christian can say in faith, "Greater is He {Christ} that is within you than he {Satan} that is in the world." {1 John 4:4]

Those First Century Apostolic Christians defeated Paganism by their faith in the blood of the Lamb and by the word of their testimony. We reiterate…They were not fighting a literal war! These Christians were used by God to defeat Pagan idolatry! Yes! By their word of testimony, they witnessed to those idol worshippers about a resurrected Saviour! They won Pagan people to Jesus Christ through their personal witness of the gospel!

- It is written in the scriptures that Christians went everywhere preaching the gospel!
- It is written in the scriptures that they loved not their lives unto death!
- It is written in the scriptures that Christians turned the world upside-down!
- It is written that the Lord confirmed the Word, which they preached with signs and wonders and miracles of healing!

**Let us review what we have learned thus far...**

The symbols have revealed the, *"Great Red Dragon"* as Pagan Rome who had deceived the whole earth through idolatry for centuries! It was the Great Red Dragon {Roman Empire} and his angels {Pagan Priesthood with their adherents} that were cast down by the power of the living Christ. We reiterate...It was the Pagan religion of the Roman Empire that was cast down or lost its deceptive power over mankind! These scriptures are telling us that Satan could no longer use Pagan ideologies in the religious realm on earth to deceive mankind. The true gospel had brought Light into the darkness and revealed the Living Christ! Historical records and the book of Acts affirm that all these things did take place... Just as the *"more sure word of prophecy"* has declared.

I would admonish every reader to review the book of Acts and hear the whole story of the conflict that took place between Paganism (The Great Red Dragon) and the Star Crowned Woman (Christianity) which the Revelation prophecy has described through this symbolic imagery. As the glorious White Horse has symbolized, Christians went forth conquering and to conquer! They conquered by relating the everlasting gospel! The book of acts records that there were four thousand people saved at one time and at another time another five thousand! What a manifestation of the power of God! Nine thousand people born into the Kingdom of God in the beginning of that Apostolic Period.

Peter writes about the fulfillment of this declaration of salvation which was made in the Revelation prophecy... "Ye are a *chosen generation, a royal priesthood, an holy nation, a peculiar people; that*

35

*ye should shew forth the praises of Him who hath called you out of darkness into His marvelous light. {1 Peter2: 9}*

An affirmation of that which was written in the Revelation prophecy…*"Now is come salvation, and strength, and the kingdom of our God and his Christ.*

**Twenty first century Christians must also realize as our first century brethren did, that our fight is a "Spiritual warfare"**

The armour of God is clearly defined in Paul's letter to the Ephesian Christians. *"Finally, my brethren, be strong in the Lord, and in the power of his might. Put on the whole armour of God, that ye may be able to stand against the wiles of the devil. For we wrestle not against flesh and blood, but against principalities, against powers, against the rulers of the darkness of this world, against spiritual wickedness in high places. Wherefore take unto you the whole armour of God, that ye may be able to withstand in the evil day, and having done all to stand. Stand therefore, having your loins girt about with truth, and having on the breast plate of righteousness; And your feet shod with the preparation of the gospel of peace; Above all, taking the shield of faith, wherewith ye shall be able to quench all the and the fiery darts of the wicked. And take the helmet of salvation, and the sword of the Spirit, which is the word of God."*

*{Ephesians 6:10-17}*

# *"Kingdom of God Established"*

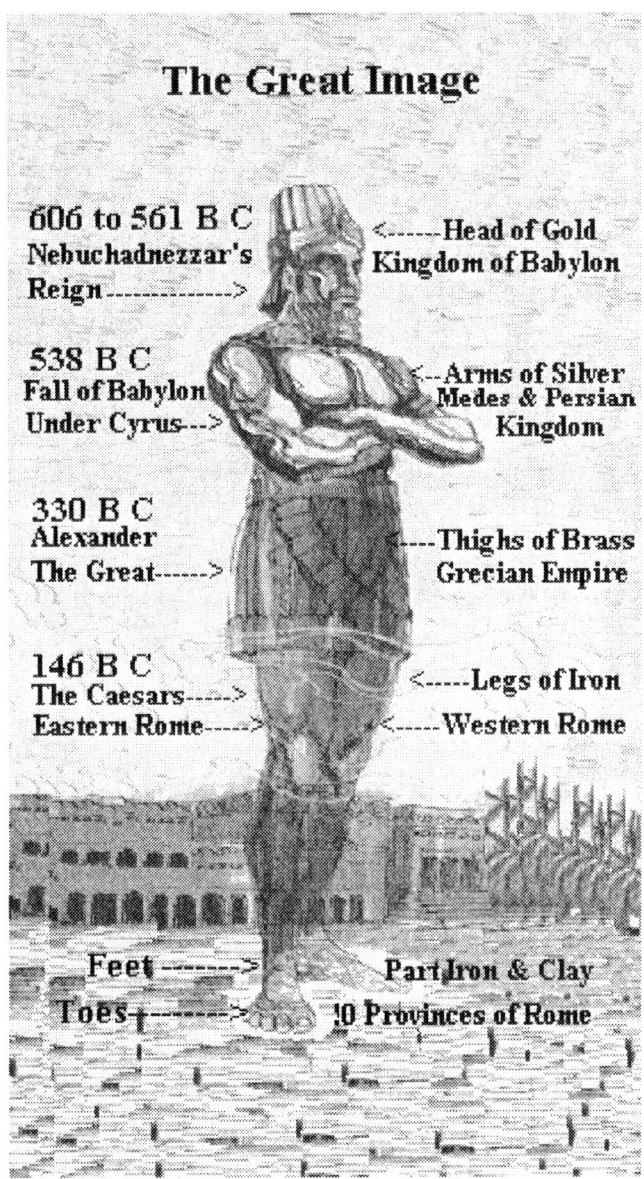

**The Great Image**

606 to 561 B C
Nebuchadnezzar's
Reign----------->
<-----Head of Gold
Kingdom of Babylon

538 B C
Fall of Babylon
Under Cyrus--->
<--Arms of Silver
Medes & Persian
Kingdom

330 B C
Alexander
The Great------>
<----Thighs of Brass
Grecian Empire

146 B C
The Caesars----->
Eastern Rome----->
<-----Legs of Iron
<----- Western Rome

Feet ------>
Toes------->
Part Iron & Clay
10 Provinces of Rome

The book of Daniel is Divinely linked to the prophecy of the book of Revelation. Daniel's writings will confirm the prophetic time of the establishment of the Kingdom of God into this world. I trust that your faith will be strengthened by these amazing prophetic truths. Here is that amazing connecting link to this Apostolic period...May I have the liberty of relating briefly this narrative in my own words...King Nebuchadnezzar had a dream. The king was much troubled by this dream. However; he could not remember what his dream was about! He called all his magicians, astrologers and soothsayers; but, none could give him the interpretation without first knowing what the King had dreamed. The king called for Daniel and ask him..."*Art thou able to make known unto me the dream which I have seen, and the interpretation thereof?*" Daniel informed him that he was in the same position as the other group, and would like to know what the dream was about. However...Daniel begins with these words of hope for the King..."*But there is a God in heaven that revealeth secrets, and maketh known to the King Nebuchadnezzar what shall be in the latter days. Thy dream, and the visions of thy head upon thy bed, are these. Thou, O King, sawest, and behold a great image. This great image, whose brightness was excellent, stood before thee; and the form thereof was terrible. This image's head was of fine gold, his breast and his arms of silver, his belly and his thighs of brass, His legs of iron, his feet part of iron and part of clay. Thou sawest till that a stone was cut out without hands, which smote the image upon his feet that were of iron and clay, and brake them to pieces. Then was the iron, the clay, the brass, the silver, and the gold, broken to pieces together, and became like the chaff of the summer thrashing floors: and the wind carried them away, and no place was found for them: and the stone that smote the image became a great mountain, and filled the whole earth. This is the dream; and we will tell the interpretation thereof before the king.*

### {The Interpretation}

*Thou, O King, art a king of kings: for the God of heaven hath given thee a kingdom, power and strength, and glory. And wheresoever the children of men dwell, the beasts of the field and the fowls of the heaven hath he given into thy hand, and hath made thee ruler over them all. Thou art this head of gold. And after thee shall arise another kingdom inferior to thee, and another third kingdom of brass, which shall bear rule over all the earth. And the fourth kingdom shall be strong as iron: forasmuch as iron breaketh in pieces and subdueth all things: and as iron that breaketh all these, shall it break in pieces and bruise. And whereas thou sawest the feet and toes, part of potter's clay, and part of iron, the kingdom shall be divided; but there shall be in it of the strength of the iron, forasmuch as thou sawest the iron mixed with clay. And as the toes of the feet were part of iron, and part of clay, so the kingdom shall be partly strong, and partly broken. And whereas thou sawest iron mixed with clay, they shall mingle themselves with the seed of men: but they shall not cleave one to another, even as iron is not mixed with clay. And in the days of these kings shall the God of heaven set up a kingdom, which shall never be destroyed: and the kingdom shall not be left to other people, but it shall break in pieces and consume all these kingdoms, and it shall stand forever. Forasmuch as thou sawest that stone was cut out of the mountain without hands, and that brake in pieces the iron, the brass, the clay, the silver, and the gold; the great God hath made known to the king what shall come to pass hereafter: and the dream is certain, and the interpretation is sure."*

{Daniel 2:28/36-45}

I am thrilled with the closing words here, that *"the "interpretation is sure."* Always keep in mind the reason for the surety of Divine interpretation…It is because that which was spoken prophetically has come to pass! Amen. Remember our confirmation of this truth has previously been given in Deuteronomy 18:20-22. Now…Let us look carefully at this connecting link that the Lord God has given to us for the certainty of the right interpretation concerning this image.

**Nebuchadnezzar's dream identifies the
four great kingdoms
that have existed on the earth.**

# 1.Babylon 2.Medeo-Persian

# 3.Grecian 4. Rome.

**Daniel identifies the first kingdom** with these words that he states to the King. ***"Thou art this head of gold,"*** symbolizing the first kingdom which was Babylon. Gold is an appropriate symbol to exemplify the richest kingdom that ever existed on the earth. History records that Babylon had erected fifty pagan temples filled with many gold statues of their deities. A fifty thousand-pound gold laden statue of Baal stood in Babylon's public square. The hanging gardens of Babylon were a part of this magnificent kingdom and are still considered one of the Seven Wonders of the World. Historians have called Babylon the "Golden City."

**The next successive kingdom that Daniel describes would have been the Medeo-Persian.** The two arms represent the two divisions {Medes and Persians} of people that had now united together to form this kingdom. The breast and arms of the image were made of silver. As each of these successive kingdoms grow weaker, the symbolic representation of the elements change. As silver is inferior to gold, so was the kingdom of the Medes and the Persians now inferior or of lesser power than the preceding kingdom of Babylon.

**As Daniel continues his interpretation concerning the third kingdom,** he tells us that the belly and thighs of the image were of brass. As history records, the kingdom that followed the Medeo-Persian was the Grecian kingdom. We notice that the elements change again. As brass is inferior to silver, so we see the interpretation again verified. This kingdom has grown weaker now in its strength and power.

Although the Grecian kingdom was in a state of weakness, Alexander the great came forth who brought back some semblance of stability to the Grecian Empire. He was known to be a fearless mighty warrior, and brilliant scholar. Alexander established the Olympic games, fine art, and Greek culture. After his death, the kingdom was divided into four districts and governed by his four previously chosen generals. Selfishness and greed between these four generals caused the kingdom to become even weaker, which gave place to an easy conquest by the Caesars of Rome.

Daniel further describes the King's image as having legs of iron, feet and toes of part iron and part clay. Daniel had already related that this fourth kingdom of Rome would be, *"strong as iron and subdueth all things."* According to historians, Rome did exactly that! Under the

Caesars, the Great Roman Empire subdued the entire world! Many historians use the term, "Rome ruled with an iron hand." A Pax-Romana was established as the armies of Rome captured all the surrounding provinces. This was in reality a "republic of slavery." This last kingdom of man was the fulfillment of the scriptures that we are reading from Daniel's writings. It was indeed Rome that bruised, broke to pieces and subdued all peoples.

As we review these scriptures from Daniel's writings, we see that the symbols accurately describe the actual events and conditions that brought about the fall of the great Roman Empire. The mixture of the elements of clay and iron identify the weakness of Rome as it began to crumble from within. It is written that this mixture of people, *"Shall not cleave to one another, even as iron is not mixed with clay."* At this time, there were Babylonians, Medes and Persians, Greeks and Romans, along with many sects of Jews and even Christians within the Empire of Rome. There was no, *"cleaving together,"* for these various ideologies, cultures, religions and life-styles. These inner conflicts finally brought about what is known as the fall of the great Roman Empire. The greed of the Caesars, the inner corruption, cultural differences and the wickedness of the people themselves were the cause of the fall of Rome! Daniel also wrote, *"The kingdom shall be divided."* We see the legs of the image, which symbolizes the two divisions of Eastern and Western Rome. The toes of the image symbolize the ten provinces that had grown out of Rome in her later history.

## These ten provinces are recorded as:
## 1.Heruli 2.Lombards 3.Ostrogoths 4.Suevi
## 5. Visigoths 6.Anglo-Saxons 7.Burgundians
## 8.Vandals 9.Franks 10.Huns.

Some commentators have mistakenly projected these ten kingdoms of the toes on the image to be somehow connected with the United Nations of this present age. How could this be? If you would measure the body of this image by the years that each kingdom reigned, beginning with the head, the chest, the loins, the legs, and the feet with the toes, you will find a perfectly proportioned body. If the toes were not to follow in proper succession, then the toes would make the image a monstrosity! The toes would measure more than

41

two thousand years long if they were supposed to represent any nations of this present age. What a misrepresentation of the body's proportions this would be! The Dispensational theory will not stand the test of these scrutinizing scriptures. Dispensationalism fails to present the…**"more sure word of prophecy."**

### Confirming the Fulfillment of
### The Kingdom of God on Earth

Immediately after Daniel's explanation of the four kingdoms, he then gives the King this promise from the Lord. *"And in the days of these kings shall the God of heaven set up his kingdom, which shall never be destroyed: and the kingdom shall not be left to other people, but it shall break in pieces and consume all these kingdoms, and it shall stand forever. Forasmuch as thou sawest that the stone was cut out of the mountain without hands, and that it brake in pieces the iron, the brass, the clay, the silver, and the gold; the great God hath made known to the king what shall come to pass hereafter: and the dream is certain, and the interpretation thereof sure."*

It is thus written: *"And in the days of these kings shall the God of heaven set up a kingdom."* What days and what kings was he speaking about? We will find the answer in Luke's gospel *2:1-2, "And it came to pass in those days, that there went out a decree from Caesar Augustus, that all the world should be taxed. And this taxing was first made when Cyrenius was governor of Syria."* The rest of this story should be familiar to all… Jesus Christ was born into this world at the time of the Caesars. It was the Caesars {these kings} that ruled the Kingdom of Rome. Imperial Rome was the existing government into which Christ was born. God announced the coming of His kingdom by sending His own Son into this world. This was His message…

*"The Spirit of the Lord is upon me, because he hath anointed me to preach the gospel to the poor; he hath sent me to heal the broken hearted, to preach deliverance to the captives, and recovering of sight to the blind, to set at liberty them that are bruised, To preach the acceptable year of the Lord.* {Then Jesus said} *This day is this scripture fulfilled in your ears."{Luke 4:18-21}*

What was that acceptable year of the Lord? It was the *"Year of Jubilee."* The Year of Jubilee meant a NEW BEGINNING AGAIN.

Yes! Jesus Christ presented Himself as the Jubilee! He brought a new beginning to all humanity, even the ushering in of the Kingdom of God. This is what Jesus meant when He said..."*This day is this scripture fulfilled in your ears.*" Mark wrote in his gospel..."*The time is fulfilled, and the kingdom of God is at hand: repent ye, and believe the gospel.*"

Christ was and still remains that King of all Kings. The power of His Kingdom did break into pieces the iron, the brass, the clay, the silver and the gold, which represented all the previous kingdoms. All of these kingdoms were incorporated in these symbols. Christ did establish His Kingdom on this earth and of His Kingdom there shall be no end! Christ was and ever shall be that "*Stone*" cut out of the mountain without man's hands. Peter writes about this Chief Corner Stone..."*Wherefore it is also contained in the scriptures, Behold, I lay in Sion {the church} a chief corner stone, elect, precious: and he that believeth on him shall not be confounded. {1 Peter 2:6}*

Through the image of King Nebuchadnezzar, the Lord had revealed to Daniel just when to expect His Kingdom. "*In the days of these kings*" or after these kingdoms of men had come to an end, the God of heaven would set up His kingdom which would never end! It is thus written: *The great God hath made known to the king what shall come to pass hereafter and the dream is certain, and the interpretation thereof is sure.*"

Jesus Christ, the King of all Kings did come into this world over two thousand years ago and He did complete His mission! He did set up His Kingdom on this earth at that time! Christ's Kingdom is a Spiritual Kingdom. He said it Himself!

Jesus spoke plainly to Pilate and to all who will hear from that time until we enter into eternity...He said, "*My kingdom is not of this world: if my kingdom were of this world, then would my servants fight, that I should not be delivered to the Jews: But now is my kingdom not from hence. Pilate therefore said unto him, Art thou a king then? Jesus answered, Thou sayest that I am a king. To this end was I born, and for this cause came I into the world, that I should bear witness unto the truth. Everyone that is of the truth heareth my voice.*" {John 18:36-37}

If you are seeking the truth, I pray that you will open your heart to this message and hear Christ's Voice concerning His Kingdom. The

Christ, the Anointed One did not fail because the majority of Jewish people rejected Him as their promised Messiah. It was "their failure" because they did not recognize that His Kingdom was to be a "Spiritual" Kingdom. They were expecting Him to be an earthly king. They were expecting the Messiah to come and deliver them from Rome's tyranny. They were expecting Him to restore them to preeminence as His chosen people. They misunderstood the nature and purpose of Christ's Kingdom and they still remain in "unbelief" to this present day.

## Will Christ return to Jerusalem?

There are many in the Christian community that have embraced this Jewish stance and are expecting Christ to return and establish a Jewish nation once again on the earth. These Dispensationalists claim that the Jewish people will rebuild what is called a "Third Temple" in Jerusalem. They teach that there will be a new priesthood raised up to make animal sacrifices once again on their altars. Some Rabbis claim that one of the things necessary for this Third Temple is the ashes of the red heifer. A group of people are supposedly breeding this lineage of red heifers for that purpose. Jesus words would be very appropriate to use here... *"If the blind lead the blind, both shall fall into the ditch."* One cannot help but wonder if these people of the "Christian faith" ever read and studied the book of Hebrews??? What a reproach to the everlasting covenant that God made through His Son's precious blood! These people are counting Christ's blood as an "unholy" thing when they want to go back to what God has DONE AWAY WITH! Dispensationalists that are caught up in this theory of error think that Christ will rule the world from Jerusalem with the Jews as God's chosen and favored people. Some where in this speculated theory, the so-called Anti-Christ will appear. Dispenationalists are divided in their speculations concerning this "postponement theory." Some predict a seven-year tribulation, a pre-tribulation; and others predict a post-tribulation. All of these speculative events and scenarios are contrary to the Word of God! The scriptures have proclaimed Christ as King of Kings and Lord of Lords and His Spiritual Kingdom is NOW! He did say… *"Its is finished."*

We have previously traced the origin of the false theory of a supposed future Millennial Age to come in our preface.

However…there is a deeper understanding that must be linked to this for complete clarity on this subject. It is this…The misconception of the Jews as the favored people of God, has been formed by a terrible distortion of Daniel's seventy weeks of prophecy. Since this particular prophecy is the foundation of truth concerning the promised Messiah, I would share this complete thesis from my learned brother in prophetic ministry.

## It is essential to hear the truth of the matter in its entirety…

### *"Daniel's 70th Week"*
### *By: Ralph Woodrow*
### *Future or Fulfilled?*

"One of the most glorious, thrilling, and wonderful Old Testament prophecies which pointed to Christ is found in Daniel 9:24-27. This is known as the prophecy of Seventy Weeks, it gives a measurement which indicated the exact year that the Messiah would be revealed! It predicted his death and the great redemption it would accomplish.

Verse 24: "Seventy weeks are determined upon thy people and upon thy holy city, to finish the transgression, and to make an end of sins, and to make reconciliation for iniquity, and to bring in everlasting righteousness, and to seal up the vision and prophecy, and to anoint the most Holy."

Verse 25: "Know therefore and understand, that from the going forth of the commandment to restore and to build Jerusalem unto the Messiah the Prince shall be seven weeks, and three score and two weeks: the street shall be built again, and the wall, even in troublous times."

Verse 26: "And after threescore and two weeks shall Messiah be cut off, but not for himself and the people of the prince that shall come shall destroy the city and the sanctuary; and the end thereof shall be with a flood, and unto the end of the war desolations are determined."

Verse 27: "And he shall confirm the covenant with many for one week: and in the midst of the week he shall cause the sacrifice and the oblation to cease, and for the overspreading of abominations he shall make it desolate, even until the consummation, and that determined shall be poured upon the desolate." {Daniel 9:24-27}

## SEVENTY WEEKS OF YEARS

This great prophecy pertaining to Daniel's people and the city of Jerusalem is linked with a time period of seventy "weeks." All Bible students recognize that these seventy weeks or 490 days are symbolic of years - each day representing a year - that is, a time period of 490 years. It was this same year – for – a - day principle that was used in Numbers 14:34. Because of unbelief, the Israelites were to wander for 40 years in the wilderness, a year for each day that the spies were absent searching out the land. This same scale was used in Ezekiel 4: 4-5 "For I have laid upon thee the years of their iniquity, according to the number of days, three hundred and ninety days: so shalt thou bear the iniquity of the house of Israel." Further, we notice that within the divine measurement of Seventy Weeks or 490years, there are three main parts: 49 years {7 weeks} then 434 years {62 weeks} and then the final 7 years {the 70th week}

## STARTING POINT

The time period was to begin with the "going forth of the commandment to restore and build Jerusalem." As is well known, at the time Daniel received the revelation of the 70 weeks, the city of Jerusalem and the temple were in ruins. His people were captives in Babylon. But Daniel knew from a study of the book of Jeremiah that the captivity would last but 70 years. {Dan. 9:2} and then a decree would go forth for their release so they could return and build again their city. The prophecy of Isaiah even told that it would be a man by the name of Cyrus who would come to power and bring these things about! "Thus saith the Lord to his anointed, to Cyrus...he shall build my city, and he shall let go my captives, not for price nor reward." {Is. 45}

All of this happened with amazing accuracy and timing. Cyrus did come to power. He did set the captives free. He did issue a decree that resulted in the rebuilding of the temple and the city of Jerusalem with houses for the thousands who returned. The decree is recorded in Ezra 1.

The going forth of the decree of Cyrus to rebuild Jerusalem ended in 70 years captivity, and began the period 7 times as long {70 times 7} which pertained to Messiah. {Dan.9: 2 & 24} The city was rebuilt. As the prophecy stated, the times were troublous when the wall and streets were built. The account of all of this is given in the Bible. This work of rebuilding occupied the first segment of seven "weeks," that is, 49 years.

The next segment of time, 62 weeks, that is, 434 years, was an exact measurement to reach unto the appearance of the Messiah. Thus the time of our Lord's first coming was definitely indicated! Later, when this time was fulfilled, those who knew this prophecy of the 70 weeks, were expecting the appearance of the Messiah, that is, the Christ, {"Christ" is the exact Greek equivalent of the Hebrew word "Messiah."} Thus when John came baptizing, "the people were in EXPECTATION, and all men mused in their hearts of John, whether he were the Christ, or not." {Lk. 3:15} In answer to this, John confessed that he was not the Christ. {John 1:20} John was not the Christ, but the time for the appearance of Christ {the Messiah} was very close – according to the prophecy. Then shortly – right at the exact time prophesied – 483 years from the proper starting point of the prophecy – Jesus came to John and was baptized! The Holy Spirit in the form of a dove descended upon Him.

The "most Holy" was anointed with the Holy Spirit to begin his public ministry as the "anointed one" – that is, the Christ, the Messiah! And so the prophecy thus far was fulfilled even to the very year. Thus Jesus, in evident reference to the time – prophecy of Daniel, said: "The TIME is fulfilled. {Mk. 1:15} The prophecy of Daniel goes on to say that the Christ, the Messiah, was to be "cut off" – he was to die - "but not for himself." And of course this was fulfilled in the death of our Saviour. Jesus died, not for his own sins _ He had done - but for US he died!

What a glorious and exact prophecy this is! We have seen how the prophecy told that Jerusalem would be rebuilt. It also revealed that later it would be destroyed again. "The people of the prince that shall come shall destroy the city and sanctuary." As is well known, Roman armies under the direction of prince Titus destroyed the city of Jerusalem and the temple in 70 A.D. On these things we have mentioned thus far, there is a general agreement among Christians. However, in comparatively recent times there has a risen a teaching which has caused a definite difference of opinion about the final "week" of the prophecy – the 70th Week. The questions involved in this are these:

## QUESTIONS

Does the 70th week pertain to CHRIST or ANTICHRIST? Has it been FULFILED or is it yet FUTURE? Bearing these questions in mind, let us look again at the passage under consideration and especially verse 27 which describes the 70th Week.

Verse 26: "Messiah shall be cut off, but not for himself: and the people of the prince that shall come shall destroy the city and the sanctuary; and the end thereof shall be with a flood, and unto the end of the war of desolations are determined.

Verse 27: And he shall confirm the covenant with many for one week; and in the midst of the week he shall cause the sacrifice and the oblation to cease." Now we notice that verse 27 starts out: "And he... "To whom does the pronoun "he" refer? This is important. In our day, there is a teaching that has become very widespread which says that verse 27 refers to

ANTICHRIST; that the antichrist will make a covenant with the Jews for seven years {allowing them to make sacrifices in a "rebuilt" temple at Jerusalem} and then half way through the seven years {the 70th week} he will break his agreement with them; that this even year period is the "great tribulation" that all of this is yet FUTURE – the 70th week being separated from the 69th week by a "gap" of almost 2,000 years! All of this is based upon the assumption that the "he" of verse 27 is the Antichrist. But how could "he" refer to the Antichrist when Antichrist is not mentioned or even indirectly referred to in the context? The context does mention a "prince" that was to bring his armies and destroy the city and the sanctuary, but such could not possibly refer to some yet future antichrist or ruler, for history abundantly shows that the armies and the people that destroyed Jerusalem and the temple were the Roman armies under the direction of Titus. This happened in 70 A.D. Moreover, the pronoun "he" could not refer to the word "prince" for the word "prince" is the object of the modifying clause "of the prince." A pronoun cannot properly have as its antecedent the object of the modifying clause. And so from the structure of the sentence and from the facts of history, we know that "he" of verse 27 cannot be linked with the clause "the people of the prince that shall come and destroy the city and sanctuary".

Taking these things into consideration, there is only one person in the entire passage to whom the pronoun "he" could possibly refer and that is to the Messiah! It is the Messiah who is the subject of the passage and to whom "he" refers, and this will become more clear as we proceed. The essence of the passage then is this: "Messiah shall be cut off...and he shall confirm the covenant...he shall cause the sacrifices and the oblations to cease." Was this fulfilled by Jesus Christ? Indeed it was. As we shall see in more detail shortly, it was Jesus who put an end to sacrifices {in God's program" by himself becoming the supreme sacrifice for sins forever! It was Jesus who confirmed the covenant! This was definitely the view of the early church and the view that has been held firmly and consistently by Christians down through the centuries. It has only been in more recent times that attempts have been made to apply the passage to the Antichrist – teaching that Antichrist will make a covenant with the Jews in a yet future seven year period {allowing them to make sacrifices in a "rebuilt" temple} and then forbidding them to do this, thus causing the sacrifices to cease! How erroneous this is. There are over 280 references to "covenant" in the scriptures and not one of them in any way introduces the idea of a covenant being made between the Jews and a future Antichrist! Yet to hear some tell it, we might suppose that this modern theory of Antichrist making a seven year covenant with the Jews is as much a Biblical fact as God's covenant with Israel at Sinai!

48

## FUTURE OR FULFILLED

Now those who teach that this passage refers to Antichrist, also teach, of course, that the 70th week is yet FUTURE. But the other "weeks" were fulfilled {as all agree} in consecutive order – each "week" following the other – up to the days of Christ. By what method of reasoning then can some separate the 70th week from the 69th and place it off in the future? Let us look again at the prophecy. Omitting the modifying clauses for the moment to get an essence of the passage, we read: From the going forth of the commandment to build Jerusalem unto the Messiah shall be 69 weeks, and AFTER" {Notice the word is not "in" but "after"} "and AFTER 69 {7 plus 62} weeks shall Messiah be cut off." Now "AFTER" 69 weeks does not and cannot mean "in" or "during" the 69 weeks! If Messiah was to be cut off AFTER the 69 weeks, there is only one-week left in which he could have been cut off – the Seventieth Week!

Think about this. Absolutely no other conclusion can be drawn. Yet supposedly great Bible teachers in an effort to apply the 70th week to Antichrist say that Christ was cut off within the 69th week and that the 70th week is yet future! Thus an attempt is made to teach something that is both inconsistent and impossible – that "after" does not mean after. And upon this erroneous idea a whole structure of prophetic interpretation has been built! Messiah was to be cut off AFTER 69 weeks, that is, during the 70th week. Therefore, since the crucifixion of Christ took place during the 70th week {and absolutely no other conclusion can be drawn from this passage!] then the 70th week can not possibly refer to a yet future seven year period of time. And by the same token, it cannot have any connection with the rule of a future Antichrist! There is just simply no way to sensibly or scripturally make the 70th week refer to some future time, for it was during this 70th week that Christ was crucified. This is past, Fulfilled. But when during the 70th week {of seven years} did the prophecy say Messiah would be cut off? "AFTER 69 weeks {7 plus 62} shall Messiah be cut off...And he {Messiah} shall confirm the covenant with many for one week" – the 70th week, only one remaining! – "and in the midst of the week" – in the middle of the seven years – "he shall cause the sacrifices and the oblations to cease."

According to this then, Christ was to confirm the covenant during the final seven years of the prophecy, was to be crucified, and in the middle of the seven years – that is, at the completion of three and a half years of ministry – he would cause the sacrifices to cease. This all happened exactly as predicted. Our savior was crucified after three and a half years of ministry, He, who was the "messenger of the covenant" did confirm the covenant and brought an end to the old system of repeated sacrifices by himself becoming the sinner's substitute and eternal sacrifice! No other sacrifice since that time has ever had any merit with God – and so, in the scriptural sense of the word, sacrifices ceased. The sacrifice of Christ was the FINAL sacrifice in the program of God. The time of our Lord's death – in the midst of the week of seven years – was an exact fulfillment of the 70 weeks prophecy!

Understanding this, we can now see the real significance in certain New Testament statements, which also speak of a definite established time at which Jesus would die. For example, concerning Jesus, we read: "They sought to take him: but no man laid hands on him, because his hour was not yet come." {Jn 7:30} In John 2:4, Jesus said, "Mine hour is not yet come." On another occasion, he said, "My time is not yet come." {Jn. 7:6} Then just prior to his betrayal and death, he said, "My time is at hand."{Mt. 26:18} and finally. "the hour is come." {Jn. 17:1 & Mt. 26:45} These and other verses clearly show that there was a definite time in the foreordained plan of God when Jesus would die. He came to fulfill the scriptures, and there is only one Old Testament scripture which predicted the time of his death – the prophecy which stated that Messiah would be cut off in the midst of the 70th week – at the close of three and a half years of ministry! And how perfectly the prophecy was fulfilled in Christ!

But those who say that the confirming of the covenant and causing sacrifices to cease in the midst of the 70th week refers to a future Antichrist, completely destroy this beautiful fulfillment and are at a complete loss to show where in the Old Testament the time of our Lord's death was predicted. The teaching that the 70th week is a yet future period of seven years is known as the "gap theory." With all due kindness to those who have taught and believed this, we must say that such a theory is unscriptural, unfounded, and contradictory. How can some so positively point out how the measurement of the 69 weeks was fulfilled in the appearance of Christ – each year following the other right on schedule – then jump over about 2,000 years and place the 70th week at the end of the age? All of the other weeks followed each other in logical sequence. Since when doesn't 70 follow 69? By what logic can anyone separate the 70th from the 69th by a gap of 2,000 years? To teach that the prophecy could have such a "gap" is to teach that we could also put gaps in other places and instead of the prophecy counting unto the Messiah – as it so wonderfully does! - It could be applied to anyone, just depending on how many years we might choose to put a "gap"! Such methods would destroy the very meaning and purpose for which the time prophecy of the 70 weeks was given. The "gap theory" could be likened to a man with a yardstick who cut off the last inch and attached a piece of elastic between the 35th and 35th inches. Then he could stretch the 36th inch out as far as he wanted! But in so doing he would defeat the very purpose for which the yardstick was intended! Yet this is exactly the same principle involved in the widely believed "gap" theory of separating the 70th week from the 69th week and placing a parenthesis or gap of approximately 2,000 years between!

## "STOPPED CLOCK"?

How then do those who hold this view – the gap theory – explain this discrepancy? In attempting to explain this, they say that God's prophetic clock stopped ticking when Christ was crucified and will not start ticking again until the Jews are back in their own land. Scofield put it like this: "Now there is a great principle concerning prophetic chronology. God never reckons time with the Jews when they are out of their land. Then there is always an interlude. With Israel out of the land, God's Jewish clock stops. It begins again when Israel is back where Israel ought to be." {Addresses on Prophecy, p. 101} BUT is it true that God only counts prophetic time when the Israelites are in their own land? For example, Jeremiah prophesied that the Israelites would be taken captive to Babylon and would "serve the king of Babylon seventy years. {Jer. 25:11-12}

Later, when it came to pass that Israel was taken captive, Daniel studied the sacred writings to determine how many years they would be in captivity and Jerusalem remain desolate: "I Daniel understood by books the number of the years, whereof the word of the Lord came to Jeremiah the prophet, that he would accomplish seventy years in the desolations of Jerusalem." {Dan. 9:2} Daniel "understood" the length of time that they would be in captivity by his study of the writings of Jeremiah! At that time, the Israelites were "out of their land." Jerusalem was desolate. Yet, obviously the prophetic clock had NOT stopped ticking, for Daniel understood the captivity would be seventy years.

But had some of our modern day "scholars" been around, they would have told Daniel in arrogant tones that he was mistaken; that since the Jews were "out of their land" that God's "prophetic clock" had stopped ticking! The passing of the years has further demonstrated the utter folly of this theory, as seen by the following facts. In 1948, a state of Israel was formed in Palestine. Now those who held the clock theory claimed that when Israel would be back in its own land, the clock would start ticking again. And since the stopped clock was the only thing that was keeping the final seven years of Daniel's prophecy from being fulfilled {according to the theory} then the 70th week should have started in 1948! Obviously this did not prove true.

The "stopped clock" theory was invented to support the "gap theory" both of which prove erroneous upon investigation. The seventy weeks prophecy was given to Daniel as something he could "understand." {V. 25}

51

He knew nothing of any gaps or stopped clocks.! The fact is that the seventieth week followed the 69th in logical order and the events of the 70th week were fulfilled perfectly and wonderfully! Let us now look at the prophecy step by step and see how each event has been fulfilled!

1. **"Jerusalem was to be restored."**
2. **"The street and the wall were to be rebuilt in troublous times."**
These first two prophecies came to pass. The account of this work of rebuilding is given in the books of Ezra and Nehemiah.

3. **"The most Holy was to be anointed."** This was fulfilled at the time of Jesus' baptism. "Now when all the people were baptized, it came to pass, that Jesus also being baptized and praying, the heaven was opened. And the Holy Ghost descended in a bodily shape like a dove upon him, and a voice from heaven, which said, Thou art my beloved Son: in thee I am well pleased." {Luke 3:21-22} Shortly after this, Jesus entered into the synagogue of Nazareth and announced: "The Spirit of the Lord is upon me, because he hath ANOINTED me." {Luke 4:18-22} Later, in Acts 10:38. Peter mentioned "how God ANOINTED Jesus of Nazareth with the Holy Ghost...who went about doing good, healing all who were oppressed of the devil." Daniel's prophecy revealed that the time period unto the Messiah would be 69 weeks {483 years} This measured to the year that Jesus was baptized and anointed to begin his ministry as the Messiah, the Christ, the "anointed one." And so this prophecy that the most Holy would be anointed was fulfilled with exact precision.

4. **"Messiah was to be cut off."** This is a plain reference to the crucifixion and death of the Lord Jesus. {Matthew 27}

5. **"To finish the transgression."** As Jesus was dying, he cried: "It is FINISHED." What was finished? At Calvary, he brought an end to transgression. He finished it by becoming sin for us. This is a wonderful prophecy, which pointed to the redemptive work of Christ. "Surely he that borne our griefs and carried our sorrows...he was wounded for our transgressions." {Is. 53:5-5}

6. **"To make an end to sins."** Here the basic thought is repeated. If we understand the glorious significance of what was accomplished at Calvary, we know that here there was truly an end made of sins.

Jesus, who came "to save his people from their sins" accomplished this when he "put away sin by the sacrifice of himself." {Mt. 1:21; Heb. 9:26} Thus an end to sin was made by the shedding of his blood. {Heb. 9:22} all of this does not mea, of course, that right at that point men quit sinning. This was not the case. But what the scriptures do mean is that at Calvary the eternal sacrifice for sin was made, so that any and all – past, present, or future – who will be forgiven of sins will be forgiven because our Lord's death over 2,000 years ago made an "end of sins."!

7. **"To make reconciliation for iniquity."** This too was part of our Lord's redemptive work. "Wherefore in all things it behooved him to be made like unto his brethren, that he might be a merciful and faithful high priest in things pertaining to God, to make RECONCILLIATION for the sins of the people." {Heb. 2:17} "Having made peace through the blood of his cross...to RECONCILE all things to himself...and you, that were sometime alienated...yet now has he RECONCILLED in the body of his flesh through death. {Col. 1:20-22} "God was in Christ, RECONCILLING the world to himself, not imputing their trespasses unto them; and hath committed unto us the word of RECONCILLIATION." {2 Cor. 5:19} Plainly, "reconciliation for iniquity" was accomplished by Jesus, for the Lord hath laid on him the INIQUITY of us all." {Is. 53;6}

8. **"To bring in everlasting righteousness."** This too was accomplished by the redemptive work of Christ! "For he hath made him sin for us, who knew no sin; that we might be made the RIGHTEOUSNESS of God in him." {2 Cor. 5:21} "Even the RIGHTEOUSNESS of God...through the redemption that is in Christ Jesus: whom God hath set forth to be a propitiation through faith in his blood, to declare his RIGHTEOUSNESS for the remission of sins that are past..." {Rom. 3:21-26}"By his own blood he entered in once into the holy place, having obtained ETERNAL REDEMPTION" – everlasting righteousness – "for u." {Heb. 9:12} This eternal or everlasting righteousness that was accomplished at Calvary is contrasted to the old sacrifices under the law which were only of a temporary nature – offered repeatedly – but Christ, once for all time, offered himself – this providing, as the prophecy of Daniel predicted, "everlasting righteousness." One only has to read the great redemptive passages of Romans, Corinthians, Colossians, Ephesians, and Hebrews to see how that an "end" of transgressions and sins – "reconciliation for iniquity" and "everlasting righteousness" – was accomplished at Calvary by our Lord Jesus Christ. Certainly there is no logical or scriptural way these "To seal things will be accomplished during a supposed future seventieth week at the end of the age. To teach such is to make the Bible contradictory and take away from the glory of that great redemption of Calvary which so beautifully and completely fulfilled these prophesies!

9. **"To seal up the vision and prophecy."** the use of the metaphor "to seal" is derived from the ancient custom of attaching a seal to a document to show that it is genuine. {See 1 Kings 21:8, Jer. 32: 10-11 cf Jn. 6:27; 1Cor.9:2} Christ "sealed" Old Testament prophecy by fulfilling what was written in the visions and prophecies of the Old Testament concerning him, and thus, he "sealed" them – showed that they were genuine. But there is

also another sense in which Christ's coming sealed up the vision and prophecy in connection with Daniel's people. In rejecting Jesus as the one foretold in the scriptures, their Bible became a closed book to them, they became spiritually blind – their vision was "sealed up." "For the Lord…hath closed your eyes: the prophets and your rulers, and seers hath he covered. And the vision of all is become unto you as the words of a book that is sealed; which men deliver to one that is learned, saying, Read this…and he saith, I cannot; for it is sealed." {Isa. 29:10-13} And to this day, there is a "blindness' and a "vale" over their eyes in the reading of the Old Testament. To such, the scriptures are sealed up – closed!

{Rom.11: 25; 1 Cor. 3:14}

**10. "He shall confirm the covenant."** When Jesus instituted the Lord's supper, representative of his shedblood for the remission of sin, he said: "This is my blood of the New Testament {covenant} which is shed for many for the remission of sins." {Mt. 26:28} the word testament means covenant, and is often translated that way. The covenant was confirmed by the death of Christ, by his shed blood. How much more shall the blood of Christ, who through the eternal Spirit offered himself without spot to God, purge your conscience from dead works to serve the living God? And for this cause he is the mediator of the New Testament." {Covenant} Jesus is called the "mediator of the new covenant." {Heb. 8:6} the "messenger of the covenant"{Mal.3:1} and his shed blood is called "the blood of the everlasting covenant." {Heb. 12:24} There can be no mistake about it. Our Lord Jesus is truly the one who through his redemptive sacrifice at Calvary confirmed the covenant! And how beautifully this harmonizes with what we have already seen.

**11. "He shall cause the sacrifices and the oblation to cease."** This too was fulfilled in the death of Jesus Christ. In the Old Testament, as we have mentioned, sacrifices were repeatedly made. Each of these was but a mere type looking forward to the time when the perfect sacrifice, the Lamb of God, would be offered. Once this would be accomplished, God would no longer require or accept any other sacrifice. The perfect sacrifice was Jesus Christ. And thus, the old system of repeated sacrifices {types} could only end at Calvary _ when Christ became the perfect, eternal, and final sacrifice. {See Hebrews 9 and 10} Further proof that this was fulfilled in Christ, is seen in the time element of the prophecy. The 69th week measured unto Messiah; AFTER the 69 weeks he would be cut off in the midst of the remaining week – in the middle of the 70th week – that is, at the close of the three and a half years. This was fulfilled by Christ – right at the exact time stated – for his ministry did indeed last three and a half years.

That this was the length of our Lord's ministry may be seen by a study of the Gospel according to John. Eusebius, a Christian writer of the 4th century, mentioned this: "It is recorded in history that the whole time of our Savior's teaching and working miracles was three years and a half, which is half a week. This John the evangelist will represent {make known} to those who critically attend this Gospel." And so, after three and a half years of ministry as the Christ – the anointed – Jesus was cut off in death, in the middle of the "week" of seven years, thus making the final sacrifice. For a few more years, the Jews did continue their sacrifices, but these were never recognized by God – and thus cannot be termed sacrifices in the true scriptural sense of the word – such sacrifices plainly ceasing with the death of the eternal and perfect sacrifice, Jesus Christ!

The prophecy stated that Messiah was to confirm the covenant with many of Daniel's people for the "week" during which he was cut off in death. When Christ came, was his ministry directed to Daniel's people – to "Israel?" Yes! {Daniel 9:20} John introduced himself as he "that should be manifest to Israel."{John 1:31} "I am not sent," Jesus said, "but unto the lost sheep of the house of Israel." {Mt. 15:24} And when he first sent out his apostles, they were directed: "Go not into the way of the Gentiles…go rather to the lost sheep of the house of Israel." {Mt. 10:5-6} The first half of the "week" of our Lord's ministry was definitely directed toward Israel. But what about the second half – the final three and a half years of the prophecy – which was also linked to Israel? Did the disciples continue for the duration of the remaining three and a half years to preach {as Christ's representatives} especially to Daniel's people – to Israel? Yes, they did! Jesus had given the great commission that they were to " into all the world and preach the gospel to every creature; "go ye therefore teaching all nations"; "Ye shall be my witnesses…unto the uttermost parts of the earth." {Mk. 16:15; Mt. 28:19' Acts 1:8} YET {and this is significant} after Christ ascended, the disciples still at first preached only to Israel! Why? We know of only on prophecy that would teach that this was to be the course followed. It is the prophecy of the 70 weeks, which indicated that after the death of Messiah there would still be three and a half years to be fulfilled in connection with Israel!

Bearing this in mind, we can now understand at least one reason why the gospel went "to the Jew first" and then later to the Gentiles. {Rom. 1:16} As Peter preached shortly after Pentecost: "Ye are the children of the prophets, and of the covenant…unto you first God, having raised up His Son Jesus, sent him to bless you, in turning away every one of you from his iniquities." {Acts 3:25-26} "It was necessary that the word of God should first have been spoken to you," {Acts 13:46} said Paul and Barnabas.

In person, Christ came to Israel. Through the disciples – for the remainder of the "week" – his message still went to Israel. But after the three and a half years of the disciples' ministry exclusively to Israel was completed, we can expect that there would be a turning of God's blessings to the Gentiles. And this is exactly what happened. As is well known, the conversion of Cornelius completely changed the missionary outreach, onlook and ministry of the church. Though the New Testament does not give the exact date when this happened, apparently the time for special exclusive blessing upon Daniel's people had drawn to a close – the seventy weeks were fulfilled. – and the gospel which had gone first to the Jews was now to take its full mission as Christ taught – to be preached to all people of all nations!

This time of changeover was marked by a heavenly visitation to Cornelius, a gentile. An angel was sent to him and told him to call for Peter "who shall tell thee words whereby thou and all thy house shall be saved." {Acts 11:14} And so he sent for Peter who had the keys to the kingdom. Peter had introduced the gospel at Pentecost to Israel; now he was to be the man to introduce the gospel to the Gentiles! It was the next day after the angel had appeared to Cornelius that his messenger arrived at Joppa where peter was staying. Right on time, God showed Peter a vision of unclean animals which, when he was made to understand its meaning, cause him to know that the gospel was now to go to the Gentiles and not to Israelites only. All these things were timed perfectly – showing that God's hand was accomplishing a definite purpose. Making then the journey to the house of Cornelius, Peter took the gospel to the Gentiles. While Peter yet preached, the Holy Ghost fell upon them and they began speaking in tongues – exactly like the Israelites had dome at Pentecost. {Acts 10: 16-47} Returning then to Jerusalem, Peter explained how God had sent an angel to Cornelius He told of the vision he had seen and how God himself confirmed it all by giving to the Gentiles the gift of the Holy Ghost! "When they heard these things, they held their peace, and glorified God, saying, Then hath God also to the Gentiles granted repentance unto life." {Acts 11:18} From this very point, more and more, there was a turning from the Jews to the Gentiles with the gospel message. God's measurement of 490 years pertaining to Israel had obviously been completed!

**12. "Jerusalem and the temple to be destroyed."** Etc. The Jewish nation having rejected the blessings offered them through their Messiah and those whom he had sent, was now marked for destruction. Shortly the prophecy would be fulfilled which said: "the people {armies} of the prince that shall come {Titus} shall destroy the city and the sanctuary; and the end thereof shall be with a flood {a scattering, a dispersion} and unto the end of the war desolations are determined." This part of the prophecy was not dated within the framework of the 70 weeks as was the appearance of the Messiah, the time of his death etc. Nevertheless, living on this side of the fulfillment, we know that this too happened, and when.

It was in 70 A.D. that the armies under the direction of Titus came and destroyed Jerusalem and the temple. This was followed by repeated invasions and desolations until A.D. 135, "the end of war." And what desolations they were! Not only was Jerusalem left desolate, but as historians tell us, "nearly all Judea was laid waste." {P. 548 Caesar and Christ, by Durant} Even as our Lord had brought his judgement upon this nation before {because of their disobedience and abominations they committed} so again, his judgements were prophesied to fall upon them.: "For the overspreading of abominations he shall make desolate, even until the consummation, and that determined shall be poured upon desolate." {verse 27} God had "determined" before just what their judgement would be: "My soul shall abhor you," he said, "and I will make your cities waste, and bring your sanctuaries unto desolation, and I will not smell the savour of your sweet odours. And I will bring the land into desolation…and I will scatter you among the heathen, and I will draw out a sword after you: and your land shall be desolate, and your cities waste." {Lev. 26:30-33} One can't help but notice that the wording here is almost identical to that of the prophecy of Daniel.

The Jewish nation had filled their cup of iniquity full, they had rejected and killed the Messiah and persecuted those that he sent unto them. Thus, that which was "determined" that which was spoken before in warning, was poured out upon them. They were left "desolate" spiritually, first of all – of their own choice! – and then came literal destruction of their city which was laid "waste" they were "scattered" and the whole land of Judah was brought into "desolation" by the judgement of God!

We have pointed out 12 basic things that were revealed in connection with the 70 weeks prophecy: (1) Jerusalem would be destroyed; {2} The street and wall would be rebuilt in troublous times; {3{The most Holy would be anointed; {4} Messiah would be cut off; {5} He would finish the transgression; {6} make an end to sins; {7} make reconciliation for iniquity; {8} bring in everlasting righteousness; {9} " Seal up the vision and the prophecy; {10} confirm the covenant; {11} Cause sacrifices to cease; and finally {12} Jerusalem and the temple would be destroyed and desolations would sweep the land.

## Consider the following chart…

**Every single one of these events
have been fulfilled.**

70 Weeks or 490 Years Were Determined To Complete God's
Dealings With Israel As A Nation {Daniel 9:24-27}

Babylonian
Captivity

70 Years

Daniel
To
Malachi

7 Weeks
or
49 Years

Remaining Prophetic
Time Until
"Messiah Prince"

62 Weeks
or
434 Years

The Gospel
Preached
To The
Jews for...

The Baptism
Of Christ

3 and 1/2
Years

Peter
Preaches
To The
Gentiles
for...

3 and 1/2
Years

69 Weeks Plus
1 Week = 490 Yrs.

Return To Jerusalem
The Walls And Temple Rebuilt

Completing The 70th. Week

*The Key To Understanding Symbolic Time Reckoning
is Found In {Ezekiel 4:4-5 ~ each day for a year}*

58

We have seen that the 70 weeks were subdivided within the prophecy in three parts: 7 weeks - 62 weeks, and 1 week which is - 49 years - 434 years and 7 years.

**The first segment** of 49 years was taken up with the work of rebuilding Jerusalem.

**The next segment** of 434 years measured "unto Messiah."

**The final segment** of time, the 7 years, was of utmost importance.

**The first half** was the time of our Lord's ministry. His death marked the middle of the seven years and brought an end to the old system of sacrifices, our Lord himself becoming the perfect and final sacrifice.

**The last half** of the 7 years included the outpouring of the Holy Spirit and the ministry of the early church in its opening glorious days.

**The end of the period** of God's exclusive favor upon Israel was marked by a turning to the Gentiles with the gospel message.

The grand theme of this prophecy is Jesus Christ! Its great fulfillment shines forth from Calvary with glory and power! Its timing is perfect. Its words harmonious. Its message satisfies the soul! To cast all this aside and attempt to apply much of the prophecy to a time yet future and to the Antichrist {instead of Christ and His redemptive work at Calvary} is, we feel a serious error. We appeal to all brethren who have taught or believed this to reconsider this interpretation in the light of the scriptures." End quote

## Christ's Purpose for His kingdom

Jesus, the Christ, the Anointed One came to deliver ALL mankind from the tyranny of Satan and sin! He did not come to destroy the Roman's and set up a Jewish kingdom. Daniel's 70th week prophecy has given us the reason why the Jews missed their Messiah! As New Covenant - New Testament believers, we are translated from the kingdom of darkness into the Kingdom of God's dear Son through the new birth. Christ's Kingdom is a SPIRITUAL Kingdom!God inspired his chosen apostle to write these eternal truths concerning His Kingdom…*"But unto the Son he saith, Thy throne, O God, is forever and ever: a sceptre of righteousness is the sceptre of thy kingdom."* {Hebrews 1:8} The entire book of Hebrews presents the fulfillment of God's Kingdom, which He established through the New Covenant. All the gospels proclaim that the time for the Kingdom of God was at hand, not in two thousand plus years later! Jesus said that the only way any one can enter into His Kingdom was through a "Spiritual" birth. Ye must be born again to enter into this Kingdom.

# Hear the Word of the Lord....

- *"And Jesus went about all Galilee, teaching in their synagogues, and preaching the gospel of the kingdom, and healing all manner of sickness and all manner of disease among the people."* *{Matthew 4:23}* *"But if I cast out devils by the Spirit of God, then the kingdom of God is come unto you."* *{Matthew 12:28}*
- *"Verily I say unto you, That the publicans and harlots go into the kingdom of God before you."* *{Matthew 21:31 b}*
- *"The time is fulfilled, and the kingdom of God is at hand: repent ye, and believe the gospel."* *{Mark 9:1}*
- *"And he said unto them, Verily I say unto you, That there be some standing here, which shall not taste of death, till they have seen the kingdom of God."* *{Mark 1:15}*
- *"And the people, when they knew it, followed him: and he received them, and spake unto them of the kingdom of God, and healed them that had need of healing."* *{Luke 9:11}*
- *"The kingdom of God cometh not with observation: Neither shall they say, Lo here! Or, lo there! For, behold, the kingdom of God is within you."* *{Luke 17:20&21}*
- *"Verily, verily, I say unto thee, Except a man be born again, he cannot see the kingdom of God."* *{John 3:3}*

Every scripture throughout the Holy Writ verifies that Christ did establish His Kingdom, which He Himself declared to be a SPIRITUAL KINGDOM! I ask everyone to please redeem the time to read the account of the two travelers on the Emmaus road who walked with Christ after His resurrection. I share a portion of those scriptures...They said, *"But we trusted that it had been he {speaking of Jesus} which should have redeemed Israel"*...Jesus answered them, *"O fools, and slow of heart to believe all that the prophets have spoken: Ought not Christ to have suffered these things, and to enter His glory? And beginning at Mosses and all the prophets, he expounded unto them in all the scriptures the things concerning himself."* *{Luke 24:21 and 25-27}*

Christ had no "postponement plan" or "gap" theory in mind as the Dispensationalists have asserted. These false theories of men have brought forth much confusion within the Christian community. Their theories have also made void the truth concerning this Revelation Prophecy as God intended it to be understood. God is not the Author of confusion! It is important for all Christians to receive this present truth concerning Christ's Kingdom.

## "Dispensationalism"
### The great misconception of men!

- **It is a theory conceived of men!**
- **There is NO Biblical foundation for this theory!**
- **There will be NO Pre-Millennialism!**
- **There will be NO Post-Millennialism!**
- **There will be NO Pre-Tribulation!**
- **There will be NO Post Tribulation!**
- **There will be NO anti-Christ in a supposed**
- **Seven-Year Tribulation!**
- **There will be NO one thousand-year reign of Christ on this earth!**

Paul affirms this as he writes..."*For the Lord himself shall descend from heaven with a shout, with the voice of the archangel, and with the trump of God: and the dead in Christ shall rise first: Then we which are alive and remain shall be caught up together with them in the clouds to meet the Lord in the air: and so shall we ever be with the Lord.*" {1 Thess.4:16-17}

There is no one thousand-year gap between these two events! Christ will NOT set foot upon this earth again! He already stood on the Mt. of Olives. Christ already fulfilled Zechariah's prophecy when He came into the world the first time. The entire fourteenth chapter of Zechariah is consumed with the promise of the coming Messiah. THE FIRST TIME! There is NO mention of these prophecies describing a "second" coming. Listen carefully... "*And his feet shall stand in that day (gospel day} upon the mount of olives, which is before Jerusalem on the east, and the mount of Olives shall cleave in the midst thereof toward the east and toward the west, and there shall be a very great valley; and half of the mountain shall remove toward the north, and half of it toward the south.*" {Zechariah 14:4}

This is "that" particular isolated scripture which is taken out of its original context to build the false teaching of Christ's return to this earth for another age. The Dispensationalists await Christ's standing on the Mount of Olives. When the remainder of this chapter is studied out, we will see from verses six through nine that the Lord has given the SPIRITUAL representation of Christ's Kingdom as it was to be established in the earth. Let us take the time to review this, for it holds the key to reproof and understanding... *"And it shall come to pass in that day, {gospel day} that the light shall not be clear, nor dark: But it shall be one day which shall be known unto the Lord, not day, nor night: but it shall come to pass, that in the evening time it shall be light. And it shall be in that day, which the living waters shall go out from Jerusalem; half of them to toward the former sea, and half of them to the hinder sea: in summer and in winter shall it be. And the Lord shall be king over all the earth: in that day {gospel day} shall there be one Lord, and his name one." {Zechariah 14:6-9}*

Jesus Christ entered into the "darkness" of this world. It is thus written... *"In him was life; and the life was the light of men. And the light shineth in darkness; and the darkness comprehended it not."* {John 1: 4-5} This "day" of Christ's entrance into the world was known only to the Lord God Jehovah. Verse eight is speaking of that "LIVING WATER" that Christ gives to all men who seek Him and receive new Life. Hear His Words... *"In the last day, that great day of the feats, Jesus stood and cried saying, If any man thirst, let him come unto me and drink. He that believeth on me as the scripture hath said, out of his belly shall flow rivers of living water." {John 7:37-38}*

*The LIVING WATERS did indeed go out from Jerusalem just as Zechariah seeks to convey through this figurative language...half of them to toward the former sea, winter and summer etc. The gospel story did cover the whole world! The Lord Jesus Christ was indeed crowned KING OF KINGS and LORD OF LORDS. He was declared to be ONE LORD by His miraculous powers, His death and His resurrection!* There is no reason to discount this truth just because the Jewish people rejected Christ! What God did, He did for ALL people! It is written, "whosoever" will believe may come and drink of the water of life freely! Zechariah's prophecy was indeed fulfilled at Christ's FIRST entrance as the Messiah! All the gospels proclaim this...Matthew 21:1& 24:3/ Luke 19:29/Mark 13:3 {check them out}

Volumes could be written from the Word of God, Old and New Testament alike to confirm this truth. However, we have gleaned out enough scriptural truths that those who would, *"hear the truth as it is in Jesus,"* may receive it.

**Let us now review all these previous events
in their chronological order as they took
place within the Apostolic Period...**

The *"White Horse and Rider"* presented the conquering faith of Christianity as it was birthed into the world. Under this symbolic scene the early Christians went forth conquering that Pagan society with the Word of God. Paganism was cast down or lost its power to deceive because of the glorious gospel of Jesus Christ through the testimony of those first century Christians.

The *"Star Crowned Woman"* appeared on the prophetic scene, which represented the church as She gave birth to the man-child. {converts to Christianity} Isaiah described the entrance of the Kingdom of God into this world as a *"nation born in a day."* Peter spoke of this Kingdom as a *"holy nation."* The saints of God shouted with a loud voice saying... *"Now is come salvation, and strength, and the kingdom of our God, and the power of his Christ."* *{Revelation 12:10}*

The *Great Red Dragon* has been identified from Daniel's prophecy as the fourth kingdom on earth, which was the Roman Empire. This is that same Great Red Dragon that is seen standing before the women who was ready to devour her child as soon as it was born. The Roman Emperors and Pagan priests were the human agents that Satan influenced and used to persecute the Christ's followers. This connecting link from Daniel to the book of Revelation gives us the Divine starting point in the establishment of the Kingdom of God. {Revelation 12:1-3}

Through Daniel's Divine connecting link, we have now established the exact time of the entrance of God's Kingdom on earth.

**History cannot be denied!**

**All these things did come to pass!**

**This is the...**

*"more sure word of prophecy."*

# The Medieval Period
## *"The Black Horse"*

*"And when he had opened the third seal, I heard the third creature say, Come and see. And I beheld, and lo a black horse; and he that sat on him had a pair of balances in his hand. And I heard a voice in the midst of the four beasts say, A measure of wheat for a penny; and see thou hurt not the oil and the wine." {Revelation 6:5-6}*

We can understand this symbolic scene with certainty as we continue to use the symbolic key, which God has given. We are looking for that which is analogous through these symbols of this Black Horse and Rider. This Rider, being a human agent, like the previous ones is representing another kingdom of religion. His steed, meaning another civil authority also supports this religious system. The color of the Horse has changed along with the actions and character of the Rider. We may also *"Come and see"* through this analogy, that the Black Horse symbolizes "darkness." This darkness entered into the world through the Apostate church calling itself Christianity during this Medieval period.

The Black Horse {Rome's civil authorities} and Rider {The Apostate Priests} did indeed eclipse the Light of the glorious gospel by replacing the Word of God with their invented ceremonies and practices of Paganism! This was all done under the cloak of Christianity.

In this brief index of information given through the opening of the third sealed scroll, the Black Horse and Rider are symbolizing the historical events that will effect God's Kingdom or true Christianity in Rome's history. We have previously related some of these events. We will have more to say later about the darkness which eclipsed the Light of Christ, as we come to Daniel's prophecy of the "Little Horn."

Let us keep in mind that we are tracing the past events of this Christian dispensation with all its conflicts and victories. In this particular vision, John saw that the Rider of this Black Horse had a pair of balances in his hand. He also heard a voice speaking about, *"a measure of wheat for a penny, and three measures of barely for a penny; and see thou hurt not the oil and the wine."* Seemingly a strange statement for us to understand! However, God's Word can always be deciphered. He has admonished us to *"study to shew ourselves approved, rightly dividing the word of truth."* This can be done! Yes, it does require a special effort. Yes, it does require many long and tedious hours of research and seeking the wisdom of God. This is why God has placed the members in the Body as it has pleased Him. It evidently has pleased Him to call me into this prophetic ministry and I have joy in that hope of my calling. However! It has required a determined effort on my part, to spend much time in serious study to rightly divide the Word of truth. I must hastily add…How could I do less than give Him my best when He purchased me with such a supreme price! I can never repay the Lord, but I can obey Him, love Him with all my heart, mind, and soul and do His will.

Let us return to this seemingly difficult passage of scripture…I have always found that a good Bible commentary will be an asset in the study of customs that are prevalent throughout the Bible. From Adam Clarke's commentary, we learn this…In ancient times land-owners were required to pay heavy taxes. Every fifteen years, a new assessment was made of the farmer's yield of corn or his vineyard of grapes. The new taxes would then be based upon what that years harvest would be. This would then become the requirement to be paid for the next fifteen years. The oppressed people adopted a method of deception in order to escape such heavy taxation. They would burn or mutilate {the word "hurt" is used in the scriptures} their crops for this one investigated year.

In doing this, their assessment would be near nothing for the next fifteen years. If the people were caught doing this however, they were put to death! Thus, the symbolic words of warning in this prophecy… *"See thou hurt not* {destroy or mutilate} *the oil* {meaning fields of corn} *or the wine."* {meaning grape vineyards}

The balances that are seen in the Rider's hand are measuring out scarcely enough barely and wheat to keep one from starving to death! The cost of the barley and wheat were a full day's wages. What is this an analogy of in the Spiritual realm? These symbols are describing a severe time of Spiritual oppression, tyranny, starvation and death imposed upon people by a religious system. Keep in mind that these are "Spiritual" truths. This is an analogy of what actuality happened during the Medieval period. We have been given an insight into the Apostate church, which is now developing.

According to unbiased historical church records, a "self exalted" priesthood had confiscated what few scriptures that were available at that time. The Word of God was replaced by the pagan ritual that was performed by the priests. This is a fulfillment of the *"measure of wheat for a penny, and three measures of barely for a penny."* The common man was not permitted to read the scriptures for himself during this "dark Age" period. Thus a time of Spiritual starvation, as the pair of balances symbolizes.

D'Aubigne's book called, "History of the Reformation" relates these circumstances concerning this Medieval period of Spiritual darkness…"The living church retiring gradually within a few solitary hearts, an external church was substituted in its place, and all its forms were declared to be of divine appointment. Salvation no longer flowing from the word, which was henceforth put out of sight, the priests affirmed that it was conveyed by means of the forms they had themselves invented, and that no one could obtain it but by these channels." End Quote

Without the glorious Light of the true gospel of Christ, Spiritual darkness filled the earth! It is interesting and miraculous to note that the Lord God spoke to the seers of ancient times about these particular events. Amos, one of God's prophets looked down through the annuls of time to foresee these very happening as he wrote… *"Behold, the days come, saith the Lord God, that I will send a famine in the land, not a famine of bread, nor a thirst for water, but of hearing the words of the Lord: And they shall wonder from sea to sea, and from the north even to the east, they shall run to and fro to seek the word of the Lord, and shall not find it." {Amos 8:11-12}*

Remembering that the seven sealed scrolls are only an index, we shall have much more within the parallel themes that will bring the detailed events of this "famine" of the Word of God.

# This "Darkness" was the actual "Spiritual" condition of all the world during what historians have come to call the…
# "Dark Ages."

# "The Star Crowned Woman In The Wilderness"

What rejoicing had been heard in the Apostolic period from the children of God as they proclaimed their victory over Satan's power! They were heard saying with a loud voice... *"Now is come salvation, and strength, and the kingdom of our God, and the power of his Christ."* {Revelation 12:10-11} However! The scene has now changed! Something has happened! The symbolic message through the Black Horse has given to us an introduction as to why this change came to be...Let us follow the righteous path of this *"Star Crowned Woman"* as she fled into the wilderness...

*"Therefore rejoice, ye heavens, and ye that dwell IN THEM. Woe to the inhabiters of the earth and of the sea! For the devil is come down unto you, having great wrath, because he knoweth that he hath but a short time. And when the dragon saw that he was cast unto the earth, he persecuted the woman which brought forth the man child. And to the woman were given two wings of a great eagle, that she might fly into the wilderness, into her place, where she is nourished for a time, and times, and a half a time, from the face of the serpent. And the serpent cast out of his mouth water as a flood after the woman, that he might cause her to be carried away of the flood. {Rev. 12:13-14} And the woman fled into the wilderness, where she had a place prepared of God, that they should feed her there a thousand two hundred and three score days."* {Rev. 12:6}

Through these scriptures, we continue to follow the plight of the woman, who symbolizes the true Christian Church. Line upon line, precept upon precept, for in this manner we will be able to understand the events that took place more clearly. The Christians were rejoicing in their newfound spiritual freedom through their faith in a Living Savior. They had experienced freedom from Satan, from their own sin, guilt and condemnation, yet they were still inhabitants on the earth. They were still subjected to the onslaughts of Satan through those who are his agents, yes, through those who do his evil bidding and deeds. This *"woe"* given to those who inhabit the earth means that something of great devastation is about to happen!

Satan is filled with wrath because he has been defeated by the blood of the Lamb and by the word of the testimony of the first century Christians. He has lost his power to deceive people through Pagan Idolatry. This symbolic language speaks to us about a severe persecution that would take place as the final effort through the Great Red Dragon's powers to eliminate Christianity from the face of the earth! Satan, knowing his time was short in using Idolatry, found a human agent to accomplish this severe persecution. It was the Emperor named Diocletian.

This *"woe unto the inhabitants of the earth"* came through this blood thirty tyrant! Diocletian was an avid Pagan himself, and still zealous for Idol worship! He had ascended to the Imperial throne in AD 274. According to historians, Diocletian's ten-year reign of terror against the Christians was the most intense and brutal of all the previous persecutions that they had endured! The noted historian Butler writes in his ecclesiastical history..."But the master piece of Diocletian's heathen policy was to seek and burn all the copies of the Word of God. The enemy had been lopping off the branches of the tree whose leaves were for the healing of the nations; now the blow was made at the root." End Quote

The symbolic language of Revelation 12: 15 affirms this historical event. This amazing prophetic fulfillment from God's truth did indeed come to pass... *"And the serpent cast out of his mouth water as a flood after the woman, that he might cause her to be carried away by the flood."* According to the previous symbolic guidelines that we have established, the *"mouth"* represents a human agent and the serpent symbolizes civil authority. As water in the natural realm destroys everything in a flood, so the water here symbolizes the same destruction in the Spiritual realm. The *"water"* symbolizing the destructive "flood" of persecution through Diocletian, as he sought to destroy every Christian and every page of the Word of God from the face of the earth!

During this time, multitudes of Christians had *"fled into the wilderness"* hiding in catacombs and forming communes to escape this extreme persecution. God had a place prepared for His Beloved for it is written that the Woman was given two wings of a great eagle that she might fly into the wilderness. {Revelation 12:14} This beautiful passage of scripture from Exodus 19:4 is alluded to..."*Ye have seen what I did unto the Egyptians, and how I bare you on eagles wings, and brought you unto myself.*" This remnant of true Christians who *"fled into the wilderness"* preserved what few scriptures there were in existence at that time. God had promised that He would *"nurture"* the woman or the true church during this prophetic season of a, *"time, and times, and half time."*

## Prophetic Time Reckoning

We continue to stand in awe at the miracle that is within God's design of symbolic language! The exact way in which all these times, places and events come together rises above the natural coincidence or mere happenings! The miracle of symbolic language is prevalent, throughout this prophetic timetable. We will notice that this same prophetic reckoning of time is used in Revelation 12:6…It is referred to in this scripture as, *"a thousand two hundred and threescore days."*

It is very important that we examine this prophetic period of time, for it has much to do with identifying, "Mystery Babylon." The Lord God Himself has established symbolic time reckoning. We will find the key to understanding the measuring of prophetic time through the writings of His servant Ezekiel. It is thus written: *"Lie thou also upon thy left side, and lay the iniquity of the house of Israel upon it: according to the number of days that thou shalt lie upon it thou shalt bear their iniquity. For I have laid upon thee the years of their iniquity, according to the number of the days, three hundred and ninety days: so shall thou bear the iniquity of the house of Israel." {Ezekiel 4: 4-5}*

We understand from this passage of scripture, that the Lord measured the time of Israel's iniquity or their backslidden condition in this symbolic time. We know that this prophecy was fulfilled in the same number of years, which the Lord told Ezekiel. Israel was in captivity for three hundred and fifty years…not three hundred and fifty days.

Now…Let us verify the same symbolic key of understanding concerning the *"time, and times and half a time."* We will also find this key of understanding through King Nebuchadnezzar's experience. The reader may examine the full account concerning King Nebuchadnezzar's haughty spirit and the discipline that God dealt to him in the fourth chapter of Daniel's writings. In this narrative, we read that the King had exalted himself above God. He took the credit for building the great kingdom of Babylon. Immediately the Lord's judgement came upon him as there fell a voice from heaven saying... *"The kingdom is departed from thee. And they shall drive thee from men, and thy dwelling shall be with the beasts of the field: they shall make thee to eat grass as oxen, and seven times shall pass over thee, until thou know that the most High ruleth in the kingdom of men, and giveth it to whom he will." {Daniel 4:32-33}*

All Bible students realize that this "seven times" represents the seven years that King Nebuchadnezzar was in a demented sate of mind with the beasts of the field. This key of understanding symbolic time reckoning, is again confirmed in Daniel 4:16. Still speaking of King Nebuchadnezzar... *"Let his heart be changed from man's and let a beast's heart be given unto him; and let seven times pass over him." Again we* reiterate that King Nebuchadnezzar's long siege of insanity in the wilderness lasted for seven years. As we have learned through Eziekiel's writings, symbolic time was reckoned as *"each day for a year."* Then through Daniel's writings, a "time" equals "one year." We can now confirm our time reckoning of the Revelation prophecy with this scriptural foundation. The word "times" then refers to "years." The Jewish calendar, which had 30 days in each month, was in use when John was given the Revelation prophecy. We adopt the same method for proper calculations.

## Prophetic Time Reckoning

| | | | |
|---|---|---|---|
| **Time** | **1 year** | **12 months =** | **360 days** |
| **Times** | **2 years** | **24 months =** | **720 days** |
| **Dividing Time** | **½ year** | | **180 days** |
| **3 ½ years** | **or** | **42 months = 1, 260 days** | |

**Please discern carefully that which is reckoned here...**
**3 ½ years, which equals 42 months, which equals 1,260 days, symbolically represents the...**
*"one thousand two hundred and sixty years"*

71

## This was the time that the true church of the Living God was in the wilderness.

## ALL history verifies the events that happened in this Medieval time frame!

As we continue to pursue the ongoing truths of this prophecy, we will learn of the many other events that came to pass during this same period of 1,260 years. They are all vitally linked together! While the Star Crowned Woman was in the wilderness for this 1,260-year period, other things were happening in the religious arena also. We will be sharing the events that took place within this Medieval time period, progressively and individually. However, we do offer this listing of scriptures in succession which confirm the events as they took place all in this identical time frame. We will repeat the first two scriptures concerning the Star Crowned Woman…

- The Woman {true church} fled into the wilderness for, *a thousand and three score days.* {Rev. 12:6}
- The Woman {true church} was nourished in the wilderness for a *time, and times, and half time,* from the face of the serpent. {Rev. 12:14}
- The Holy City, {true church} was trodden down by the Apostate church for, *forty and two months.* {Rev.11:1-2}
- The Two Witnesses, representing the Word and the Spirit prophesied for, *a thousand two hundred and three score days,* clothed in sackcloth during the Dark Ages. {Rev. 11:3}
- Blasphemies and power were given to him {meaning the developed Papacy} to continue, *forty and two months.* {Rev. 13:5}
- Great words were spoken against the Most High and the man of sin sought to change times and laws during this prophetic time of a, *time and times and the dividing time.* {Daniel 7:25}

All these events are covering the same time span during the Medieval period. This time span is also referred to as the Dark Age Period. We need to keep in mind that we are following the course of events that John has laid out for us as he wrote… *"After these things."* We are following the historical events of Christianity as they came to

72

pass throughout what is called the Gospel Dispensation. We affirm that the Revelation prophecy is the historical trace of the true church of the Living God.

### Let us look at the overall events which had come to pass in the Roman Empire...

• The *"Woman"* or the Remnant of the true church had previously fled into the wilderness. They had formed communes and established dwelling places. These persecuted Christians held what few scriptures there were at this time in their protection. Remember the prophecy told us it was the, *"remnant which kept the word of God."*

• Christianity...so-called...had now become the accepted state religion of Rome. However! It had become Apostate! The priesthood was a sought after position. This self-exalted priesthood began to usurp authority over the common man as local church congregations were formed. What few scriptures that remained had fast become the possession of this, "self-exalted" ministry and were not available to the common man. They had become the "possession" of the Apostate church.

• Very few truly born again believers had remained in the market place of Rome's society. The greater society of these Roman citizens were void of the pure truths of the gospel. Why was that? It was because the exalted leadership had devised other methods and means of entering into this Apostate church. The true gospel of Christ had been perverted and changed! This perversion and change is symbolized as John is given another vision and the analogy of...

# *"Measuring the Temple of God"*

*"And there was given me a reed like unto a rod: and the angel stood, saying, Rise, and measure the temple of God, and the altar, and them that worship therein." {Revelation 11:1}*

In this vision, John was given a *"rod"* to measure the temple of God, the altar, and them that worship therein. As we examine these symbols, we will see that he will be measuring "Spiritual" things, not a physical structure. He will be measuring them with a "rod." As we mentioned previously in our discourse about the man-child in Revelation 12:5, this *"rod"* symbolizes the Word of God. We will find that this present scene is analogous to the Old Testament temple worship. Keep in mind that these symbols are now relating the events that came to pass as the Apostasy began to develop in this Medieval period.

**John was to *"measure the temple."***

Let us consider briefly the typology of the Old Testament temple or tabernacle. We may then clearly discern the anti-type of this analogy. Let us visualize the Jewish tabernacle as it had been designed for the Old Testament worship. It was built with three courts. The court for the Israelites; the court for the attending priests; and the court of the Gentiles. There was an altar in the court of the priests. This priest was ordained to offer the burnt sacrifice for the sins of the people. Within this court was the entrance into the porch which then opened into a room called the, *"holy place."* {I would admonish my readers to redeem the time to study the book of Hebrews that you may receive a full understanding of the type and anti-type that is seen in this pattern. We will however, use these key verses throughout the ninth chapter of Hebrews for our basic understanding..."*Then verily the first covenant had also ordinances of divine service, and a worldly sanctuary. For there was a tabernacle made; the first, wherein was the candlestick, and the table, and the shewbread; which is called the sanctuary. And after the second veil, the tabernacle which is called the Holiest of all; Which had the golden censer, and the ark of the covenant overlaid round about with gold, wherein was the golden pot that had the manna, and Aaron's rod that budded, tables of the covenant; And over it the cherubims of glory shadowing the mercy seat; of which we cannot now speak particularly. Now when these things were thus ordained, the priests went always into the first tabernacle, accomplishing the service of God. But into the second went the high priest alone once every year, not without blood, which he offered for himself, and for the errors of the people: The Holy Spirit thus signifying, that the way into the holiest of all was not yet made manifest, while the first tabernacle was yet standing: Which was a figure for the time present, in which were offered both gifts and sacrifices, that could not make him that did that service perfect, as pertaining to the conscience; Which stood only in meats and drinks, and diverse washings, and carnal ordinances, imposed upon them until the time of reformation. But Christ being come an high priest of good things to come, by a greater and more perfect tabernacle, not made with hands, that is to say, not of this building; Neither by the blood of bulls and calves, but by his own blood he entered in once into the holy place, having obtained eternal redemption for us. For if the blood of bulls and goats, and the ashes of an heifer sprinkling the unclean sanctifieth to the purifying of the flesh: How much more shall the blood of Christ, who through the eternal Spirit offered himself without spot to God, purge your conscience form dead works to serve the living God? And for this cause he is the mediator of the new testament, that by means of death, for the redemption of the transgressions that were under the first testament, they which are called might receive the promise of eternal inheritance.*" {*Hebrews 9:1-15*}

These scriptures are describing or *"measuring"* the literal *"worldly sanctuary"* as the past dwelling place of God. This is the worship pattern that God gave through His servant Mosses concerning Old Testament worship. In the Revelation prophecy, John is now measuring the temple of God through the anti-type. This brings it into the "Spiritual" realm, which Christ has provided, through the New Testament worship. As believers in God's New Testament, WE have become His earthly tabernacles. WE are NOW His temples. Listen to these scriptures of assurance...*"Howbeit the most High dwelleth not in temples made with hands; as saith the prophet, Heaven is my throne, and the earth is my footstool: what house will ye build me? Saith the Lord: or what is the place of my rest? God that made the world and all things therein seeing that he is Lord of heaven and earth, dwelleth not in temples made with hands; neither is worshipped with men's hands, as though he needed anything, seeing he giveth life, and breath, and all things. Know ye not that ye are the temple of God, and that the Spirit of God dwelleth in you?"*
*{Acts 7:48-49/17:24-25/1 Corinthians 3:1}*

In our beginning key scripture, John was given a "rod" which represents the "word of God" to measure the Spiritual temple. This meant that the Word of God was to be the ONLY pattern or measurement to be used for the establishment of the New Testament church. We have shared briefly how the preaching of the gospel defeated Paganism through those first stalwart Christians in the Apostolic age. That gospel was the power of God unto salvation to all who believed! These *"measuring rod"* messages were spoken by Christ Himself and continued by the apostles as they wrote the Epistles.

Let us begin with the Master's message of the great commission to His disciples...*"Go ye therefore, and teach all nations, baptizing them in the name of the Father, and of the Son, and of the Holy Spirit: Teaching them to observe all things whatsoever I have commanded you: and, lo, I am with you always, even unto the end of the world. Amen"* *{Matthew28:19-20}*

The commission to believers was that they teach others to observe all things that Christ had commanded them. Those things which He taught them are called, *"doctrines."* Measuring the temple then means, the acceptance of the pure Word of God. It begins with salvation. Let us consider what Jesus taught about salvation. *"The Spirit of the Lord is upon me, because he hath anointed me to preach the gospel to the poor; he hath sent me to heal the broken hearted, to preach deliverance to the captives, and recovering of sight to the blind, to set at liberty them that are bruised, To preach the acceptable year of the Lord. And he closed the book, and he gave it again to the minister, and sat down. And the eyes of all them that were in the synagogue were fastened on him. And he began to say unto them, This day is this scripture fulfilled in your ears." {Luke 4:18-21}*

In this very brief sermon, Christ proclaimed Himself to be *"salvation."* He began to *"measure"* the new temple by offering Himself as the only means of salvation! The Jews in the synagogue were offended by His announcement from the beginning! However, all the gospels and the epistles still affirm that He was, He is and ever shall remain mankind's only salvation. Listen to Peter's use of the *"measuring rod"* in this stirring message he preached about so great salvation... *"Then Peter, filled with the Holy Spirit, said unto them, Ye rulers of the people, and of the elders of Israel, If we this day be examined of the good deed done to this impotent man, by what means he is made whole; Be it known unto you all, and to all the people of Israel, that by the name of Jesus Christ of Nazareth, whom ye crucified, whom God raised from the dead, even by him doth this man stand here before you whole. This is the stone which was set at naught of you builders, which is become the head of the corner. Neither is there salvation in any other: for there is none other name under heaven given among men, whereby we must be saved." {Acts 4:8-12}*

After the people had heard the Word that Peter preached concerning Christ's crucifixion and that He was indeed the Lord, this is how it affected them... *"Now when they heard this, they were pricked in their heart, and said unto Peter and the rest of the apostles, Men and brethren, what shall we do? Then Peter said unto them, Repent, and be baptized every one of you in the name of Jesus Christ for the remission of sins, and ye shall receive the gift of the Holy Spirit. {Acts 2:37-38}*

**Keep in mind that we are "measuring" the temple or the pattern of acceptance into the Kingdom of God.**

The book of Acts continues to record the wonderful works that God accomplished through the, *"measuring rod"* of His Word. Paul's letters to the churches were all filled with the *"measuring rod"* of God's word. Just listen to these stirring words inspired by the Holy Spirit as Paul wrote… *"The word is nigh thee, even in thy mouth and in thy heart: that is, the word of faith that we preach; That if thou shalt confess with thy mouth the Lord Jesus, and shalt believe in thine heart that God hath raised him from the dead, thou shalt be saved. For with the heart man believeth unto righteousness; and with the mouth confession is made unto salvation…For whosoever shall call upon the name of the Lord shall be saved. So then faith cometh by hearing, and hearing by the word of God." {Romans 10:8-10/13/17}*

**The Apostate Church did not use the "measuring" of God's Word during this era!**

## John was to *"measure the altar"*

Under the Old Testament tabernacle worship, the priest placed an animal sacrifice on the altar to atone for the sins of the people. In this glorious New Testament age of grace, mercy and love, we no longer need an earthly priest to minister the blood of bulls and goats for sin. We now have an high priest in Christ who offered Himself once for the sins of all mankind. Jesus laid Himself on the altar of sacrifice and God accepted His sacrifice. He was and is that perfect atonement for man's sin!

This is our blessed assurance… *"But God commendeth his love toward us, in that while we were yet sinners, Christ died for us. Much more then, being now justified by his blood, we shall be saved from wrath through him. For if, when we were enemies, we were reconciled to God by the death of his Son, much more, being reconciled, we shall be saved by his life. And not only so, but we also joy in God through our Lord Jesus Christ, by whom we now have received the atonement."* {Romans 5:8-11}

As believers in Christ, we may now enter into the Holy of Holies in perfect fellowship with our God. The blood of bulls and goats could never accomplish this! The blood of the Lamb of God cleanses us from all sin! This is why Christ spoke these words... *"Then said he {Jesus} Lo, I come to do thy will, O God. He taketh away the first covenant, that he may establish the second. By the which we are sanctified through the offering of the body of Jesus Christ once for all." {Hebrews 10:9-10}* As born again children of God we now have access into this grace wherein we stand through Christ. We have been made the righteousness of God in Christ!

**The Apostate Church did not use the "measuring" of God's Word during this era!**

## John was to measure...

## "them that worship therein"

Who were these who were able to worship therein? These worshippers represent *ALL* the blood washed ones who have been "measured" by the Word of God. Those who accepted Jesus Christ as the Way, the Truth and the Life. Believers become the temples of God by being born again of His spirit, through their acceptance of Christ as their personal Savior. These are the people who have heard God's call to repentance and have responded by faith to His perfect salvation through Christ. These are the people who have had a repentance experience not to be repented of. These are people who have bowed the knee before their Creator with a broken and a contrite heart. These are the people who have forsaken all sin!

Believers are conformed into the image of Christ through their acceptance of God's Holy Spirit. The indwelling Presence and power of God's Holy Spirit keeps their lives holy. John measured these that worship therein as true believers who had been delivered from all sin and Satan's power! They had accepted Christ's salvation through His sacrificial atonement. They were worshipping God in Spirit and in Truth. They had been "measured" by the Word of God.

The scriptures affirm this glorious truth... *"For the grace of God that bringeth salvation hath appeared to all men, Teaching us that, denying ungodliness and worldly lusts, we should live soberly, righteously, and godly, in this present world; Looking for that blessed hope, and the glorious appearing of the great God and our Saviour Jesus Christ; who gave himself for us, that he might redeem us from all iniquity, and purify unto himself a peculiar people, zealous of good works. These things speak, and exhort, and rebuke with all authority. Let no man despise thee." {Titus 2:11-15}*

Believers now come to God by this new and living way, which Christ has consecrated for us. He is that eternal ever living High Priest over the house of God, whose house we are. {Hebrews 3:6} He has washed us from our sins in His own blood, and made us kings and priests unto God and His Father. {Revelation 1:6} The scriptures are the only "measuring rod" that will lead us into all truth and keep us on the right path that leads us to our eternal home. *"All scripture is given by inspiration of God, and is profitable for doctrine, for reproof, for correction, for instruction in righteousness: That the man of God may be perfect, throughly furnished unto all good works."*
*{2 timothy 3:16-17}*

Many other scriptures are available on this subject, but the ones that we have shared should be ample in giving us understanding concerning the measuring of the temple. The measuring of the temple of God, and the altar, and them that worship therein is a symbolic scene. It was meant to show the difference between the true church of the Living God and the heresies of the Apostate Church. I remember hearing one of the old reformers preach it this way. He said, The measuring of the temple is...One Bible wide, one Bible high, one Bible long and one Bible deep. I can say "amen" to that!

As we continue with John's instructions, we find that he was told NOT to measure the, *"court of the Gentiles."* In other words it was NOT to be included or recognized as a part of God's plan. John wrote...that these Gentiles would, *"tread under foot the holy city for forty-and two months."*

# *"The Holy City Trodden Down"*

John was given these instructions…*"But the court which is without the temple leave out, and measure it not; for it is given to the gentiles; and the holy city shall they trod under foot forty and two months. {Revelation 11:2}*

We have considered the measuring of the temple and found that this measuring was symbolizing the true instructions that God had given through the doctrines of His Son Jesus Christ. The church of God was and always will be measured by the Word of God. The Word is that which brought the church into existence, and it is by the Word of God that it continues to exist! In these continuing instructions, John is told to leave out the Gentile court and measure it not.

Let us consider this analogy from its beginning. Under the Old Testament Temple worship, Gentiles were considered unbelievers. They had no place designated in the original Temple for them to participate in Jewish worship. However, during King Herod's time, he rebuilt the temple in Jerusalem for the Jewish people with many subtle changes. Historical records tell us why these changes were made in the literal structure of the temple. When King Herod rebuilt this temple for the Jews, he made additions to please ALL the people. King Herod added an outer court which he called the "Court of the Gentiles" thus permitting them to have access into the temple also. This addition was one of the many changes that he made as the temple was built over a period of years. Matthews Henry's complete commentary has this to relate concerning the…

## Court of the Gentiles.

The question is ask…"Why was the outer court not measured? This was no part of the temple, according to the model given either of Solomon or Zerubbabel, and therefore God would have no regard to it. He would not mark it out for preservation; but it was designed by the Gentiles, to bring pagan ceremonies and customs and to annex them to the gospel churches, so Christ abandoned it to them, to be used as they pleased." End Quote

Our present symbolic scene in the Revelation prophecy has revealed the events perfectly that came to pass in the "Spiritual" realm. This is what the symbols are declaring. The self-exalted leadership of the Apostate church had permitted Pagan ceremonies and unbelievers to enter into the church. The Apostate church would not come under the preeminence of Christ. It had no use for the "measuring" of the Word of God! It had devised its own dogmas and Idolatrous ceremonies during this era. This is why it was written that John should not, *"measure the Court of the Gentiles."*

This Apostate church, which had developed, was NOT to be included in this measuring. It was NOT accepted of God. The Apostate church had devised it's own hierarchy with a supreme head called the Pope with its prelates, cardinals, bishops, and priests as attendants. As the Papacy developed, each Pope usurped the authority of God by adding his own dogmas to the tenants of the Roman Catholic Church down through the ages. Their origin was from Paganism!

The Word of God was rejected as the, *"measuring Rod"* by the Apostate Church of Rome. Thus it is written: *"the court which is without the temple leave out."* God would not accept this Apostate church as HIS CHURCH! We are assured of this truth because of the actions that were attributed to this *"Gentile"* church. It is written that, *"they trod underfoot the holy city."* The "they," as we have found out are called, "Gentiles" meaning unbelievers in God's true pattern for His church. The "they" that John was seeing through this vision was the Apostate Church of Rome.

The *"holy city"* is symbolizing God's true church. To…*"trod under foot the holy city,"* means to do great injustice and abuse to God's true temple, His Word and His church. Did this happen? Yes! It is written that the *"Gentiles"* symbolizing the Apostate church abused the true church of Christ. They *"Blasphemed"* God and His temple. Remember the word blasphemy means usurping the authority of God. This Apostate church usurped the authority of God. They changed the original pattern, which Christ had established through the prophets, and the apostles, Jesus Christ Himself being the chief cornerstone.

Did this abuse happen to God's people physically also? Yes! History verifies both the Spiritual and the physical abuse of God's true saints during the Dark Age period. We will relate those heinous crimes that were committed against God's people as we move into our further subject of the reign of the "Little Horn." We affirm that God's true temple; His true church is built through His Divine pattern, which He has given through His written Word. When Jesus our Lord walked among us, He always reminded His followers... *"The words that I speak unto you, they are Spirit and they are life."* These prophetic messages are relating the Spiritual experiences and events pertaining to the Kingdom of God.

### Let us summarize these circumstances...

At its birth into this world, the true church of God was composed of born again believers. These Christians were the visible Body of Christ, which reflected and identified the true church. The book of Acts verifies this! This was God's pure church, which means it's people were, *"measured by the Rod of God."* They were a holy people! They were born again believers! NO unbelievers dared "join" them. This was not a mixture of saints and sinners carrying out the rituals of an organized institutional church!

According to the Revelation prophecy, the Woman symbolizing God's true church had fled into the wilderness. {Rev. 12:6 & 14} This would have been close to the end of the second century. With the absence of these true believers, Satan now had an opening to initiate the falling away that took place! This falling away gave rise to the great apostasy. The development of the Papacy proved to be the fulfillment of the *"holy city being trodden under foot."* {Rev. 11:2}

If you will notice, on our previous outline of prophetic time, the Woman's seclusion in the wilderness was to be 1,260 years. We take notice that this is the same time period that the holy city was to be trodden under foot. Proving once again the *"More sure word of prophecy."* Sufficient to say, and history does also record that God kept His true church pure and nurtured Her during this prophetic time. We will follow through on the fulfillment of her immerging from that wilderness experience in the connecting parallel theme of The Two Horned Beast.

According to most historians, the decayed state of the Apostate church is dated from about the year 270 AD. How could this apostasy have happened? Let us investigate these circumstances and we will know...The apostle Paul had written this warning to the infant Christian church... *"Take heed therefore unto yourselves, and to the flock, over which the Holy Spirit hath made thee overseers, to feed the church of God, which he hath purchased with his own blood. For I know this, that after my departing {after his death} shall grievous wolves enter in among you, not sparing the flock. Also of your own selves men shall rise, speaking perverse things, to draw disciples after them." {Acts 20:28-29}*

Evidently, the people did not heed his warning, for these things that Paul spoke about did came to pass. As we have related from the historical record, men did arise within the infant Christian church and draw others to themselves. By the latter part of the third century, many Pagan practices and Idolatry had become accepted within this Apostate church, calling itself "Christian." These circumstances again affirm the fulfillment of the symbolism of the, *"holy city being trodden down."*

## The Falling Away or Apostasy

The historian Dowling writes this vivid description of the Apostate church... "The scholar, familiar as he is with classic descriptions of ancient mythology, when he directs his attention to the ceremonies of papal worship, cannot avoid recognizing their close resemblance, if not their absolute identity. The temples of Jupiter, Diana, Venus, or Apollo, their altars smoking with incense box, and attending upon the priests, their holy water at the entrance of the temples, with their aspergilla or sprinkling brushes, their thuribula, or vessels of incense, their ever burning lamps before the statues of their deities, are irresistibly brought before his mind, whenever he visits a Roman Catholic place of worship and witnesses precisely the same things." A quote from the "History of Romanism." End quote

These Pagan practices were the *"perverse things"* that Paul was speaking of that came through this "self appointed" ministry. During this period of time, the Woman, the true church was not permitted her God ordained place in the world. The preaching of the gospel; of believing in Christ through repentance; of turning from sin; of being born again in an experience of salvation was not preached as the Way to God. The first perversion that appeared in, *"the court which is without the temple,"* was the acceptance of unconverted people into the Apostate church through the ritual of a baptismal ceremony. Infants were even being baptized into this Apostate church! God's Word tells us to "BELIEVE" and be baptized. A baby cannot be a candidate for Biblical baptism. A baby cannot "believe" on the Lord Jesus Christ and be saved. Infants are under the grace and protection of God's blood covenant through Christ. They are ALL accepted of Him into Heaven if they die.

The Emperor Constantine had pronounced Christianity the State religion as a political maneuver in the early part of the third century. Many Pagan and Jewish proselytes now "joined" this socially accepted Apostate church professing itself to be Christianity. However these people languished in the absence of their Pagan and ceremonial rituals of worship which they had been accustomed to. These unconverted church members brought their ceremonial worship and Idolatry with them into this State Church...The burning of candles in prayers for the dead; using vessels of incense; sprinkling brushes; praying on beads, using the so-called holy water at the entrance of the temples etc. etc.

## The simplicity of the gospel of Christ was being "trodden under foot."

Those in leadership positions accepted and adopted these Pagan ceremonies to accommodate their adherents and keep them within the walls of the church. Why did they do this? The answer...It was because the church had become socially accepted and financially prosperous. Those in leadership positions depended upon the members of the church for their financial support. It is a recorded historical fact that "Bishoprics" would even be bought and sold for financial gain during this time. These events would prove to be the preparation for the...

## "Man of Sin"

to come forth and be revealed or seen openly. The apostle Paul wrote about this very deception. *"Now we beseech you, therefore brethren, by the coming of our Lord Jesus Christ, and by our gathering together unto him, That ye be not soon shaken in mind, or be troubled, neither by spirit, nor by word, nor by letter from us, as that the day of Christ is at hand. Let no man deceive you by any means: for that day shall not come, except there come a falling away first, and that man of sin be revealed, the son of perdition; who opposeth and exalteth himself above all that is called God, or that is worshiped; so that he as God sitteth in the temple of God, showing himself that he is God. Remember ye not, that, when I was yet with you, I told you these things? And ye know what witholdeth that he might be revealed in his time. For the mystery of iniquity doth already work: only he who now letteth will let, until he be taken out of the way. And then shall that Wicked be revealed, whom the Lord shall destroy with the spirit of his mouth, and shall destroy with the brightness of his coming: Even him, whose coming is after the working of Satan with all power and signs and lying wonders, And with all deceivableness of unrighteousness in them that perish; because they received not the love of the truth, that they might be saved. And for this cause God shall send them a strong delusion, that they believe a lie: That they all might be dammed who believed not the truth, but had pleasure in unrighteousness."*

*{2 Thessalonians 2:1-12}*

Although this is a lengthily portion of scripture, we need to understand the full meaning of what Paul is relating, for it has a direct bearing on our understanding of, *"Mystery Babylon the Great, The Mother of Harlots."* The believers here in the Thessalonian church were concerned about the Lord's soon return. They were expecting Him to return momentarily. When they met together, they were always talking about when He would return. In fact, everytime they met one another, they would speak the word "parousia" which meant His presence with them or...Will He return today? They were expecting Jesus to come back momentarily. They didn't know it would be two thousand plus years as we have been waiting for His return!

Paul is correcting their thinking here in the second verse, as he begins to let them know that some events will take place before the Lord's return. He tells them that there will first come a falling away. Many commentators have placed this *"falling away"* in the "end time." No! That is not what Paul has said. He is speaking of the time that these Christians were living in. The remaining scriptures follow this line of thought, for he speaks of a *"man of sin"* that will be revealed. What does the word reveal mean? It means that he would be visibly known! He would be seen openly! The description that Paul then gives identifies this man of sin as the son of perdition. That is the same name that was used to identify Judas. Judas meant a traitor, so also, this man of sin would be in that same category. He would prove to be a traitor to the Lord's truth!

Consider these things...In verse six, the apostle Paul makes a statement that the church knew what it was that was withholding this man of sin from being revealed. Through the truths of this prophecy, we have already learned that the Pagan religion was still in force at the time of Paul's writing. The *"man of sin"* could not come forth because of Paganism withholding. This mystery of iniquity that was already at work would be the transferring of the Pagan seat and authority into the hands of the developing Apostate church. {Rev.13: 2b} Paul continues to tells us... *"And then shall that Wicked be revealed."* According to history, we have seen these very events come to pass through the rise of the Papacy and verified through the Revelation prophecy. Paul's further description in these remaining scriptures confirm what the prophecy reveals about this Apostate church. We will keep these circumstances in mind, for Paul's summary of these events will be more clearly seen as we continue to pursue...

# "The Two Witnesses Clothed in Sackcloth"

*And I will give power unto my two witnesses, and they shall prophesy a thousand two hundred and three score days, clothed in sack cloth."{Revelation 11:3-6}*

We cannot leave this prophetic scene until we identify these two important witnesses. First of all, we need to note that these "Two witnesses" prophesied in sackcloth for the same period of time that the "Holy City" was trodden down by the Gentiles. {Revelation 11:2b} We will see the connection between these two events as we proceed. We may with confidence identify these two witnesses as the, "Word of God and the Spirit of God." How can we be so sure of this?

John gives the analogy in the concluding scriptures which identity them. It is thus written... *"These are the two olive trees, and the two candlesticks standing before the God of the earth. And if any man will hurt them, fire proceedeth out of their mouth, and devoureth their enemies: and if any man will hurt them, he must in this manner be killed. These have power to shut heaven, that it rain not in the days of their prophesy: and they have power over waters to turn them into blood, and to smite the earth with all plagues, as often as they will."* {Revelation 11:4-5}

The analogy John was given is referring to the power of the Spirit and the Word of God. We recognize that these events mentioned here are referring particularly to the Old Testament miracles of God.

- We recall that the Lord God Almighty through His Spirit of power opened the earth with fire and devoured His enemies. It is written that the Lord opened the earth with fire and swallowed up Dathan and covered the whole company of Abiram when they opposed Mosses.
- We recall that Elijah was fed by the hand of the Lord in the time of his exile at the brook Kidron. It is written that, *"the heavens were shut up and it rained not for the space of three and a half years."*

• We recall the plagues that the Lord God sent during Pharaoh's rebellion in Mosses' time. The waters were turned into blood along with all the many other plagues that were sent. This analogy that is given in our present Revelation scene is identifying the power of these Two Witnesses.

## The "Two Witnesses" are the
## Word of God and the Spirit of God

The prophet Zechariah further identifies these witnesses... *"And the angel that talked with me came again, and waked me, as a man that is awakened out of his sleep, And said unto me, What seest thou? And I said, I have looked and behold a candlestick all of gold, and a bowl upon the top of it, and his seven lamps thereon, and seven pipes to the seven lamps, which are upon the top thereof: And two olive trees by it, one upon the right side of the bowl, and the other upon the left side thereof. So I answered and spake to the angel that talked with me, saying, What are these, my lord? Then the angel that talked with me answered and said unto me, Knowest thou not what these be? And I said, No, my lord."*

### Again Zechariah asks in verses 11through 14...

*"What are these two olive trees upon the right side of the candlestick and upon the left side thereof? And I answered again, and said unto him, What be these two olive branches which through the two golden pipes empty oil out of themselves? And he answered me and said, Knowest thou not what these things be? And I said, No, my lord. Then said he, These are the two anointed ones, that stand by the Lord of the whole earth."*

According to verse six of this same chapter, the Lord is being even more specific concerning these, *"two anointed ones."* He reiterates...*"Not by might, nor by power, but by my spirit saith the Lord of hosts."* Last but not least, the book of Hebrews records this statement concerning these two witnesses...*"Wherein God, willing more abundantly to shew unto the heirs of promise the immutability of his counsel, confirmed it by an oath: That by two immutable things {the Word and the Spirit} in which it was impossible for God to lie, we might have a strong consolation, who have fled for refuge to lay hold upon the hope set before us." {Hebrews 6:17-18}*

Returning to Revelation 11:3b…It is said that these Two Witnesses shall, *"prophecy a thousand three score days clothed in sackcloth."* What does the sackcloth symbolize? In Old Testament times, the Lord's prophets clothed themselves in sackcloth and walked through the cities to mourn the spiritual condition of Israel's bondage. This analogy is used in the Revelation prophecy, to show that the Word and the Spirit of God were in grief or mourning because of the apostate condition that existed. It was now the New Testament Israel that was in bondage. This is why the Two witnesses are shown clothed in their sackcloth. The Two Witnesses could not prophesy and work openly representing God's true church during the Dark Age period.

## The Two Witnesses were secluded in the wilderness church, which is represented by the Star Crowned Woman.

## The time periods of these

## prophetic events are the same…

- *The holy city shall they {the Apostate church} tread under foot forty and two months = 1,260 years {Revelation 11:2b}*

- *And I will give power unto my two witnesses, and they shall prophesy a thousand two hundred and threescore days, clothed in sackcloth = 1,260 years {Revelation 11:3b}*

**The miracle of the "more sure word of prophecy"
is seen once again in the prophetic agreement
of the perfect timing of all these events.**

We will now follow through with the detailed explanation of these prophetic events as they came to pass in what has been identified by all historians as the "Dark Ages." Why are these circumstances and events so important for us to know about today? It is because all these prophetic scenes are connected together and will ultimately reveal the truth concerning, *"Mystery Babylon"* and her final hour! It is because God will definitely involve every one of His children in making an eternal decision through the hearing of this Revelation prophecy! Let us continue on in our historical trace of God's church through this Medieval age. The stage has now been set for the great apostasy that will mushroom and envelop the world for ages to come with the appearing of the....

# *"The Diverse Leopard Beast"*

*"And I stood upon the sand of the sea, and saw a beast rise up out of the sea, having seven heads and ten horns, and upon his horns ten crowns, and upon his heads the name of blasphemy. And the beast which I saw was like unto a leopard, and his feet were as the feet of a bear, and his mouth as the mouth of a lion: and the dragon gave him his power, and his seat, and great authority. And I saw one of his heads as it were wounded to death: and his deadly wound was healed: and all the world wondered after the beast. And they worshipped the dragon which gave power to the beast, saying, Who is like unto the beast? Who is able to make war with him? {Rev. 13:1-4}*

We are striving to bring all these historical events in a chronological nanner that the reader may follow a certain pathway in understanding these prophetic truths...The analogies of the Holy City being trodden under foot and the Two Witnesses prophesying in sackcloth comes to a fruition in this Leopard like Beast. We recall in Revelation 12:17 that Satan's wrath was against the, *"remnant that keep the commandments of God and the testimony of Jesus."* It was written that Satan went to make war with her seed. Remember! Satan must have a human agency to work through! At this period of time, the Woman's seed, converts to Christ, the true church were in the wilderness. In our past discourse, we have described briefly the apostate condition of the "so-called" Christian church.

Our question now is this...How could Satan make war against the TRUE church after he had been cast down and lost his power to deceive. Let us keep in mind that Paganism was that religion which had been cast down, or lost its power to deceive the people through Idolatry. Satan has now found another human agency to work through. He has found another power to use to make war against the Woman.

As we follow this symbolic imagery, we will find that Satan is making war on the Woman's seed with an even greater deception than Paganism, which preceded it! We will find that this "Diversified Beast" which we see rising up out of the sea or abyss, is a continuation of the preexistent Empire of Rome. We know this because the crowns were no longer on the heads, for the seven consecutive heads had fallen. We now see that the crowns are on the horns. These horns symbolize the powers of the ten lesser kingdoms that came into existence in Rome's later history. We will speak in detail concerning the one head that was wounded to death whose deadly wound was healed later.

## The appearance of this Beast...

is now seen with some definite character changes. Let us examine these changes which will verify that this is one and the same preexistent Beast or Kingdom representing Rome...

The *Leopard*, being a spotted animal is symbolizing the mixture of the various cultures and peoples who now live in the Roman Empire. The kingdom now consisted of Babylonians, Medes and Persians, Grecian and Romans.

The *Bear* symbolizes the Medes and Persians themselves. Daniel's prophecy also identifies this Bear as the Medes and Persian kingdom. {Daniel 7:7:5} History speaks explicitly about the cruel bear like nature of the Medes and Persians.

### John said of this Diversified Beast that,
### *"his mouth was as the mouth of a Lion."*

Daniel identifies the Kingdom of Babylon in this same symbolic language. He connects this feature with the first kingdom of Babylon. {Daniel 7:4}

It is said that the *Dragon* gave this Diversified Beast his power, and his seat, and great authority. The intermingled beasts within this Diverse Beast are showing us the diversified but continuing existence of the Empire of Rome. Let us again employ Lord's method of conveying truth..."*Line upon line, precept upon precept,*" It is evident that the Beast now has the name of *"blasphemy"* written on his heads. It will be needful for us to consider the Bible definition of blasphemy. Listen to Christ's own words..."*I and my Father are one. Then the Jews took up stones again to stone him. Jesus answered them, Many good works have I shewed you from my Father; for which of these works do you stone me? The Jews answered him, saying. For a good work we stone thee not; but for blasphemy; and because that thou, being a man, makest thyself God."* {John 10:30-33}

93

We understand then from these scriptures that blasphemy means usurping the authority of God. It means claiming to be God or do the works of God. This Diversified Beast is the culmination of ALL blasphemies that have come forth from the Apostate church! In our next subject of, "The Reign of the Little Horn" we will see the fruition of these blasphemies and heresies through Daniel's connected prophecy. We will keep this expression of "blasphemy" uppermost in our minds as we pursue the truth concerning *"Mystery Babylon."* She is seated on this same Beast at a later time pictured as full of the names of blasphemy. *{Revelation 17:3}*

As we return to our present scripture, we will consider the transfer of power that is spoken of in Revelation 13:2 b. The scriptural symbols tell us that the power, seat and great authority of the former Beast {Paganism} were now given over to this new administration. We will discover that a new Head or rather a revived Head will now take this place. This Head will be likened unto the old Imperial form of government under Rome. As we review what John saw through the symbols, let us consider this change of authority. *"And I saw one of his heads wounded to death; and his deadly wound was healed."* *{Revelation 13:3}*

## We have previously established that these 7 heads represented the 7 consecutive forms of government of Rome.

## A brief history lesson here will help us to understand these events...

When Emperor Constantine moved his literal seat to Constantinople in the third century, this left that seat or office in Rome vacant. The bishop of the Apostate church took advantage of this situation and claimed Constantine's seat of authority there. The so-called Popes actually attained their authority by degrees. In the fourth century, the Emperor Valentinian recognized Leo as the official head of this state church, by conferring on him the tittle, "Bishop of Rome." This gave Leo unlimited authority and power over the entire Roman Empire. This prestigious position earned Leo the name of "Papa" by the people. Each man who has been elected the head of the Roman Catholic Church has received and adopted this name since that day. He is still called the Papa or Pope. "Viva La Pappa" still rings out in chants by the Popes faithful adherents! This same Leo of the fourth century became known as, "Leo the Great" and is revered to this day by the Roman Catholic Church as one of their greatest Popes!

Looking back into history, we know that the Supreme Pagan Priest called, "Pontifix Maximus" ruled together with the Emperors that governed Imperial Rome. This Imperial form of government was the sixth political Head of Rome. The union that took place here in the fourth century between the Emperor Valentinian and Pope Leo, was simply the revival of the old Imperial rule. The overthrow of the Lombardian kingdom under the reign of Pepin opened the way for the Apostate church to have even greater power and authority. The Lombardian kingdom included the Heruli and Ostrogoths. This is that same overthrow which Daniel wrote about concerning the, *"three horns* {or powers} *which were uprooted."* We will elaborate on this event in more detail under the subject of, "The Reign of the Little Horn."

As history progressed, the Pope crowned Charlemagne a Patron Saint and the Emperors and the Popes reigned together supremely over the people of the Roman Empire once again. Thus, the fulfillment of John's vision...*The "deadly wound was healed"* by reviving the old Imperial head. The Apostate priesthood calling itself Christianity now replaced the Pagan priesthood. The Popes even assumed the tittle of Pontifix Maximus as the Pagan priests before them were called! They also adopted the same elaborate magnificent paganistic kingly attire. It all remains the same today in the year 2002.

John continues to elaborate on this same subject matter in these connecting scriptures. *"The beast that thou sawest was, and is not; and shall ascend out of the bottomless pit, and go into perdition: and they that dwell on the earth shall wonder, whose names were not written in the book of life from the foundation of the world, when they behold the beast that was, and is not, and yet is."* {*Revelation 17:8*}

We also can behold this Beast through the eye of symbolic language...The former *beast that was* {existed as Imperial Rome} *and is not* {ceased to exist} *and yet is* {has been revived as the Patrician form.} The symbols continue to confirm these same events in Revelation 17:10-11. *"And there are seven kings*: {7 heads of

Rome's government} *five are fallen* {five had already fallen in John's lifetime} *and one is* {referring to the Imperial head when John was living} *and the other is not yet* come; {which would be the Patrician} *and when he cometh, he must continue a short space. And the beast that was,* {Imperial head} *and is not,* {ceased to exist} *even he is the eighth, and is of the seven,* {or a repeat of the same form} *and goeth into perdition."*

These symbols clearly define the seventh and eighth heads as representing one and the same form of government only under a different name. The development of the Papacy is the fulfillment of the eighth Head that John has described, for they have all followed chronologically.

As we return to our key scripture in Revelation 13:4, let us rehearse the detailed circumstances that were to accompany this, "Diverse" beast. We now read that, *"all the world wondered after the beast...and that they worshipped the dragon which gave power to the beast.* We have previously mentioned the transfer of power that the bishop at Rome assumed when Constantine moved his seat from Rome to Constantinople. We are continuing in the development of what historians have called the "Dark Ages." We are seeing another great religious kingdom immerging through this Diverse Beast. This was in essence the same beast {Rome} but was now garbed in the cloak of Christianity! John writes that... *"they worshipped the dragon which gave power unto the beast: and they worshipped the beast, saying, who is like unto the beast? Who is able to make war with him?"* {Revelation 13:4}

It is stated that "they" speaking of the deceived people within the Apostate church, worshipped the dragon and they worshipped the beast. How could this be? These symbols are telling us that the very nature, rituals and ceremonies of their worship were liken to the Dragon worship which preceded it. What was that worship? It was Paganism! It was Idolatrous! The esteemed historian Newton has expressed well this transfer of worship and power. I would quote this interesting observance from his book...

## "On the Prophecies."

"This beast of Revelation {Rev.13: 1-10} introduces a new species of idolatry, nominally different, but essentially the same. Now, it is the worship of angels and saints instead of gods and demi-gods of antiquity. No kingdom or empire was "like" that of the beast! It had no parallel on earth, and it was in vain for any to resist or oppose it. It prevailed over all; and "all the world" in submitting to the religion of the beast, did effect submit again to the religion of the Dragon." End Quote

Remember…John wrote, *"Who is like unto the beast? Who is able to make war with him?"* No one was able to stand against the tyranny of the Papacy during the prophetically related 1,260 years called the Dark Ages. During this period, the Beast was to prevail, practice and to prosper. As it is written… *"ALL that dwell upon the earth shall worship him, whose names are not written in the book of life."*
*{Revelation 13:8}*

Many stalwart Christians rose up and tried to oppose the tyrannical Papacy, but they all met the same fate! Martyrdom! John Huss preached in Bohemia a century before Martin Luther preached in Saxony. Huss spoke out against the Pope's blasphemies who took upon himself the pompous tittles of "Lord God the Pope, King of the world, Holy Father, King of Kings and Lord of Lords, Vicegerent of the Son of God." Huss also spoke out against the Pope's blasphemies exposing his extravagant claims to have the power to dispense with God's laws, to forgive sins, to release from purgatory, to damn, and to save. He preached that the Pope blasphemes God's tabernacle or true church, by denouncing them as heretics and then makes war on them. The Pope blasphemes *"them that dwell in heaven"* {glorified saints and angels} by impious adoration and idolatrous worship. This bold witness for Christ and His truth, John Huss was burned at the stake July 6 1415 by order of the General Council of Constance. When the fagots were pilled up around him ready for the torch, he said to the executioner…

"You are now going to burn a goose; {Huss signifies goose in the Bohemian language} but an a century you will have a swan arise whom you can neither roast nor boil." This was a direct prediction of the next forerunner of the Reformation who was Martin Luther. {Luther's name signifies swan}

Martin Luther was an Augustinian monk who taught theology at the University of Wittenberg in Germany in the beginning of the 15th Century. He was known to be a learned and devout Christian. Luther had begun to seriously question some of the doctrines of the Catholic Church. During an official visit to Rome, his spirit was grieved because of the moral corruption that was so prevalent there. This Apostate church lived in the depth of open iniquity including their Priests and Popes! A personal search may be done at any public library to follow the UNHOLY lineage of the papacy! A few unbiased history books should still be available.

I would share this account from
F.G. Smith's commentary of ...

## The Revelation Explained:

"Pope Benedict IX was guilty of such scandalous crimes that he became the object of public aborrence and finally sold the Popedom. One of his infallible {?} successors in the papal chair, Pope Victor III, pronounced this infallible profligate a person "abandoned to all manner of vice. A successor of Simon the Sorcerer, and not of Simon the Apostle. Baronius, the popish annalist, confesses that Pope Sergius III, receded the acts of Pope Formosus. This same Pope has a son named John by an infamous prostitute named Marozia. Through the influence of his licentious Mother John ascended the papal throne, under the name John XL...So the unlawful deeds of Sergius produced this infallible link in the holy chain of uninterrupted apostolic succession! It must be remembered that the Popes have for ages laid claim themselves to be infallible!" End Quote

During this "dark Age" period, the Apostate church denied the scriptural right of having a wife for their Priests. The Catholic Council of Toledo decreed that the Priests could live openly with a concubine, provided that they were content with one and that they should not be condemned.

Wadington's History speaks thus..."The ecclesiastical records of fifteen centuries contain no name so loathsome, no crime so foul as Rodrigo Borgia who ascended the Papal throne under the tittle Alexander VI. He publicly coabated with a Roman matron named Vanozia, by whom he had five acknowledged children. Neither in his manners nor in his language did he affect any regard for morality or for decency; and one of his earliest acts of his pontificate was to celebrate with scandalous magnificence, in his own palace, the marriage of his daughter Lucretia. On one occasion this prodigy of vice gave a splendid entertainment within the walls of the Vatican to no less than fifty public prostitutes at once, and that in the presence of his daughter Lucretia, at which entertainment deeds of darkness were done over which decency must throw a veil; and yet this monster of vice was, according to papists...the Vicar of Christ upon earth, and was addressed by the tittle of "HIS HOLINESS!" End Quote

Alexander VI was the crowned and anointed head of the Catholic Church in their boasted chain of holy apostolic succession for eleven years! Surely a fulfillment of John the Revelator's description...

## MOTHER OF HARLOTS AND
## ABOMINATION OF THE EARTH

Is it any wonder that this pious Priest, Martin Luther was so overtaken with grief at these conditions! As historians relate..."While ascending the sacred stairs of the Lateran on his knees, Luther seemed to hear a voice thundering in his soul, *"The just shall live by faith."* This scripture was in all probability the "seed" that began the Reformation."

When Leo X was elected Pope, the church needed money to build St. Peter's Basilica. A Papal bull was issued that would grant indulgences to people if they gave a sum of money into the coffers of the church. {In the Catholic Church, Indulgences are given as a remission for sins committed or punishment due the person for a specific sum of money} Leo sanctioned this operation and gave the authority to a Dominican friar whose name was Tetzel to carry it out. Tetzel went into the streets as a town crier carrying this message..."Indulgences are the most precious and the most noble of God's gifts. There is no sin so great that an indulgence cannot remit...only let him pay well, and all will be forgiven him. Come I will give you letters, all properly sealed, by which even the sins that you intend to commit may be pardoned. I would not change my privileges for those of St.Peter in heaven; for I have saved more souls by my indulgences than the Apostle and his sermons. The Lord Omnipotent hath ceased to reign; he has reigned all power to the Pope." Source: D'Aubigne

When Tetzel came to Germany with his indulgences, Luther confronted him and opposed him openly! Luther printed up what is his well known ninety-five theses against the sale of these indulgences and all the abuses he saw within the church. He nailed these theses to the door of the church at Wittenberg and invited any scholar to compare God's Word with the errors of the Church Fathers. Luther and his followers scattered this printed page everywhere. It brought about utter chaos and soon the whole continent of Europe was in controversy! The Pope immediately excommunicated Luther and branded him an heretic! As a public reply, Luther burned the Papal bull at the door of Wittenberg. Thus...the fulfillment of prophecy continued on, opening the way for the 16th century reformation!

Another episode in history, which verifies these truths which are related within the prophecies..."In the year 27 BC Marcus Agrippa built a huge circular arena, which was called the Pantheon. This arena was dedicated to all the gods and the goddesses of the Roman Empire. Pagan statues of their various gods were placed inside this circular Pantheon to accommodate all who visited Rome from the surrounding provinces. In the year 610 AD this same arena came into the possession of Pope Boniface IV. This Pope confiscated it for a "Christian" edifice. The engraved inscription over the entrance of the Pantheon had previously read, "To all the Gods and Goddesses of Rome." The Pope had a new inscription etched over the door which now read, "To the Blessed Virgin and all the saints." The original pagan idols remained! Only the names had been changed! From that time on, Roman Catholic people as they began to be called, went into the same Pagan arena and bowed themselves down to the same stone status and prayed to them." End Quote

This Pantheon still stands as a relic of the past Apostasy. This huge domed Pantheon is even now being considered by historians to be selected as the eighth wonder of the world. What a deception to identify this Idol worship with Christianity! Thousands of Roman Catholic adherents still make their pilgrimages to these various Idol shrines today, expecting some miracle to happen as they bow themselves down before a stone statue. Many are seen kissing the feet of a stone statue! What a disgrace to the true and living Christ! God's Word still says..."*Thou shalt not make unto thee any graven image and thou shalt not bow thyself to them.*" This commandment may have has been removed from the Catholic version, but it still remains in God's Book called the Bible!

I have purposely incorporated these pertinent facts from well-recognized historians concerning these events that took place regarding Christianity and the Apostate church. I trust that these historical facts will give an added credibility to this writer's composition of prophetic truth.

*This interpretation concerning*
*"Mystery Babylon"*
*is not an invention of my own thinking*
*or a private interpretation.*
*It is God's "more sure word of prophecy."*

We have previously identified the perpetual *"man of sin"* and have taken a brief look at his rise to power. As we enter into our next subject of the *"Reign of the Little Horn,"* we will be shown that the two are identified as one in the development of Papacy of Rome...

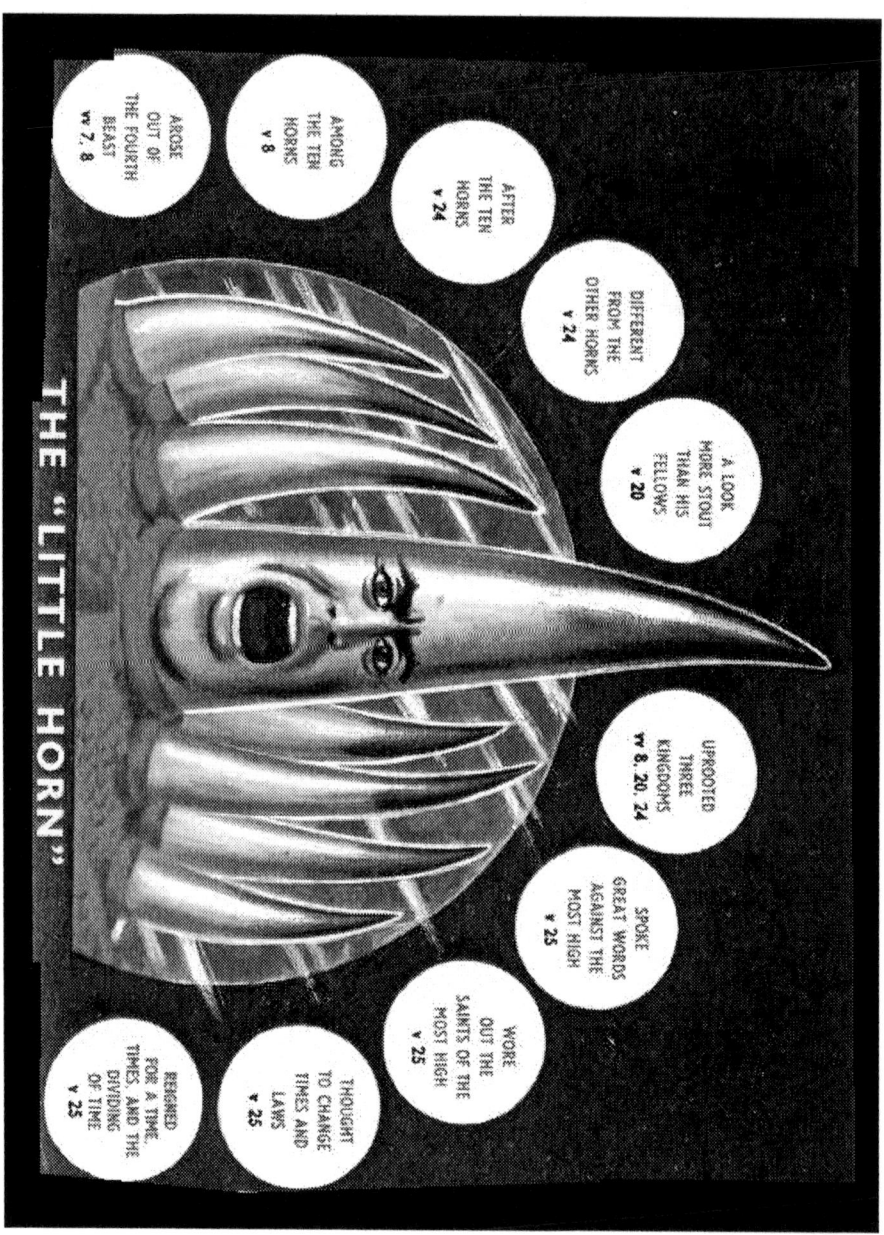

# *"The Reign of the Little Horn"*

The previous picture chart gives all the scriptural references that enumerate the events that came to pass through the reign of the "Little Horn" or the Papacy. I trust that the reader will redeem the time to read and affirm these vital scriptures from Daniel's prophecy... *"I considered the horns, and, behold, there came up among them another little horn, before whom there were three of the first horns plucked up by the roots: and, behold, in this horn were eyes like the eyes of a man, and a mouth speaking great things." {Daniel 8:8}* Daniel then tells us exactly what these *"horns'* represent...*"And the ten horns out of this kingdom are ten kings that shall arise: and another shall rise after them; and he shall be diverse from the first, and he shall subdue three kings." {Daniel 7:24}*

Horns always represent the power of civil authorities. Daniel affirms that these "horns" are symbols of "power." He tells us that they are "ten kings." He relates their intent and purpose and history verifies that which Daniel speaks of. In our previous subject of the Diverse Leopard Beast, we presented a brief history lesson. If you will review this lesson, you will find there the full details of the overthrow of the Lombardian kingdom, which included the Heruli and the Ostrogoths. These are the three kings that were subdued by the "diverse king" spoken of in Daniel's prophecy. Who was this "diverse" king? The Papacy! Who was the "little horn" that came up among the others and plucked up by the roots {destroyed} the other three? It was the Papacy!

We affirm then that this *"little horn"* represents the Papacy that uprooted these three kingdoms. According to unbiased historical accounts, the Popes themselves were more powerful than the Emperors during this Medieval period. The Emperors even bowed themselves down before the Popes to maintain their political positions. The mystical religion that the Popes and the Apostate church had devised held the people in superstition and fear! This condition is affirmed in the concluding description of the judgement of Mystery Babylon the eighteenth chapter of Revelation, verse eight...*"And the woman which thou sawest is that great city, which reigneth over the kings of the earth."* These two powers, ecclesiastical

103

and civil were united in a reign of tyranny and oppression upon the entire then known world! The *"little horn"* that Daniel is considering is a duel symbol. The horn itself is symbolizing the civil power of Rome, yet it has human characteristics. It is written that this horn had, *"eyes like the eyes of a man, and a mouth speaking great things."* These human characteristics identify this horn also as an ecclesiastical or religious king. This is why Daniel said that it was "diverse" or different from the others.

### Daniel wrote that this "horn" had the eyes of a man = The Holy See.

This Apostate church assumes the position of being the all "Seeing Eye" of God through the Pope. Yes, the Roman Catholic Church calls herself, "The Holy See." Since the Papacy emerged about the middle of the 4th century, every Pope has claimed to be the voice of God unto the whole world. This is why the word "Catholic" is used. The word Catholic means "Universal." The Pope claims to have universal power over the entire world!

### The *"Little Horn"* of Daniel and the *"Diverse Beast"* of Revelation both represent the same ecclesiastical power.

We have previously considered this Diverse Beast that stood upon the sand of the sea in the first four verses of Revelation thirteen. To refresh our minds…This was that Beast which had received the transfer of power from Paganism. This was that Beast that came forth clothed in the cloak of Christianity as another deception from Satan. Remember that this Beast is representing the continuing saga of the Roman Empire, now operating under the guise of Christianity. This is God's prophetic truth which history bears witness to.

Now we will carefully and prayerfully make the Divine connection and comparisons between Daniel's prophecy and Revelation 13:5-9…*"And there was given to him a mouth speaking great things and blasphemies; and power was given unto him to continue forty and two months. And he opened his mouth in blasphemy against God, to blaspheme his name, and his tabernacle, and them that dwell in heaven. And it was given unto him to make war with the saints, and to overcome them: and power was given him over all kindreds, and tongues, and nations. And all that dwell upon the earth shall worship him, whose names are not written in the book of life of the Lamb slain from the foundation of the world. If any man have an ear to hear, let him hear."*

We have identified the *"him"* in this scripture as the perpetual reign through the Papacy. The Roman Catholic Church has always affirmed that the "Chair of St. Peter" as they call it is singular. This means that they have always considered it as "one" since they proclaimed Peter as the first Pope. The Popes of every age have usurped the power of God and opened their mouths in blasphemy against God's Word.

**These are the blasphemies that the
Revelation prophecy is speaking of...
The Popes have ascribed to themselves the same names as the true
and Living God!**

## The Holy Father

## The Vicar of Christ

## Lord God of the Universal Catholic Church

• The Popes have always adorned themselves in magnificent, costly, elaborate kingly robes, which are a duplicate of the ancient Pagan priest's attire. As we have previously mentioned, the Popes have used the same tittle of the Pagan priest, Pontifix Maximus down through the ages. The name "Pontiff" is still used officially today to address the Pope.

• In every age, the Popes have presented themselves to be "worshipped" by the people. Their adherents bow down to them, kissing their hands and oftentimes even their feet! The Popes always make their grand appearances with great pomp and ceremony as kings or potentates, with their elaborate entourages in attendance! The prophetic scriptures relate this very happening.

*"And they worshipped the beast, saying,
Who is like unto the beast?"*

May I ask the reader this simple question…Do the gospels present the lowly Nazarene traveling into cities with this great pomp and ceremony like these self appointed Potentates? Did Jesus adorn Himself with the eloquence of a great king with an elaborate entourage? I will leave this to the reader to examine the scriptural portrait of Christ to receive the answer.

Daniel continues his description of this ecclesiastical king or the *"little horn"* which is that fulfillment of the Papacy…*"And he shall speak great words against the most High…and think to change times and laws: And they shall be given into his hand until a time and times and a dividing time." {Daniel 7:25}*

The usurping of God's power and authority by one man opened the way to a dictatorship in this Apostate church. The heresies began to multiply! With each new Pope, more invented Paganistic dogmas were added. The dogmas of the Popes became the final authority, even above the Word of God! Let us make some comparisons here…God's Word offers freedom to all people through grace. It is written in the Bible, *"By grace are ye saved through faith."* The Apostate church placed people under bondage to their religious institution by adding the mass; auricular confession of an earthly priest; penance; sacraments; holy days; feast days; fast days; pilgrimages; praying the rosary; vain repetitious prayers; and many other rituals having no scriptural foundation whatsoever. A fulfillment of that message which the Lord God gave to Daniel.

***"And there was given to him a
mouth speaking great things."***

## The Heresies

- **The sacrifice of the Mass**...was instituted in the later part of the third century. The priests now supposedly ministered salvation to the people, rather than a personal act of faith in each believer. This Catholic dogma teaches that the so-called, "Holy Eucharist" is the perpetual act of the bloody sacrifice of Christ. This heretical doctrine teaches that the bread and the wine actually become the physical body and blood of Jesus. Through this Mass, Jesus Himself is offered again and again and again as a perpetual sacrifice for sin.

## WHAT BLASPHEMY!

God's Word refutes this heresy! It is written..."*Jesus, who needeth not daily, as those high priests, to offer up sacrifice, first for his own sins, and then for the people's: for this he did once, when he offered up himself.*" *{Hebrews 7:27}*

• **The exaltation of Mary...** is another blasphemy against God by this Apostate Catholic Church. Mary is not the Mother of God! Mary was born in sin and needed a Saviour like all humanity. She was surely highly favored of God. She was a faithful handmaiden chosen of the Lord God to give birth to His Son. Mary's devotion to God in offering herself for this miraculous event was admirable. However, nowhere do the scriptures place her in a position to be worshipped or idolized and prayed to.

• **The assumption of the Virgin Mary...**another Catholic doctrine, which falsely claims that Mary is in Heaven as an intercessor with Jesus Christ. God's word tells us that there is only ONE MEDITAOR between God and man, the man Christ Jesus. {1 Timothy 2:5} Only Christ has been resurrected from the dead! Mary still awaits the resurrection at Christ's return with all other faithful believers.

• **Praying to the dead...** The Pagan religion exalted their great men after they died by a process that they called "deification." They proclaimed them to be eternal and prayed to them as they burned incense in their honor. The Catholic Church adopted the same process that Paganism used, calling their process canonization. They exalt their dead and proclaim them to be able to hear and answer prayer as "patron saints." The Bible tells us that there is no communication between the living and the dead. In fact, the Bible calls praying to the dead "divination" and condemns the act.

- **Praying on rosary beads...**In the tenth century, one called Peter the hermit introduced the rosary beads used in counting the Stations of the Cross. He copied this practice from the Hindus and Mohammedans. The vain repetitious prayers of the "Hail Marys" and the "Our Fathers" to the so-called, "Mother of God" are contrary to the word of our Lord Jesus Christ. In fact...He warned His followers NOT to use vain repetitions as the heathen do!

- **The Roman Catholic church is filled with Paganistic rituals...**The wearing of medals or scapulars for protection from danger or injury; the act of the sign of the cross; the crucifix itself is venerated and kissed; the veneration of relics; the burning of incense and candles; the so-called holy water; praying on beads; holy days and feast days are all adopted from the former "Red Dragon" of Paganism! The Roman Catholic religion is not Biblical Christianity! You will find NONE of the afore mentioned rituals within the pages of the Bible. You will not even find them in the Duey version of the Bible that Catholics claim as their own.

### We have heard the fulfillment of what Daniel has written...

*"And he shall speak great words against the most High, and shall wear out the saints of the most High, and think to change times and laws."*
*{Daniel 7:25}*

Other actions besides the blasphemy of God's Word are attributed to the *"little horn"* of Daniel and the Diversified Beast of Revelation. Let us consider the portion of this scripture that I have highlighted along with what Daniel had previously written in this same chapter verse 21...*"I beheld, and the same horn made war with the saints, and prevailed against them.* Then John wrote...*"And it was given unto him to make war on the saints, and to overcome them: and power was given him over all kindreds, and tongues, and nations. And all that dwell upon the earth shall worship him, whose names are not written in the book of the Lamb slain from the foundation of the world." {Revelation 13:7-8}*

This scripture in Revelation is describing the same ecclesiastical power that Daniel is writing about. Why did the Papacy make war against the saints, which are God's true people? It was because they would not bow down and worship "his holiness" through Pagan rituals. How did the Papacy "make war" against the saints? How did the Papacy "overcome" the saints? We are speaking of TRUE Christians as "saints." The Bible refers to God's children as "saints" throughout the letters that are written to the churches.

Multitudes of Christians today are not even aware of the atrocities that this Apostate church committed! Let me share some facts of history concerning this holocaust against the true church. I am quoting the introductory paragraph of Foxe's Book of Martyrs...

"Thus far our history of persecutions has been confined principally to the Pagan world. We now come to a period when persecution, under the guise of Christianity, committed more enormities than ever disgraced the annals of Paganism. Disregarding the maxims and the Spirit of the true gospel, the papal church, arming herself with the power of the sword, vexed the church of God and wasted it for several centuries. This period is most appropriately termed the Dark Ages. The kings of the earth gave their power to the "beast" and submitted to be trodden on by the miserable vermin that often filled the papal chair, as in the case of Henry, Emperor of Germany. The storm of persecution first burst upon the Waldenses in France." End Quote

These severe persecutions were done through this Apostate religion calling itself Christianity! The Emperors aligned themselves with the Popes and empowered them with all the civil forces needed to carry out their heinous crimes upon ALL who would not worship the Beast! {Papacy} We may trace the diminished and suppressed testimony of the true gospel of Jesus Christ during the Dark Ages through these various bodies of people...The Waldenses; the Cathari; the Lollards' the Vandois; the Leonists; the Albigenses and the Lombards.

Let us look closely at the scriptural description of those who worshiped this Beast of the Papacy. It is written that, all that dwell upon the earth worshiped him whose names are not written in the book of the Lamb! {Revelation 13:8} That means that ALL those who had their names written in the Lamb's book of life DID NOT worship the beast. These were the true *"saints of God"* that the Diverse Beast or the "Little Horn" made war against! The previously mentioned groups of people were branded as heretics because they would not worship through the Papal church. They would not bow down to the Pope's preeminence.

This is how the tyranny was carried out against these people that were branded as "heretics." Criminals, who had been imprisoned, formed what Catholic historians call the "Holy Crusades." Their history is very biased and presents a distortion of the true events that really happened. Here is the truth of the matter concerning these so-called "Holy Crusades." The Papacy offered freedom to any prisoner who would join their so-called "Holy Crusades." Their orders were to hunt down and murder these groups of people who had fled into the wilderness. Yes! Murderers were pardoned by an edict from the Pope, backed up by the civil power of the Emperors to do these dastardly deeds!

The Inquisitions were also used by this "Diverse Beast" or "Little Horn" in fulfillment of that which was written. "He" still referring to the Pope, *"wore out the saints; made war on them and overcame them; and prevailed against them."* Few people are aware of what took place under the guise of Christianity through these Catholic Inquisitions during the Dark Ages! Here is the story of the Inquisitors…Pope Innocent III authorized certain monks to act as Inquisitors. The power of these Inquisitors was unlimited and without question! We could liken them to the Gestapo agents of Hitler's time in Nazi Germany.

The process against any accused person was short, for an accusation was considered adequate from an inquisitor as certain guilt! Among the monks that Pope Innocent authorized to be an inquisitor was a man called Dominic. He was passionately devoted to the Pope, and extremely zealous against those who were opposing the Papacy. An order of monks called, the Dominican Friars, were organized by this over zealous monk. The members of this order became the chief inquisitors and were the ones that carried out the execution orders of the Pope. Trials were never granted to the accused, so the punishment was swift and without mercy!

Going to any reputable library and selecting an unbiased history book on this subject matter will corroborate all these accounts and many more. For the sake of God's prophetic truth, which He has called me to write, I must relate these accounts from the annals of history. As a born again child of the True and Living God, I am personally indebted to these stalwart saints who endured such persecution to keep the true faith alive.

## Recorded incidents from Foxe's book of Martyrs

"A respected clergyman who had denied the Catholic faith, one called Adrian Chalinski, was roasted alive in a slow fire; Almericus and six of his disciples were ordered to be burned in Paris for asserting that God was no otherwise present in the sacramental bread than in any other bread; and that it was idolatrous to build shrines to saints and that it was ridiculous to offer incense to them.

*Francis Bibard had his tongue cut out for speaking out in favor of the reformed; afterward he was burned to death. Hundreds of the reformed persuasion were beaten, racked and scourged, and also roasted to death in a slow fire. Their crime was saying that the Mass was a denial of the death and passion of Christ. One of the monks, being of a savage and cruel nature, requested the cardinal, that he might have the opportunity of shedding some of the blood of these people at his own hand. His request being grated, he took a large sharp knife and cut the throats of the fourscore men, women and children, with little remorse, as a butcher would have killed many sheep. After this atrocity was done, every one of the bodies were quartered, and the quarters were placed on stakes, and then fixed in different parts of the country for thirty miles around. This was supposed to be a warning to other heretics.*

*Sixty women were racked so violently that the cords cut into their bones, yet they returned them to prison. What a death they died. With wounds, mortified with infection and pain. Women were ravaged before their husbands; the knife was taken into pregnant woman's stomachs; swords were literally thrust down into the throats of hundreds who would not recant their true faith in Christ! Men, women and children by the thousands were loaded on to boats riddled with holes and set out to sea to drown." End Quote*

112

This was indeed the "Holocaust" of the Papacy during the Dark Ages! Historians estimate that fifty million so-called heretics were murdered in cruel and heinous manners under the supremacy and tyranny of the Papal church.

## This was the fulfillment of the prophecies...

*"I beheld, and the same horn made war with the saints, and prevailed against them...*

*And he shall speak words against the most High, and shall wear out the saints of the most High, and think to change times and laws: and they shall be given into his hand until a time and times ad the dividing time."* {Daniel 7: 21 & 25}

*"And there was given unto him a mouth speaking great things and blasphemies: and power was given to him to continue forty and two months."* {Revelation 13:5}

## All these events took place within the

## Prophetic time of 1,260 years of darkness.

# The Sectarian Period
## *"The Pale Horse and Rider of Death"*

*"And when he had opened the fourth seal, I heard the fourth creature say, Come and see. And I looked, and behold a pale horse: and his name that sat on him was Death, and Hell followed with him. And power was given unto them over the fourth part of the earth, to kill with the sword, and with hunger, and with death, and with the beasts of the earth." {Revelation 6:7-8}*

Each of the four apocalyptic horses has represented a supporting power for their Riders. Each one of the horses has been presented with their own particular symbolic color, which has identified their characteristics and purpose.

• **The first horse was "White"** symbolizing the purity and righteousness of true Christianity. The authority of the Kingdom of God and His Christ was the supporting power.
• **The second horse was "Red"** symbolizing Pagan Idolatry and the supporting power of the Kingdom of Rome.
• **The third horse was "Black"** symbolizing the "Dark Age" period of the Apostate church whose supporting power was the Roman Emperors.

In our present prophetic scene, we see a "Pale" horse now coming forth. This Pale Horse will prove to be the supporting power that will come from an earth born religious kingdom of men. This "Pale" color is symbolizing the pale light of the emerging gospel, which had been hidden by the Apostate church for centuries. Not dark or light, but a cloudy time for the reappearance of true Christianity.

The Prophet Zechariah foretold of this time as he looked down through the annals of time…He wrote: *"And it shall come to pass in that day, that the light shall not be clear, nor dark: But it shall be one day which shall be known to the Lord, not day, nor night…"{Zechariah 14:6-7a}*

The duel symbols of the Pale Horse and then the Rider called death present a rather strange paradox. The Pale horse appears to have good intentions, yet the accompanying symbols of the character of the Rider show a merging into an evil intent. This vivid portrayal of the Rider tells us that his name was *"death and Hell followed after him."* We will understand what this death and hell means as we enter into the more detailed parallel theme next of the Two Horned Beast.

According to the symbols given, the actions and characteristics of this Rider appear to be as heinous as the Rider of the Red Horse. This Rider also killed with the sword and then with hunger and death! He also employed the beasts of the earth, representing the civil authorities, to assist him in his dastardly deeds! This Rider will prove to be another religious system emerging which will have rule in the earth. The previous power of the Papacy ruled the entire earth! The scope of the operation of this new emerging Rider was not nearly as far-reaching as the previous religious kingdom, for it is said that his power was only over the *"fourth part of the earth."*

We keep in mind that the seven sealed scrolls are only an index or a brief introduction to the more detailed events that will follow. This Rider's actions connect with the parallel theme of Two Horned Beast. We will see these symbols fulfilled through his appearance next on the prophetic scene. To lead into this connection, let us refer back to the concluding scriptures of the Diverse Beast in Revelation 13:8-10. You may want to return to those scriptures and refresh your memory by reading the entire passage. In conclusion John wrote…"*He that leadeth into captivity shall go into captivity: he that killeth with the sword must be killed with the sword. Here is the patience and the faith of the saints."{Rev.13: 10}*

The "He" that is mentioned in this scripture is referring to the Papacy and the Apostate Church of Rome. John tells us that in God's time, through the patience and faith of His true saints, there would come a time when the Apostate church itself would be driven into captivity. We are now entering into that prophetic and historical period of time as we look at…

## *"another beast coming up out of the earth."*

115

# "The Two Horned Beast"

*"And I beheld another beast coming up out of the earth; and he had two horns like a lamb, and he spake like the dragon. And he exerciseth all the power of the first beast before him, and causeth the earth and them that dwell therein to worship the first beast, whose deadly would was healed. And he doeth great wonders, so that he maketh fire come down from heaven on the earth in the sight of men, And deceiveth them that dwell on the earth by the means of those miracles which he had power to do in the sight of the beast; saying to them that dwell on the earth, that they should make an image to the beast, which had the wound by the sword, and did live. And he had power to give life unto the image of the beast, that the image of the beast should both speak, and cause that as many a would not worship the image of the beast should be killed."* {Rev. 13:11-15}

The patience and faith of the saints had endured the long dark night of Papalism! Daniel affirmed this same patience and faith of the saints that came after the *"horn"* made war on them. He also wrote... *"Until the ancient of days came, and judgement was given to the saints of the most High; and the time came that the saints possessed the kingdom."* {Daniel 7:22}

The Apostate church and the developed Papacy had held the world in Spiritual darkness, superstition and captivity for the 1,260 years which had been prophesied. Now...just as Daniel had prophesied, judgement was given to the saints of the most High. This judgement came to pass through the, *"Lamb-like Beast"* that now appears on the prophetic scene. We shall see that the time had come for the saints or the true children of God to possess the Kingdom! John had also written... *"He that leadeth into captivity shall go into captivity."* Historian's record that when the Pope lost his supreme temporal authority he exiled himself to a part of Rome called Vatican City. He was forced into captivity himself!

Notice in John's opening words that he calls this *"another"* beast. {Rev. 13:11} This is not a continuation of the Roman lineage of the Dragon {Paganism} and the Beast {Catholicism}. This was *another* Beast, which symbolized *"another"* separated religious kingdom. However, as we examine each of the characteristics of this Two Horned Beast, we will see that there was a reference made to the

Dragon. John said, *"he spake as a dragon."* Let us begin our examination of these symbols and let God speak His understanding to our hearts…First, John saw this Two Horned Beast *"coming up out of the earth."* This Beast or kingdom of religion was "earth born," meaning that man birthed it or brought it into existence. It was not Heaven born! God did not birth this religion! He did not bring it into existence! He did not sanction it! How do we make this determination? We determine this by following the historical accounts of Christianity just as we have been doing.

On the positive side, we will find the fulfillment of this Two Horned Beast in the 16th century Protestant Reformation. On the negative side, it will have its fulfillment in the development of the many schisms and sects that have emanated from man's designed Protestant institutions. Let us look at the symbolic features of this Beast. The "two horns" on this Beast represent the "two civil powers" that gave their support to the 16th Century Reformation. Germany was the *"horn"* symbolizing the civil power that supported Luther as he protested and stood against the Roman Catholic Church. Martin Luther was the catholic priest who defected from the Apostate church of Rome. The other *"horn"* or civil power was England, which supported Zwiggle's efforts. He was another stalwart reformer who came forth also protesting the heresies of the Popedom.

These two powerful men of God along with thousands of their adherents from Germany and England broke forth from the tyranny of the Papacy. They "protested" the Papacy and declared their freedom to worship God according to the dictates of their own hearts through the scriptures. Thus the name "Protestantism" was formed. The 16th century Protestant Reformation was progressive and on going. After the death of Luther and Swiggle, God raised up John Calvin. He began what was called, "The Reformer's Party." Over two thousand congregations of "Protestants" were established in France, Italy, Germany, Holland, England and Scotland. Thus…Another religious kingdom began to take root in the earth. As John had written…It was "earth born."

John also had told us that this Beast *"had two horns like a lamb.* This Two Horned Beast, as a new kingdom of religion put on an appearance of being a *"Lamb"* trying to represent the true Lamb of God. However, some of his characteristics deny this! Does a lamb in the natural have horns? I think not! As we have mentioned, those two horns are symbolizing the civil powers that sustained this Beast or this earth born religion. Does the true Lamb of God need civil powers to sustain His Kingdom? No! John also wrote that this Beast *"spake as a Dragon"* meaning that there were things spoken, taught and accepted that came forth from Paganism. Does the true Lamb of God speak as the Dragon? Does the true Lamb of God teach and accept that which comes forth from Paganism? I think not! The Dragon always represents Paganism and Idolatry.

This Two-Horned Beast also exercised the same power as the first Beast whose deadly wound was healed. {Revelation 13: 12} As strange as it may seem, after fighting to get free from the oppression of the Papacy, this Two Horned Beast is now seen exercising the same power over humanity as the previous Beast. It is said that this Two Horned Beast also caused multitudes to worship the first Beast!

How could this happen? John is telling us through these symbols that this earth-born Beast caused the people to worship in much the same manner, ritual or pattern as the first Beast was worshipped. John calls it an "Image" in his continuing description. On the positive side...Great wonders are attributed to this Beast! {Rev.13:13} It is written that, *"fire came down from Heaven."* What was this fire from Heaven? What were these great wonders? As we have stated, this Two Horned Beast has duel characteristics that appear to be paradoxical. Some good and some evil tendencies are symbolized in his mannerisms and actions. These *"Great wonders"* were seen as the Holy fire from Heaven, or the anointing of God that fell upon the stalwart Reformers who came forth protesting the Apostate Church of Rome. The first reformers preached the everlasting gospel wherein people could be born again of God! Yes! God did work through these men to accomplish His purpose in restoring the truth of salvation and exposing the darkness of the Apostate Church. God worked these miracles and sent the fire from heaven BEFORE the "Image" began to appear and sect making began.

More explanation is given concerning the events that came to pass as John writes that an..."*Image was made to the beast, which had the wound by a sword, and did live."* {Revelation 13:14} We affirm that this Beast which had the wound by a sword, and did live, still represents the original first Beast which existed as Paganism. As we have followed the symbols, we found that Paganism transferred its power to the Diverse Beast, which was the Papacy. We know this because John said that this Beast still lived. That means this religion still had supporters "people" who continued to serve and worship through this religion. They kept it alive! The Catholic Church lives on and on and on...still in its Apostate state! In their ignorance of the Word of God, Catholic adherents still keep this Apostate Church alive!

We have learned from John's description of this Two Horned Beast or Kingdom of religion that it had a duel personality. It not only *"doeth great wonders"* but it also *"deceived them that dwell on the earth."* What was this deception? It was the *"Image"* that was made. No! It was not a physical image, but an image in the Spiritual realm. This Two Horned Beast re-produced a Spiritual likeness of the previous Beasts. Their "worship" was an image or a copy of the same ceremonies, rituals, forms and traditions of the Apostate church. They did not continue to *"search the scriptures"* for the TRUE pattern of worship! They just walked in the "pale" light that had been revealed in fragments from their reformers.

## The Second Stage of Apostasy

As we continue to follow the course of history, we will see that this "Two Horned Beast" was indeed a second stage of apostasy! It is written in Rev 13:11, that this Two Horned Beast *"spake as a dragon."* Meaning that Pagan ideologies and practices still remained in their forms and rituals of worship. We will see this when we examine the "Image" that was made. The symbols also tell us that this Two-Horned Beast exercised all the power of the previous Beast and caused all the earth to "worship" through their designated way. The Revelation prophecy proclaims that these events happened! The history of Protestantism confirms it!

## Let us reflect on these events ...

We wonder how these things could have taken place after God had blest the reformers with such a wonderful deliverance from the bondage and captivity of the Papacy! The reason was that they did not discern the nature of the true scriptural church of God. They were limited to only a "pale" light after immerging from the darkness of the

Apostate Church. This second stage of the apostasy also happened because the reformers and their followers became divisive among themselves. The followers of Martin Luther believed strongly in his foundational doctrine of *"The just shall live by faith."* They separated themselves to become "Lutherans." And so it went with all the other reformers. Luther himself denounced Zwingli as a heretic, and the Calvinists would have nothing to do with the Lutherans. Then we have Calvin at Geneva sanctioning the burning of Servetus because of his different views on Christianity. Crammer consenting to the execution of two anti-Baptists. Even John Knox held the view that all Roman Catholics in Scotland ought to be put to death. Anglican Protestants actually waged cruel and relentless war against all Protestants who refused to conform to the established church of England.

After their respective leaders died, the followers of each of the reformers began to separate themselves into hostile sects. Each sect tenaciously adhering to what specific doctrine their founder had brought forth. As Protestantism settled down into its various sects and schisms, each held their own adherents in a "Spiritual bondage" with their particular stance. Each creating their own particular forms, creeds, rituals and ecclesiastical rule.

As the fourth sealed scroll was opened, the symbols described these events of this Rider and the Pale Horse…*"And I looked, and behold a pale horse: and his name that sat on him was death, and Hell followed with him. And power was given unto them over a fourth part of the earth, to kill with the sword, and with hunger, and with death, and with the beasts of the earth." {Revelation 6:8}*

# We see again that history has confirmed the…
## *"more sure word of prophecy."*

This Pale Horse and Rider is symbolizing Protestantism as a whole and the beasts of the earth represent the civil authorities who supported their warfare. Protestants did actually wage war against each other because of their different doctrinal beliefs! Yes! Each of their respective countries were involved in this so-called holy war, fighting one against the other! This war lasted for thirty years! In fact, historians' have branded this the "Thirty Year War" of Protestantism.

These historical events are the fulfillment of what John wrote about in *Revelation 13: 15...* "*And he had power to give life unto the image of the beast, that the image of the beast should both speak, and cause that as many as would not worship the image of the beast should be killed.*"

Life comes through the support of people who have loyalty to their belief system. What any religion speaks becomes their belief system and brings forth life. Yes! It also brings death! Many so-called "Holy wars" have been fought in the name of religion. I would like to make a profound statement right here! The true and Living God and the Father of our Lord Jesus Christ has never taken part in any of these so-called holy wars! Jesus said, "*He who takes up the sword shall die by the sword.*"

## Understanding the Spiritual Image which Protestantism made...

**1. The Apostate Church of Rome denied the Divine Theocracy of God.** "Theocracy" means being governed by the Lord Jesus Christ through His Word {His Bible Doctrine} and by the power of the Holy Spirit. The Beast {Catholicism} has usurped the authority of God by instituting a monarchy ruled by one man called the Pope as the head of their church. Throughout the past centuries, these Popes have replaced the pure Word of God with their dogmas and traditional practices, which are actually rooted in Paganism and Idolatry. They have mixed just enough of the Bible into their teachings to deceive people.

## The "Image" made by Protestantism

Every Protestant denomination has made its own administrative head or ecclesiastical hierarchy, thus making an image to the Beast or Catholicism, which existed before it. They have also rejected the "Theocracy" of God. As we have learned from our past symbols, this lamb like Two Horned Beast also "*spake as the dragon,*" incorporating many of the same idolatrous practices.

# Ecclesiastical systems

**Episcopalians**...Rule by Superior order of Clergy
**Rule of Elders** ...Presbyterianism
**Ministerial Assemblies**...Democratic rule
**Fellowship Conferences**...Congregationalism

The Lord Jesus Christ is the only designated Head of His church in the earth. He said...

*"I will build my church and the gates of hell shall not prevail against it."*

He is still building it His designated way, for those who will believe and accept it through the written Word of God. God places the members in the Body of Christ as it pleases Him through their calling by the Holy Spirit. God will call true shepherds to Pastor His flocks...IF...people will have faith and permit Him to do so. Nowhere in the scriptures will you find that the sheep are searching for a Shepherd through a pulpit committee. Amen? No record is given in any of the epistles about boards or committees governing God's church. We read that the Holy Spirit was the ONLY One who did all the administration that was needed. This was and still is the Divine pattern of instruction God has given for ALL generations to follow...*"And he gave some, apostles; and some, prophets; and some, evangelists; and some, pastors and teachers; For the perfecting of the saints, for the work of the ministry, for the edifying of the body of Christ: Till we all come into the unity of the faith, and of the knowledge of the Son of God, unto a perfect man, unto the measure of the stature of the fullness of Christ."* {Ephesians 4:11-15}

**2.   The Apostate Church substituted church membership and baptism** in place of a true experience of salvation. The Priests baptized infants as an entrance into this Apostate church. They also followed up with "catechism" classes and "confirmation ceremonies" of indoctrination to hold their adherents' captive for life.

## The "Image" made by Protestantism

Protestantism has reproduced its various means of "church joining" which has also replaced the personal salvation that God offers. Many Protestant sects have embraced the infant baptism of the Apostate church. Others employ a "sprinkling" ritual as an induction into their particular persuasion. The more liturgical churches have used the "catechism" indoctrinating process. Most evangelical sects have a formal "church joining" service for those adherents who choose to become members. Many congregations simply welcome their new members with the, "right hand of fellowship." Some denominations have people sign a commitment card for membership into their organization.

Joining a church will never save anyone! Joining a church will never bring Christ's salvation! Joining a church will never atone for sin! Joining a church will never get anyone into Heaven! Joining a church will never keep anyone out of Hell! Why is church joining an intricate part of the denominational system? It is because membership obligates people to be "loyal" to that particular persuasion in financial support and participation. This is a "fleshly" concept of loyalty! Loyalty to Christ comes through His Spirit of Love within and it will prompt true fellowship in the Body of Christ apart from membership contrived of men.

The Word of God tells us that *"whosoever believes and is baptized shall be saved."* The Lord added to the church daily those that were saved. The Word tells us that we are accepted of God through His Son Jesus Christ and all baptized into His Body by that self same Spirit as believers.

Jesus said, *"Ye must be born again to enter into His church or into His kingdom."* According to the word of God, the joining of an earthly institution divides the Body of Christ. The apostle Paul wrote these words of reproof and correction to the Corinthian church…*"Now I beseech you, brethren, by the name of our Lord Jesus Christ, that ye all speak the same thing, and that there be no divisions among you; but that ye be perfectly joined together in the same mind and in the same judgement…Now this I say, that everyone of you saith, I am of Paul; and I of Apollos; and I of Cephas; and I of Christ. Is Christ divided? Was Paul crucified for you? Or were you baptized in the name of Paul?" {1 Cor. 1:10-13}* This message is as relevant today as when it was written. God is more than able to govern His Church apart from the confusion of men's ideologies. In fact, He will accept no other way!

**3. The Sacrifice of the Mass**, and the vain repetitious chanting of prayers as their form of worship, has been instituted by the Roman Catholic religion. This is a complete distortion and utter misrepresentation of the sacrifice of Jesus, which He made on Calvary!

## A brief explanation of the Mass

The Roman Catholic Church believes and teaches that in every Mass, in every church, throughout the world {estimated at up to 200,000 Masses a day} Jesus Christ is being offered up again, physically, as a sacrifice for sin to benefit not only those who are alive, but the dead as well! Every Roman Catholic Mass is a recreation of Jesus' death for the sins of the world. Not a symbolic re-creation...but a literal, actual offering of the flesh and the blood of our Lord Jesus Christ to make daily atonement for all the sins that have been daily committed since Jesus was crucified over 2,000 years ago. This is why the bread and the wine must physically become Jesus' body and blood – so they can be offered for sin: the Holy Eucharist is the perpetual continuation of the act of sacrifice and surrender of our Lord. According to the dogma of Rome, the Mass is identical to Calvary —it is a sacrifice for sin – it must be perpetuated to take a way sin." End Quote

{Selected from the Catholic Chronicles}

**According to the Word of God...**Christ completed the atonement in one sacrifice. It is written: *"Who needeth not daily, as those high priests, to offer up sacrifice, first for his own sins, and then for the people's. This he did once, when He offered up Himself."* {Hebrews 7:27}.

It is interesting to note that the Catholic adherents are denied their Biblical right to partake of the wine, which represents the "Blood Covenant" of Christ. Only the priests are permitted to partake of the wine. As the Mass is said, a Catholic prayer book orders their worship services. The priest and the congregation chant in unison back and forth in a vain repetitious litany. Auricular confession to an earthly priest, who supposedly gives them absolution from their committed sins, is also a part of this so-called worship. The Apostate church has devised all these Spiritual innovations! You will find NONE of them in the Bible!

## The "Image" made by Protestantism

As the Catholic Church has their pre-programmed prayer book to guide their participants, so a pre-programmed church bulletin orders and instructs most every Protestant worship service in today's religious institutions. Like the Catholic Church, the partaking of what is unscripturally called the, "Holy Communion" is the central part of most liturgical worship services.

Most denominations offer their "Holy Communion" in regimentation on a weekly or monthly timetable. Christ would hardly recognize this mode of operation as that which He ordained while sharing the "Last supper" with his disciples. The gospel narrative presents an entirely different portrayal of this remembrance supper! It was meant to be a time of fellowship. You will never find the term "Holy Communion" written in the scriptures when referring to the "Lord's Supper." That which makes the communion "Holy" is our relationship with God through Christ. According to the scriptures, this supper was ordained as an invitation to believers only.

The scriptural presentation of the "Lord's Supper" is God's pattern for His church who are the redeemed. Multitudes of faithless unbelievers partake *"damnation to their souls,"* even as the Apostle Paul mentions in his letter to the Corinthian church because they do not discern the Lord's Body and Blood. {1 Corinthians 11:29} Believers and unbelievers are placed on the same plane in this Protestant ritual. The elements of the wine and bread are passed in an offering plate to all the people as they are seated in their pews, or as the recipients line up in grocery style fashion to partake at the altar. The "bread" has been replaced with a fish food like wafer for convenience and given with a thimble of juice from a plastic throwaway container.

The Protestants use the same litanies, forms and rituals, in their worship service as the Apostate church embraces. Generally speaking these litanies consist of the vain repetition of the Lord's prayer; ministers reading prayers; people chanting in unison scriptures back to the minister and perhaps a recitation of the Apostles Creed. In many Protestant congregations, open confession for sins is practiced, which is read in unison from their hymnal. This is a copy or an "image" of the auricular confessional booth used in the Catholic persuasion. Jesus rebuked the Pharisees of His time for these very same actions as He spoke these words... *"This people draweth nigh unto me with their mouth, and honoureth me with their lips; but their heart is far from me. But in vain they do worship me, teaching for doctrines the commandments of men."* {*Matthew 15:8-9*}

He also spoke emphatically that those who worship God must worship Him in Spirit and in truth. This means a born again experience! You must be born again to even see the Kingdom of God. It is evident that this Two-Horned Beast of Protestantism has also substituted their forms and rituals for the scriptural New Testament church. God's original design was spontaneous worship coming from the hearts of true believers prompted by the Holy Spirit.

This is written concerning their simple style of worship... *"And they continued steadfastly in the apostles' doctrine and fellowship, and in breaking of bread, and in prayers. And fear came upon every soul: and many signs and wonders were done by the apostles. And all that believed were together, and had all things in common. And they continuing daily with one accord in the temple and breaking bread from house to house, did eat their meat with gladness and singleness of heart, Praising God, and having favour with all the people. And the Lord added to the church daily such as should be saved."* {*Acts 2:42-47*}

The scriptures record this simplicity in worshiping Christ. Search the book of Acts...You will never find the counterfeit worship of the Institutionalized Churches or Catholicism recorded there! You will never find any record of fragmented Christians governed by various hierarchies of men in the Holy Writ! Christians were ONE in doctrine.

When the first century Christians met together...one had a psalm, one had a word of praise, one had a testimony and the Word of God was preached and studied. They broke bread together had prayer, sung a hymn together and went out to witness and bring others to Christ. Worshiping God was not a pre-programmed set of rituals and forms for the first century church. All worship was guided by the Holy Spirit and done in decency and in order. God is calling His people back to Biblical Christianity through this Revelation prophecy IF they will *"hear what the Spirit and the Word saith unto the churches."*

**4. The Holy Sacraments,** a term used by the Apostate church claims these as a necessary means for salvation. The Holy Eucharist; the endless ceremonies of feast and fast days; Ash Wednesday; Good Friday; Passion Week; Holy days; pilgrimages to shrines; the Lenten season etc etc. All these are projected as a necessity for their complete salvation. Through this false concept, the Apostate church denies the grace of God, which is all sufficient through the shed blood of Jesus Christ. The scriptures let us know that Christ alone is our Life and our salvation. Nothing is to be added! We are complete in Him! These scriptures will be more than sufficient to let us know that the errors of additions are NOT acceptable to God... *"Beware lest any man spoil you through vain philosophy and vain deceit, after the tradition of men, after the rudiments of the world, and not after Christ. For in him dwelleth all the fullness of the Godhead bodily. And ye are complete in him, which is the head of all principality and power....Let no man therefore judge you in meat, or in drink, or in respect of an holy day, or of the new moon, or of the Sabbath days: which are a shadow of things to come; but the body is of Christ. Let no man beguile you of your reward in a voluntary humility and worshipping of angels, intruding into those things he hath not seen, vainly puffed up by his fleshly mind, And not holding the Head, from which all the body by joints and bands having nourishment ministered, and knit together, increaseth with the increase of God. Wherefore if ye be dead with Christ from the rudiments of the world, why, As though living in the world, are ye subject to ordinances, Touch not; taste not; handle not; Which all are to perish with the using; after the commandments and doctrines of men? Which have a wisdom in will worship, and humility, and neglecting of the body; not in honour to the satisfying of the flesh." {Colossians 2:8-23}*

### The "Image" made by Protestantism

The so-called Lenten Season; Passion Week; Maundy Thursday; Good Friday; are now being observed in most liturgical Protestant churches.

**5. The Catholic Hierarchy,** from the Pope down through the Cardinals, Monsignors and Priests all adorn themselves in lavish, elegant and expensive kingly attire. These garments are the exact duplicates of those that were designed and worn by the Pagan Priests of antiquity.

## The "Image" made by Protestantism

In like manner, the majority of Protestant clergy have now adopted some fashion of sacerdotal attire. They also appear in their lavish velvet robes of elegance. Many add the wearing of expensive gold crosses around the neck or draped about the waist. Others distinguish themselves with a white color on backwards in black attire. All of this attire is a show of worldly pride, pomp and ceremony, unlike the lowly Nazarene. Jesus walked among men "unnoticed" in the same apparel as the disciples. He did not "elevate" Himself in any manner to be distinguished above others. In most Protestant churches even the choir members are now elaborately adorned in their robes of elegance to appear for their performance. As altar boys are used to assist the Catholic Priests in performing their ritual, so in many liturgical Protestant persuasions acolytes are used in the lighting of the candles and in assisting their bishops.

**6. The Roman Catholic Church invented** a self-styled place called, "purgatory" which offers another time to receive mercy and salvation from God. The Word of God declares *"NOW is the accepted time; behold, NOW is the day of salvation."* No future time is promised in the scriptures of getting in right standing with God. In fact, John the Revelator wrote these words of warning. *"And there shall in no wise enter into Heaven anything that defileth, neither whatsoever worketh abomination, or maketh a lie: but they which are written in the Lambs book of life." {Rev. 20:27} "He that is unjust, let him be unjust still: and he which is filthy, let him be filthy still: and he that is righteous, let him be righteous still: and he that is holy, let him be holy still." {Revelation 22:11}*

## The "Image" made by Protestantism

Protestantism has also devised and presented another time for the mercy and salvation of God, like the invention of purgatory. They call this time, "The Millennial Age." They speak of another age to come when the Jews are again to be especially favored with God's salvation. They speak of another time when through a so-called "Great Tribulation" time, others will be saved. This deception gives many people a false hope of being saved at another time. We have gone into great detail under the past subject of the Kingdom of God concerning this false theory of a Millennial Age to come.

We found through the scriptures that God has dealt with the Jewish nation once and for all! He sent His Son and they rejected Him as their Messiah and Saviour. Jesus made this clear as he said… *"O Jerusalem, Jerusalem, thou that killest the prophets, and stonest them which are sent to thee, how often would I have gathered thy children together, even as a hen gathereth her chickens under her wings, and ye would not! Behold, your house is left unto you desolate."*
*{Matthew 23:37-38}*

The Jewish people had their opportunity and rejected it! God has nowhere promised that they will be a "chosen" people and have a second opportunity to accept His salvation! NOW is the day of salvation for "whosoever" will. There is no more Jew nor Greek, bond nor free, but all are one through faith in Christ. {Galatians 3:26-29} Since Christ came, we have entered into the New Covenant dispensation of grace.

## "The Mark of the Beast"

Let us resume our investigation of the other activities that this Two Horned Beast is engaged in… *"And he causeth all, both small and great, rich and poor, free and bond, to receive a mark in their right hand, or in their foreheads: And that no man might buy or sell, save he that had the mark, or the name of the beast, or the number of his name. Here is wisdom. Let him that hath understanding count the number of the beast: for it is the number of a man; and his number is 666."* *{Rev. 13:16-18}*

Tim LeHay…and other popular T V celebrities in the religious field have written a variety of books bordering on the ridiculous to the sublime on this particular subject of the mark of the Beast. These books are heralded as Biblical, yet they are filled with science fiction scenarios. These strange speculations, theories, fantasies and fictions do not come from God! We must keep focused on God's key of symbolic language based on analogy. This is the only means we have of receiving God's truth through this prophetic message.

We are investigating the Two Horned Beast of Protestantism. It is stated that this religious system caused ALL, meaning all their members or adherents to receive a mark. What is this mark that they are to receive? Come, let us reason together again…Mankind has used this familiar terminology of being "marked" throughout the ages. We still use the expression in our modern day vernacular. We say, "He is a marked man." Does this mean that someone has tattooed a message on his forehead, or upon his hand? No! Does this mean that a person has a microchip embedded in his flesh? No! Being a marked person is a verbal expression to note some particular misdeed that he or she has done.

Let us see the analogy in these scriptures concerning this "mark." Protestant church members are "marked" with their particular denominational name. They are identified by what they have believed in and have acted upon it by joining that particular persuasion. If you ask them, "What church do you belong to?" They will tell you, I am a Baptist…or I am a Methodist…or I am a Nazarene…or I am a Presbyterian…or I am a Greek Orthodox…or I am a Lutheran and the list goes on and on! They are telling you their "mark." They have been "marked" with the brand name of their religion. The scriptures tell us that these church members received this, *"mark in their right hand, or in their foreheads."* What does this symbolize? Let us look more closely at the analogy presented here.

## Evangelical Denominations

Most evangelical denominations do not require a catechism class, but simply give their prospective members the "right hand of fellowship." This induction is done before the congregation in a designated membership service. Some congregations vote their approval or disapproval upon the candidates who would become members. The minister is usually the one who gives the right hand of fellowship in a handshake, meaning a bond of fellowship or acceptance. John was referring to these particular adherents of the Beast who received the mark, *"in their hand."* These people have been welcomed into another "earth born" religious sect. By their act these people have now received their particular "Mark of the Beast."

### Ecclesiastical Denominations

The more formal ecclesiastical churches in Protestantism expect a potential member to attend their catechism classes in order to learn their particular doctrines. After a series of lessons concerning the history, traditions and beliefs of that particular denomination, they are received as members. The potential member has accepted these traditional doctrines *"into their mind"* and acted upon what they have believed. Therefore, we conclude that these more liturgical denominational adherents receive the "mark" in their forehead. They have now received the "Mark of the Beast." Keeping in mind that the "Two Horned Beast" symbolizes this earth born kingdom of religion. In order to participate in any official capacity within each denomination, it is usually mandatory that one must become a member. Thus the continuing fulfillment of what John wrote... *"no man might buy or sell, save he that had the mark, or the name of the beast, or the number of his name."* {Rev.13: 17}

God's Word confirms this mode of operation. *"I will put my laws into their mind, and write them in their hearts."* {Hebrews 8:10} True believers go through the same process by receiving the doctrines and teachings of Christ. God has written His laws in our minds and in our hearts. Does He do this in a literal way? Does He use a micro-chip? Does He tattoo us on our forehead? No! We receive His Word into our spirits. John also verified that God's true children have His name written in their foreheads. {Rev. 14:1b} We recall that God's prophets of old referred to the mind as the "forehead." As believers, we have the mind of Christ.

## Buying and Selling

Many false interpretations have been brought forth concerning the meaning of, *"buying and selling."* Most of them are pretty bazaar! We will keep our minds focused upon the scriptures, rather than relating the strange and bazaar suppositions of Dispensationalism! First and foremost, we need to understand just what we are buying or selling here? The Lord has given to us this wisdom through His prophet Isaiah as he wrote... *"Ho, every one that thirsteth, come ye to the waters, and he that hath no money; come ye, buy, and eat; yea come, buy wine and milk without money and without price." {Isaiah 55:1}* Was Isaiah writing about a grocery order, like buying a gallon of milk or some foods to eat? Of course not! We recognize that he was referring to "Spiritual" things. He is referring to the "Water of Life," and the "Bread of Life" even Jesus Christ. Believers desire the sincere milk of the Word that they may grow thereby. {1 Peter 2:2}

The symbolic scriptures from this present passage in Revelation 13:17 are referring to those things that pertain to the Spiritual realm. These inspired words from the Lord through Isaiah are assuring all who believe that they may come to the Lord's table and partake of the water of Life freely and eat of the Living Bread. More wisdom is given to us on the subject from the book of proverbs...*"Buy the truth, and sell it not; also wisdom, and instruction, and understanding." {Proverbs 23:23}* As Christian believers, we are *"buying truth, wisdom, instruction and understanding from God."* Buying means accepting it! We receive or accept truth, wisdom and understanding by faith into our hearts and yet it is given to us as a gift. We have been invited to come without money and without price to feast at the Lord's table. God's Word and His Spirit deal with a "Spiritual" exchange, not a material or physical exchange!

This Two-Horned Beast has something to sell also. He is selling his "earth born" religion. Yes! Protestant religion is operating in the Spiritual realm also. Each sect is "selling" their own traditions, rituals, doctrines, dogmas and teachings. Their adherents are "buying" what they are selling or these churches would not have life. It takes a great deal of money to keep the mega churches of today supplied. Sincere people and yes, many true believers have bought what their particular sect has sold them and have given millions of dollars for their support. Million dollar edifices grace the landscapes of most all our suburban countryside's now, offering every social activity to be desired. Remember John wrote these words concerning this Beast. *"And he had power to give life unto the image of the beast."* This continuing life comes through the loyalty and financial support of the members of every denomination.

Let me explain further...Each Protestant sect has built their own seminary or school of divinity. This college training is a requirement if anyone would minister within this religious system. At the completion of this training, they are ordained in a formal ceremony. This ordination permits them to minister within their chosen denomination. He or she has now received their particular brand name or "Mark of the Beast." Keep in mind, God has called these Beasts "kingdoms." We have shown that the prophecy is referring to a kingdom of religion. These "ordained" ministers have now been marked by their own denominational preference. Each minister must have their proper credentials of ordination to be permitted to *"buy or sell"* their specific doctrines within each sect. Each seminary perpetuates their own particular doctrines and beliefs through their ministry. Each Denomination is very protective of their territorial boundaries.

Here is the truth! Think about this...The Catholic Church will not interview an ordained Methodist clergyman for their parish priest. The Lutherans will not hire a Nazarene minister to be their bishop. The Pentecostals will not seek an Episcopalian bishop to be their preacher. Neither will the Presbyterian Church hire a Pentecostal preacher. The Church of Christ will not be looking for a woman minister (*-*) to pastor their flock. As we have previously related through the scriptures, God proclaims these churches as schisms. Every sect of man is a schism and to join one is to add to the sin of division.

**I do acknowledge that there are true children of God in every sect or denominational system of man.**

If this were not true, God could not be "calling" for HIS people to come out of Babylon. I realize that many of God's people have never heard the truth concerning His Divine plan for His church. They have never known any other way than the denominational systems! All have been taught this vain philosophy by the "False Prophet." {Rev. 19:20} Christians have been programmed to believe that it doesn't really make any difference what church they belong to. It is just a matter of choice. God is ever trying to gain the attention of His true people in this end time to hear this vital Revelation prophecy! This is the reason why Satan has worked diligently to distort the truth of this prophetic message! This is also the reason why Jeanne Trovato is striving diligently under the anointing of God to gain your attention! IF...you are a true child of God or IF... you are a sincere seeker of God's truth, He wants you to know this prophetic truth. He wants to gather His true church again through this promised RESTORATION.

Again I must hasten to say...that when God brings this understanding to those who are His children, a decision will have to be made. Catholicism, Protestantism, Sectarianism was never God's design for His people! According to present day statistics, there are now about four hundred or more recognized denominations or so-called non-denominational churches in America. God has called all sectarianism, Babylon. Babylon means confusion! Every denomination is speaking a different spiritual language. God's command is to eliminate ALL traditional religion and return to the WORD AND THE SPIRIT of God. Nothing added! Nothing taken away! This will bring a visible representation of God's FINAL RESTORATION of true Christianity.

Let me make this profound statement! It is NOT the doctrine of Christ that has brought confusion! God is not the Author of confusion. It has always been the TRADITIONAL doctrines which men propagate that have produced the confusion. Peter penned these words that confirm my statement..."*Wherefore also it is contained in the scripture, Behold, I lay in Sion a chief cornerstone, elect, precious: and he that believeth on him shall not be confounded. Unto you therefore which believe he is precious; but unto them which be disobedient, the stone which the builders disallowed, the same is made the head of the corner. And a stone of stumbling, and a rock of offence, even to them which stumble at the word, being disobedient: whereunto also they were appointed.* {1 peter 2: 6-8}

The so-called "theologians" of the denominational systems stumble at the true Word, rejecting the chief cornerstone. We will have more to say later concerning Babylon's confused state. It is my express desire to be a worker-writer together with God that His people will hear this prophetic message and that He may accomplish His purpose..."*That They All May be One*"

**As we return to the concluding scriptures in our present chapter, we will be able with certainty to identify this...**

### "Two Horned Beast"
### as it connects with the
### man of sin whose number
# 666

Christ has given the message and John has written it with exactness... *"Here is wisdom. Let him that hath understanding count the number of the beast: for it is the number of a man; and his number is the number of a man; and his number is Six hundred threescore and six." {Revelation 13:18}*

John has provided us with a strong clue when he tells us that we may count the number of this Beast. How can we count numbers and get a name? God tells us... *"Here is wisdom, let him who hath understanding count the number of the beast."* Certain letters of the alphabet are derived from Latin and Phoenician sources, which possess numerical value. The only way we can count numbers and get letters to find a name is through Roman numerals. We know that each Roman numeral has a designated letter of the alphabet. Agreed?

We have been receiving our understanding through God's symbolic language, and if we proceed in this fact of faith, we shall know the truth. Let us pursue this avenue or key that God has given to us if we would know the name of the man whose number is 666. The first original Beast {The red Dragon} has been fully identified from our previous symbols as the Kingdom of Pagan Rome. This Pagan religion transferred its' civil and temporal power to the Apostate church which was the developed Papacy. {Revelation 13:1-2} Then the Two Horned Beast of Protestantism came forth and was birthed into existence by the image that was made. All of these religious kingdoms have come forth through the lineage of Pagan Rome.

The word "Lateinos" also refers to the Latin Kingdom or the Roman Empire. Now that we have made all the proper connecting links, let us pursue the counting of the original Beast...Let us first count the number of the name of the Kingdom of Rome which gave birth to the original Beast or the religion of Paganism...

# L=30 A=1 T=300 E=5 I=10 N=50 O=70 S=200=666
## LATEINOS = 666

Who was the religious potentate who received the transfer of power to rule the Latin Kingdom? None other than the Pope of Rome. Since the Patrician reign each Pope has been officially crowned as, VICARIUS FILII DEI.

In the English language these words translate as, VICAR OF THE SON OF GOD. According to the Bible, the word "Vicar" applies to the HOLY SPIRIT.

Let us count the number of the man whose name is…

## VICARIUS FILII DEI = 666
### V=5 I=1 C=100 A=0 R=0 I=1 U=5 S=0
### F=0 I=1 L=50 I=1 I=1 D=500 E=0 I=1 = 666

*{A note of explanation: the "0" means no value}*

Now we may more readily understand the
graphic description given to the Beast of Revelation
in chapter thirteen. It was written…

***"And upon his heads the name of blasphemy."***

What blasphemy from a mere man to usurp the very name of the Holy Spirit! In our previous examination of the Two Horned Beast, we have surely found ample proof that this kingdom of religion shares fully the number 666 with the Papacy!

I must relate this unusual portion of scripture from John's gospel that the Lord directed my attention to some years ago. I believe it is very relevant and appropriate to relate at this point…A little background first for understanding. Christ had been expounding on His being the "Living Bread"to His disciples. He made this statement, *"Whoso eateth my flesh, and drinketh my blood, hath eternal life; and I will raise him up in the last day. For my flesh is meat indeed, and my blood is drink indeed. He that eateth my flesh and drinketh my blood, dwelleth in me, and I in him. As the living Father hath sent me, and I live by the Father: so he that eateth me, even he shall live by me. This is that bread which came down from heaven: not as your fathers did eat manna, and are dead: he that eateth of this bread shall live forever...Many therefore of his disciples, when they heard this, said, THIS IS AN HARD SAYING; WHO CAN HEAR IT?"*

I would interject this relevant thought...This Revelation prophecy also falls into that category. This is also a *"hard saying, who can hear it."* Unless it were given him of God the Father, it is impossible! Let us continue with the similarity of this situation that is so unusual. Jesus continued on...*"It is the spirit that quickeneth; the flesh profiteth nothing: The words that I speak unto you, they are spirit and they are life. But there are some of you that believe not. For Jesus knew from the beginning who they were that believed not, and who should betray him. And he said, Therefore said I unto you, that no man can come unto me, except it were given unto him of my Father.*

## {Listen carefully to the conclusion}

### *"From that time many of his disciples went back, and walked no more with him."*

This is not the end of the story yet...Do you realize what chapter and verse from John's gospel that this is? It is...

## 6:66

It seems more than just a "coincidence" that this discourse captures the whole theme of unbelief associated with the Mark of the Beast whose number is also 666! Then to find that the key verse is numbered John 6:66 is amazing! Known unto God...Let us hear the conclusion of the matter. *"Then said Jesus unto the twelve, Will ye also go away? Then Simon Peter answered him, Lord, to whom can we go? Thou hast the words of eternal life."*

I pose this question to every believer and seeker of truth as you continue to read this vital prophecy...Will you also go away? I pray not! I can say with Peter of old... *"To whom can we go Lord, thou has the words of eternal life."* As for me, I am going with Christ!

From the very beginning of this prophecy, we have discovered that the first Beast of Paganism has been kept alive by an ongoing program of Satan's deception through Apostate religions. This includes the second stage of Apostasy through Protestantism. There is much yet to be revealed about this Two-Horned Beast that will confirm this statement as we consider...

# *"The Two Witnesses Slain"*

*"And when they shall have finished their testimony, the beast that ascendeth out of the bottomless pit shall make war against them, and overcome them. And their dead bodies shall lie in the street of the great city, which spiritually is called Sodom and Egypt, where also our Lord was crucified. And they of the people and kindreds and tongues and nations shall see their dead bodies three days and a half, and shall not suffer their dead bodies to be put in graves. And they that dwell upon the earth shall rejoice over them, and shall make merry, and shall send gifts one to another; because these two prophets tormented them that dwell on the earth."*
*{Revelation 11:7-10}*

We have previously identified these Two Witnesses as the Word of God and the Spirit of God. We have also related that the Word and the Spirit were suppressed during the Dark Age period when the Woman {the true church} was in Her wilderness experience. The truth of the glorious gospel could not be preached openly because of the persecutions from the Papacy. During this "Dark Age" time period, the Two Witnesses were seen prophesying in sackcloth. As we have followed the scriptures, the next Beast that came forth was the Two Horned Beast out of the bottomless pit. This was after the Two Witnesses had finished their testimony clothed in sackcloth, which was during the Papal reign. What religious kingdom came forth and developed after the Papacy had ruled over the earth? According to the prophecy and history, it was the Protestant Kingdom of traditional religions. The origin of this Two Horned Beast was made known to us in our opening scriptures. It is written that this Beast *"ascended out of the bottomless pit."* What is a bottomless pit? How could it be a pit, if it had no bottom? A bottomless pit would be one that had no foundation or no bottom to it. This symbolism is describing the earth-born religions of men that have no scriptural foundation of truth to stand upon. It is bottomless, void, nothing there!

Next, we read that this Two Horned Beast was to, *"make war against them, {the two witnesses} overcome them and kill them."* The symbols are relating a "Spiritual" attack upon these Two Witnesses. We are seeing another analogy of what is happening to the Word of

140

God and the Spirit of God. Let us analyze this situation...How do you make war on the Spirit and Word of God? It is accomplished by rejecting the theocracy of God and Christ's preeminence over His church. It is accomplished by rejecting Christ's doctrine and replacing it with traditional dogmas.

We have previously shown the "Image" that Protestantism made likened to the Catholic hierarchy. The Image brought forth various forms of governments throughout the denominational systems. This war or conflict against the Two Witnesses came as these religious systems rejected the whole council of God. They rejected God's true way of worshipping Him is in Spirit and in truth. There was no scriptural foundation laid in Jesus Christ as being the ONLY preeminent Head of His church! God's way was made void, without purpose by the traditions and dogmas of men. To make void is death! Jesus told the Pharisees of His time. You have made void the Word of God because of your traditions. These two witnesses were denied their proper place of authority in this Protestant religion to prophesy or to preach the pure unadulterated gospel! Men were preaching their own traditional doctrines. This is the reason the scriptures present these Two Witnesses as slain! This was indeed the second phase of the apostasy, which was brought about through the Harlot daughters. Yes! It is thus recorded...

### *"MYSTERY, BABYLON THE GREAT, THE MOTHER OF HARLOTS AND ABOMINATION OF THE EARTH."*

This is very graphic language, but our God has a justifiable purpose in using it! This woman is called the *"Mother of Harlots"* so she has to have daughters! Come, let us reason together saith the Lord...As the Apostate Mother Church rejected Christ as her husband, so all the daughters of Protestantism have done the same. They have rejected His preeminence in Theocracy, doctrine and His name also! They have NO husband! Each have taken their own names that identify them. Each Protestant sect takes the name of their founder or their ecclesiastical government rather than the true husband's name.

### Examples:

Lutherans; St. John's Episcopal; Baptists; Methodists; Presbyterians and others too numerous to mention! The prophecy has clearly identified Protestantism as *"another beast"* or kingdom of religion. Remember...As we have previously related, Protestantism made an *"Image"* to the Beast before it. As Catholicism replaced the Word and the Spirit with their Hierarchy, their church dogmas and the Catholic Mass, so Protestantism has replaced the Word and the Spirit by their pre-planned formal Worship Services, their own traditions and their ecclesiastical governments.

In gaining this symbolic understanding, we may now look back and make the connection with the activities of the Pale Horse. As we opened the 4th Sealed Scroll, we read that the Rider on the Pale Horse was named, *"Death and hell followed with him."* Death and hell follows religion where there is no complete salvation offered through the true gospel! Death and hell follows a "form of religion" denying the power thereof to save from sin and death! The truth of the gospel alone can bring Life. It is the power of God unto salvation to all who will believe! God's word declares that, *"there is a way that seemeth right, but the end thereof is death."*

It is written that, *"hell followed with this Rider."* This means that FEW people are actually saved within this Great City of religion. The majority of these "church members" have never experienced God's salvation from sin through the power of the risen Christ! Their eternal destiny will be Hell unless they are awakened to their lost condition!

In our religious society of today, we may readily see by the sinful fruits of people's lives that an unconverted ministry has birthed an unconverted church world! This is not a personal conclusion of mine! It is an evident fact! I stand with the Lord in righteous judgement...

*"Beware of false prophets, which come to you in sheep's clothing, but inwardly they are ravening wolves. Ye shall know them by their fruits: Do men gather grapes from thorns, or figs from thistles? Even so every good tree bringeth forth-good fruit; but a corrupt tree bringeth forth evil fruit. Every tree that bringeth not forth good fruit is hewn down, and cast into the fire. Wherefore by their fruits ye shall know them."* {Matthew 7:15-19}

The religious world professes "Christianity" but few POSESS the Christ of Christianity. Few are walking in holiness and righteousness which God's salvation brings to those who really believe! The Bible still says,

**"Without holiness no man shall see the Lord."**{Hebrews 12:14}

Multitudes of unconverted "church members" continue in their sin, expecting God's grace to abound. This is the very situation that the symbols present through the Rider on the Pale Horse. Only a "pale" presentation or a portion of the Word of God is heard. The whole council of God with true salvation, which alone can save from death and Hell is not the focus. This Rider identifies the many professed ministers within the institutional churches who are not truly saved; born-again; Spirit filled Christians themselves. Many up to date statistics affirm this to be the Spiritual condition of the modern church of today.

## I offer these statistics for your evaluation

**One hundred ministerial students were selected at random for a sampling of young divinity scholars...**

Nearly one third were Methodists...

15% were Baptists

11% were Episcopalians

10% were Presbyterians

6% were congregational

6% Lutheran.

The remaining 22% included Church of God Denominations, Church of the Brethren, Pentecostal, and others who were uncommitted. One-half of these students agreed with the "Pike Heresy." What is the Pike heresy? The Reverend James Pike an Episcopal Bishop {now deceased} declared that he did not believe in the Biblical account of the virgin birth of Christ. He stated that it is a primitive myth and that Joseph, Mary's husband was probably the physical father of Jesus. Dean Pike also named other "religious myths" such as, Adam and Eve and the Garden of Eden and the existence of a sky-high heaven and a red-hot hell.

143

- Only 44% of these ministerial students believed in the virgin birth of Christ.
- Only 29% believed there was a real Heaven or Hell.
- Only 46% believed that Jesus ascended physically whole into Heaven after his crucifixion.
- Only 2% of those interviewed were even interested in discussing the subject of "original sin."
- Only 2 % believed in the immortality of man.
- Only 1% were convinced there will be a second coming of Christ.

These statistics verify the fulfillment of that which the prophecy has already related! Protestantism has presented a "pale" presentation of Christianity from the beginning of its earth born existence. These abuses and deceptions are the reason why this Revelation prophecy is so important for all people to, *"Hear what the Spirit and the Word saith."* This is the reason I am writing these prophetic truths! It is not God's will that one of us should perish, but that all should come to repentance and to the true Biblical faith in our Lord Jesus Christ. I reiterate! This message is the truth spoken with the Love of Christ through the sincerity of my heart!

## The Summation

A pre-planned program given through a church bulletin will be acted out with precision and accuracy every Sunday morning in the multitude of Protestant churches around the world. About the only changes that will be made from one Sunday to the next, is who may be on the program to sing or a different congregational hymn. Formalism KILLS the Word and the Spirit of God! There is no liberty or freedom for God to work through formalism! God has never needed a "structure or format" to work through. Throughout the scriptures, God has manifested Himself apart from the aid of man most effectively! God desires to manifest Himself spontaneously through His Spirit and His Word...not through a three-point sermon based on worldly philosophies! Unless the Word of God is preached with the anointing of God, there will be no Spiritual Life coming forth. *"Preach the Word"* was the admonition given by the Holy Spirit through the pen of His servant Timothy.

As we return to our present scriptures under consideration concerning these Two Witnesses. John wrote that, *"their dead bodies shall lie in the street of the great city."* {Revelation 11:8} We have learned that this "Great City" is symbolizing the earth born religions professing Christianity! We are not looking to see two physical bodies laying in a city street somewhere! We are not looking at two corpses that no one will bury! Let us keep focused on the analogy presented through these symbols. Let us remember that these Two Witnesses represent the "Word of God and the Spirit of God."

In verse nine, John continues to elaborate on the circumstances of these Two Witnesses. *"And they of the people and kindreds and tongues and nations shall see their dead bodies three days and an half, and shall not suffer their dead bodies to be out into graves."* We have previously presented the formalism that has encompassed most all Protestant church services. Let us visualize that formalism within any given congregation. We see a visible representation of various objects and things that might represent Christianity.

In today's word vernacular the "building" itself is being called the "Church." The scriptures tell us that "God's people" are the church NOT a building or denominational name. "People" are the ecclesia {meaning the called out of God} or the Body of Christ. This is the Church of the Living God!

**John wrote...**
**"They shall see their dead bodies**
**three days and an half and shall not suffer**
**their bodies to be put in graves."**

145

**You *SEE* a big opened Bible displayed on
a communion table at the front of the
Sanctuary in most church edifices.**

**You SEE the gold cross-centered between the
two elegant gold candles on the communion table.**

**You SEE the visual aids that are supposed
to remind one that this is a "Christian" Church.**

In our religious society, our minds have been schooled to expect the elegant stain glass windows or the look of a Crystal Cathedral. The elaborate pipe organs, the padded pews, the lavish carpeting, and the pictures of Christ are supposed to represent Christianity. Visual aids are a necessity!

**You SEE the outward appearances
or symbols of Christianity**

However! If the Word and the Spirit have been denied their place and ritualism has replaced them...they are dead! Only the outward appearances of the Two Witnesses are seen.

**We reiterate...**

# You SEE the open Bible
## representing the Word and the Spirit.

They are not put out of sight. They are not buried or put into a grave! Yet! It is said that these Two Witnesses lay dead in the streets or sanctuary of this Great City of religion. They are seen as "dead" because they are not given their rightful place to prophesy. To prophesy means that the Word of God must be preached from the one standing behind the pulpit. The Word and the Spirit have been replaced with a, *"form of religion denying the power thereof."* There is no preeminence given to Christ as the Lord of His church within these ecclesiastical churches of men's design!

An analogy is also given in these scriptures of symbolic time concerning the *"three days and an half."* {Remembering our symbolic reckoning of time means each day for a year} When Christ entered into this earth to present Himself as the expected Messiah and Lord, the majority of Jews rejected Him. They rejected Him because of their religious traditions! Some thought that He might be a prophet, others a good man, but few accepted Him as the LORD of all. He ministered unto them for a period of three and a half years trying to convince them of His Lordship. This sad statement is recorded in the gospels… *"He came unto His own and his own received him not."*

Here is the analogy as it relates to this situation within the great kingdom of men's religions. Protestantism may speak of Jesus Christ as a Savior, however, the system that they have created rejects His Theocracy as the LORD. Likewise the majority of Protestant adherents have refused Him as the LORD of their personal lives. Unless the Word of God is heard, there will be no power of God manifested! Oh yes…I understand and recognize that a few scriptures may be read. Oh yes…the congregation may mimic the scriptures back and forth, but little if any of the glorious gospel will be heard! Little if anything will be spoken about sinners needing to be saved! Little if anything will be heard about repentance; of turning from sin; of really believing and accepting the Lord Jesus Christ as the Lord of all life; of being born-again of the Spirit of God; of departing from the pleasures of sin for a season; of living a holy lifestyle; of a Heaven to gain and a Hell to shun!

There can be no change in the lives of people who attend a church service unless they hear the truths of the glorious gospel preached! Timothy wrote this warning to ALL believers... *"This know also, that in the last days perilous times shall come. For men shall be lovers of their own selves, covetous, boasters, proud, blasphemers, disobedient to parents, unthankful, unholy, without natural affection, trucebreakers, false accusers, incontinent, fierce, despisers of those that are good, traitors, heady, highminded, lovers of pleasure more than lovers of God; Having a form of godliness, but denying the power thereof" from such turn away."* {2 Timothy 3:1-5}

"Religion" does not deliver mankind from all the above mentioned evils! Yes! Timothy was writing about religious people professing Christianity! People who have a form of godliness but deny the power thereof! These people are going through the motions of religion! They are void of the true gospel of Christ, which brings deliverance from ALL sin and makes us holy as God is holy. Please consider reviewing what Peter wrote concerning the holiness that Christians may enjoy. {1 Peter 1:15-23}

The Two Witnesses representing the Word and Spirit will bring holiness and righteousness to all...if...they are given their proper place in any given Christian congregation. Amen. The institutionalized churches, with their earth born hierarchies, rituals, traditions and forms have made void the Word and the Spirit. The whole council of God is denied!

In verse ten of our present chapter, John speaks of a rejoicing that went on among the hierarchies of men, because these Two Witnesses lay dead in the streets. The ministry and people were merry making, gifts were being sent to one another because these Two Witnesses who had tormented them were no longer alive! In using God's key of understanding through this analogy, we will come to know the true meaning. Come, let us reason together... Without the Word of God and the Spirit of God, Satan has an open field for deceiving even the very elect if possible! Amen! Without people hearing the Word of God and the Spirit of God, the ministry of this great religious city has the freedom to project their own visions and or views to their adherents. If the Word and the Spirit are no longer present, there are no comparisons that can be made to discern the truth.

148

This is the reason that there was rejoicing, especially among the leadership within this great religious city. If the "social gospel" or a *"form of godliness denying the power thereof"* is all that is going forth, everything will be coming up roses. This is why John spoke of these Two Prophets as "tormentors." Now, they were no longer able to torment the unconverted ministers, or as we would say in our modern day vernacular, they could no longer give the professional ministry a hard time. The Word and the Spirit had been replaced with the dead formality that had an appearance of being "religious."

John also said that these religious leaders would *"send gifts one to another."* What were these gifts? They would have to be found in the "Spiritual" realm. An analogous word for gifts would be "compliments." They sent compliments one to another. Grand tittles were sent to exalt one another like... Holy Father, Priest, Cardinal, Reverend and Most Reverend, Bishop and Doctor, just to name a few! One receives his "masters" degree or his D. D. degree and is lauded as a great dignitary. The Word of God tells us to call NO MAN "Father." The Word tells us that ALL Christians are called priest and kings unto God, not an exalted few. {Rev. 1:6} There are NO specially called group of priests in God's kingdom to lord it over His heritage. The Word tells us that there is only One that is to be called "Reverend." His name is God. The Word tells us that believers are to be called, "brethren." I have read The Book through many times, and I have never found the afore mentioned exalted titles anywhere in it's pages to identify true Christians. Peter was never addressed as, "Pope Peter." The apostle Paul was not "Doctor Paul." John did not have a D.D. degree and Stephen was not called a priest. James was not called "Reverend James."

The Apostate Church that includes Protestantism, has invented these names to impress the world with their prestigious positions. This is that Great City which John was writing about in the Revelation prophecy. You will find no scriptures in the Bible that present Christ or His disciples as exalted earthly kingly dignitaries. In fact, it is written concerning Peter and John that they were ignorant and unlearned men...however...it is also written that the onlookers who saw them raise the cripple man to his feet, took notice that they had been with Jesus. This may have developed into a long sentence, but it says it pretty well.

I like to tell people who have wanted to address me "Reverend Jeanne" right up front, that I am not a Reverend. I have my Master's degree, which I received from my only Master whose name is Jesus. It is called a P. H. D. That means <u>P</u>ast <u>H</u>aving <u>D</u>oubts.

## The Analogy of Sodom

John wrote: *"And their dead bodies shall lie in the street of that great city, which spiritually is called Sodom and Egypt, where also our Lord was crucified."* {Rev.11: 8} Why does God compare this Great City of religion to Sodom and Egypt? Remember, he specified "SPIRITUALY." An analogy is given here concerning Sodom and Egypt, which describes the Spiritual state of this Great City of religion. What and where was Sodom? The Old Testament writer's tell us that Sodom was one of the wicked twin cities of antiquity. Sodom and Gomorrah were places where that every degregated sin was socially acceptable. God is letting us know that within this "Great City" of religion called Protestantism, SIN is an accepted practice. Yes! People who are "church members" {ministers included} will openly admit that they ALL sin. They will be quick to point out that no one is perfect to excuse their sin. They are taught by the "False Prophet" to confess their sins and then sin again and confess their sins and confess again…and on and on it goes! Sins of the flesh such as, smoking, drinking, gluttony and adultery are practiced openly and without apology! Sins of the Spirit such as jealousy, hatred, malice, strife, envy are openly manifested among those who "profess" Christianity. Paul tells us in his epistle to the Galatians that these people will not inherit the kingdom of God. {Galatians 5:21}

• The Christianity that is presented in the Bible, whose Author is Christ, teaches us that true believers are delivered FROM sin. *"Giving thanks unto the Father, which hath made us meet to be partakers of the inheritance of the saints in light: Who hath delivered us from the power of darkness, and translated us into the kingdom of his dear Son: In whom we have redemption through his blood, even the forgiveness of sins."* {Colossians 1;12-13}

• The Christianity of the Bible promises that all believers may live a victorious life over sin, the flesh and Satan. *"For whatsoever is born of God overcometh the world: and this is the victory that*

*overcometh the world, even our faith. Who is he that overcometh the world, but he that believeth that Jesus is the Son of God."*
*{1John 5:4-5}*

• The Christianity of the Bible keeps all believers free from sin, Satan and self by the indwelling presence of the Holy Spirit of God. *"This I say then, Walk in the Spirit, and ye shall not fulfil the lust of the flesh. For the flesh lusteth against the Spirit and the Spirit against the flesh: and these are contrary the one to the other" so that ye cannot do the things that ye would. But if ye be led of the Spirit, ye are not under the law."* {Galatians 5:16-18}

• The Christianity of the Bible promises believers, that we are more than conquerors through Christ who dwells with us. *"I can do all things through Christ who strengtheneth me."* {Philippians 4:13}

According to John's writings, *"He that committeth sin is of the devil; for the devil sinneth from the beginning. For this purpose the Son of God was manifested, that he might destroy the works of the devil. Whosoever is born of God doth not commit sin...In this the children of God are manifest and the children of the devil."* {1John 3:8-10} Please consider also the entire sixth chapter of Romans for further affirmation of a life free from sin.

Now let us return to investigate this graphic analogy concerning Sodom in greater depth. Within the ranks of today's Protestant and Catholic ministry, there are admitted homosexuals. Yes! Various main line denominations have even ordained homosexuals to fill the pulpits of their churches! Yes! There are many churches who openly declare that they are specifically homosexual congregations! According to the Lord, homosexuality was the abomination of Sodom and He has not changed His view!

Other deeds of darkness have been practiced by Priests within the Roman Catholic Church behind cloistered walls for centuries! According to legitimate and unbiased historians, thousands of babies have been aborted, as the Priests impregnated the nuns. In today's religious world, we now have a flood of reports from many children who have been sexually molested by Priests. Pedophiles in the churches! Who could believe this! Why has this happen? In my studied opinion, the number one reason for this abnormal behavior would be the abnormal restricted sexual life, which has been imposed upon the Catholic Priesthood. Celibacy is surely not God's doctrine or design. It is a heresy invented through the dogmas of the Papacy.

Many ministers within Protestantism have also committed these abominations before God! Why are these evils so prevalent today? According to Romans 1:24-31, it is because they refused to retain God or God's ways in their minds so He gave them over to their unnatural affections. Statistics have been given through recent Christian publications that 30% of today's ministers are now addicted to Internet pornography! Surely we are seeing these things that were written come to pass in this, "End Time" prophecy.

## The Analogy of Egypt

The Israelites, who were God's chosen people in ancient time, were held captive as slaves in Egypt for four generations. Until the Lord sent Mosses as their deliverer, these Israelites had never known any other way of life but captivity. In our present Revelation scene, we are viewing the analogy of the "Spiritual" captivity of many of God's chosen people that have been held captive within this Great City of religion. Most Denominational people have never known the true way of worshipping God. They have all been taught by the False Prophet. All they have ever known is the so-called formal worship service or the litany. This is the very reason why God has chosen to use the analogy of likening this Great City of religion, "Egypt." The name implies and represents a place of captivity.


• The ministry of this "Great City" uses another word for captivity. They call it loyalty. Yes! They bind their adherents with loyalty to a particular denomination through church membership.
• They indoctrinate their members in a cult like manner to hold them in this spiritual captivity.
• They place them in leadership positions within the structure of their hierarchy and there they remain, generally for life!
• Many of God's people have never known the freedom and liberty that comes through the Spirit of God having preeminence in their midst.
• Many of God's people have never been taught the *"whole council of God."* They have never received their full inheritance as joint heirs with Jesus.

- Many of God's people have never known what it is to live the victorious life in Christ through the Holy Spirit's indwelling presence.

This is exactly why God refers to the leadership of this Great Religious City as the, "False Prophet." {Rev.19: 20} God's people have only heard a "pale" presentation of the Word of God in this Spiritual depraved captivity. They have only known the lifeless forms and rituals of a pre-programmed service. In His great love, mercy and grace, God has somehow sustained those who have truly accepted Christ. Only by the abounding and understanding grace of God do some survive! Some are scarcely saved! On the other hand, multitudes are lost!

Included in our present symbolic scene is "gift giving." {Revelation 11: 10} Let us examine just what John is referring to here...There is also a monetary gain that is to be had within the corporate Church world of our day. The Institutional Church of today presents a very attractive money package for those who would choose Christian ministry as a profession. Since God's Biblical design has been forsaken in which ALL members are placed in the Body to function in order, a C.E.O. is now needed. Congregations are willing to invest BIG money to get the best for their investment. The affluent church has become a vital part of the social morality of today. Family Centers, as many church edifices are called have become the hub of suburban living. They offer every activity from the cradle to the grave to entertain, pacify or comply with the desires of their faithful parishioners. These religious institutions perform much like a glorified W. M. C. A. Association or a lavish County Club.

This Great City of religion has become like a megga corporate business. There are corporate ladders to climb and excellent salaries to be made. Included are many perks... Insurance benefits and lifetime pension plans; parsonages are provided; automobiles and gasoline expenses are included in these attractive financial packages. The scriptures call this arrangement a "hireling ministry." According to available and reliable statistics, few ministers in this Great City of religion profess a "Divine calling" from God to preach His Word. Like any other chosen profession, they simply choose a seminary to attend, study the required time and "learn" how to be effective in their chosen profession. As in the corporate business world, the more degrees that they obtain, places them on a higher level for advancement.

Before continuing on, we need to clarify the phrase, in this present chapter of Revelation 11:8. John wrote these descriptive words... *"that great city where also our Lord was crucified."* Let us reflect on this scripture from the book of Hebrews, which will help us to understand this symbolic phrase. *"For it is impossible for those who have once been enlightened, and have tasted of the heavenly gift, and were made partakers of the Holy Spirit, And have tasted of the life to come, If they shall fall away, to renew them again to repentance; seeing they crucify to themselves the Son of God afresh, and put him to open shame." {Hebrews 6:4-6}*

This scripture confirms what we have been relating that did come to pass prophetically, historically and actually within Protestantism. The "sin you will, sin you must" doctrine is almost universally believed within the whole realm of Protestantism today! This damnable heresy puts Christ to open shame as the Saviour of the world! It is written that He came to save His people FROM their sins, not IN them! Matthew writes... *"And she shall bring forth a son, and thou shalt call his name JESUS: for he shall save his people from their sins." {Matthew 1:21}* The Holy Spirit also makes this statement through His anointed writer, the Apostle Paul... *"But If, while we seek to be justified by Christ, we ourselves also are found sinners, is therefore Christ the minister of sin? God forbid." {Galatians 2:17}*

### In plan words...
### God forbids sin in a believers life!

Again, we turn to the book of Hebrews for more confirmation on this subject of sin... *"For if we sin willfully after that we have received a knowledge of the truth, there remaineth no more sacrifice for sins, But a certain fearful looking for of judgement and fiery indignation, which shall devour the adversaries. He that despised Mosses' law died without mercy under two witnesses. Of how much sorer punishment, suppose ye, shall he be thought worthy, who hath trodden under foot the Son of God, and hath counted the blood of the covenant, wherein he was sanctified, and unholy thing, and hath done despite unto the Spirit of grace." {Hebrew 10:26-29}*

You do understand what God is saying here in these scriptures to all mankind? He has let us know that If people do not believe, accept and act upon the promise of Jesus Christ's sacrifice for deliverance from sin, they are counting the blood of Christ an unholy thing. In other words, counting the blood of Christ no better than the blood of bulls and goats, which could never take away sin. Let us reflect back upon the 16th Century Protestant Reformation and the effect it had upon people...The Christian's protest against Catholicism brought forth an enlightened people! The scriptures were again available to the common man to read and study! Many became true believers and were born again of the Spirit of God. They were made partakers of the Holy Spirit!

The "Revival Years" as historians' term them burned brightly, and finally brought forth a holy people. These people of faith had tasted of the good Word of God, and of the powers of the world to come, but they *"fell away."* As it is written, *"they made an "Image"* of their own design. It was not an image of Christ or of Bible Christianity...thus crucifying to themselves the Son of God afresh. Yes! This "Great City" of religion professing Christianity has put Christ to open shame! They have rejected His truth concerning His blood Covenant!

- **They have created their own ecclesiastical rule and rejected the Theocracy of God.**
- **They have rejected the Word of God and the Spirit of God, which produces "Holy living."**
- **They have laid another foundation by their traditional stances rather than building upon Christ's foundation through the Holy Writ.**
- **They have put Christ to open shame by denying the power of the shed blood that God has provided through His Atonement to save to the uttermost.**
- **The Word of God and the Spirit of God have been denied their place of preeminence in this Great City professing to be "Christian."**

The only way these people can be renewed is by forsaking what God calls Babylon {confusion} and begin anew upon the sure foundation of Christ. I have previously mentioned that it is God's purpose and express desire to awaken His people by this Revelation prophecy. I have also mentioned that God will require His people to make their decision concerning this prophetic truth after they hear it. In His infinite Wisdom, Love and Grace, God has gone to great length to convince His people of this prophetic truth. As we reflect back upon all these miraculous prophetic visions, the *"more sure word of prophecy"* can be easily recognized.

## As the sixth angel begins to pour out his vial,

## {judgement}

## this entire theme continues to expand in our next subject...

# *"The Battle of Armageddon"*

Christ's true church has fought three great Spiritual battles throughout her history. The first war or conflict we learned about was with Paganism in that first century Apostolic Period. The symbols gave us the full account of the "war" that took place between the "Old serpent" as he used the Great Red Dragon's civil and religious powers against Christianity. {Revelation 12}

The next battle the true church fought was against the Leopard like Beast, who clothed himself in the garments of Christianity. We learned that the Great Red Dragon of Paganism gave his power, his seat and great authority to this Beast. This Beast was identified as the Apostate Church of Rome, which developed into the Papacy. This Apostate Church took on the guise of Christianity, yet rejected the Word of God and supplanted Pagan rituals. {Rev. 13:1-10} Next, in God's appointed time, the true church {the Woman in Revelation 12:6} came forth out of the wilderness and rose to the occasion through the 16th Century Reformation. She fought Her second great battle against the Papacy and came forth triumphant.

We then learned that *"another"* Beast came forth which *was "earth-born."* {Rev. 13:11-16} This Beast proved to be the great system of religion, which developed into Protestantism. It is written that this "earth born" Beast also *"spake as a dragon,"* meaning that there were ideologies that had come from Paganism itself. This Two Horned Beast made an "image" liken unto the Beast, which existed before it. This Image developed into the Apostate religion of Protestantism.

We have now entered into the End Time, when the true church is being encompassed about by all three of these enemies! According to the prophetic word, this battle is called the battle of, *"that great day of God Almighty"* or more commonly referred to as, "The Battle of Armageddon." {Rev. 16:16} Although this battle has been unscripturally presented by the Dispensationalist's literal interpretation, we will continue to abide in the symbolic truths that have proved to be the *"more sure word of prophecy."* We state unequivocally that this battle, like the previous battles is also a SPIRITUAL battle.

As we review the following scriptures, we will understand that this analogy reflects the Spiritual conflict with these Three Unclean Spirits... *"And the sixth angel poured out his vial upon the great river Euphrates; and the water thereof was dried up, that the way of the kings of the east might be prepared. And I saw three unclean spirits like frogs come out of the mouth of the dragon, and out of the mouth of the beast, and out of the mouth of the false prophet. For they are the spirits of devils, working miracles, which go forth unto the kings of the earth and of the whole world, to gather them to the battle of that great day of God Almighty. Behold, I come as a thief. Blessed is he that watcheth, and keepeth his garments, lest he walk naked, and they see his shame. And he gathered them together into a place called in the Hebrew tongue Armageddon. {Rev. 16:12-16}*

There is much to be said symbolically speaking in these few verses. Again, it will be advantageous for us to use the Lord's method again of, *"line upon line precept upon precept"* if we would see the content clearly. It is written in Rev 16: 12 that... *"the sixth angel poured out his vial."* {A vial means a judgement} This "angel" symbolizes the human messengers that were sent by God to expose this great deception. These human messengers {preachers of righteousness} were to bring judgement on this Great City of Babylon. It was written that the... *"water thereof was dried up, that the way of the kings of east might be prepared."* The expression *"the kings of the east"* alludes to wisdom. The gospel message verifies that wise men came from the east, searching for the Saviour. Many other Old Testament scriptures refer to those bringing special wisdom as coming from the east. In this present Revelation theme, the *"kings of the east or "angel"* are symbolizing a prophetically called ministry. A prophetically called 6th seal ministry would come forth to bring wisdom and knowledge. This message would offer freedom to God's Spiritual Israel {New Testament Church} from their captivity in Spiritual Babylon. Their judgement vial of truth and wisdom was analogous to the attack of King Cyrus, only in the Spiritual realm. Their offer of deliverance was analogous of the offer of King Cyrus also in the Spiritual realm.

# This prophetically called 6th seal ministry...

obeyed God by preaching of the whole council of His Word! God's truth dried up the water to expose the deceptions of the Three Unclean Spirits. These slimy frogs representing men's doctrines had been hidden beneath the water. The judgement preaching of a called ministry reproved the errors of traditional religion. The deceptions of these Three Unclean Spirits could now be readily seen or discerned. These preachers of righteousness, of wisdom and truth, offered spiritual deliverance to the true people of God who were being held captive in "Spiritual Babylon."

According to John's record, this vial is being poured out upon the great river Euphrates. The location is an important symbol, for it will reveal the circumstances of the events we will be considering in this present Revelation scene. Let us look back into the Old Testament to gain the understanding of this analogy. In ancient Babylon, the river Euphrates surrounded the city of Babylon. No one had been able to conquer great Babylon, because of this protective channel, which surrounded it. However! King Cyrus had a plan that brought great Babylon to defeat! During King Belshazzar's notable drunken feast, the armies of King Cyrus diverted the riverbed and marched into the city unhindered. They captured the impregnable city of great Babylon!

A notable and an unusual invitation was given to the Israelites by King Cyrus after he had captured Babylon. He gave all the Israelites, who had been held captive under Belshazzar's reign an opportunity to return to their own land and rebuild their temple in Jerusalem. Some rejoiced and returned. Not all of the Israelites however chose to return to Jerusalem and worship the true God of their ancestry. Why did they refuse this opportunity? Here are the reasons...They had married into idolatrous families, they had houses and lands and were comfortable and prosperous in Babylon in spite of their captivity. Many Israelites had become an accepted part of Babylon's society that they chose to remain there.

Now, let us apply this type with the anti-type given as an analogy in our present Revelation message. Let us consider the "Spiritual" reality of what is taking place as we near the close of the ages of this present Christian dispensation. These "kings of the east" or prophetically called ministers offered God's people the opportunity of returning to "Spiritual Jerusalem" to rebuild the temple, meaning the New Testament church. We need to make the proper connection with "Spiritual" things in order to place all these truths in their proper perspective.

As we search the scriptures to see if these things be so, we find that the book of Hebrews brings us this understanding... *"But ye are come unto mount Sion, {Zion} and unto the city of the living God, the HEAVENLY JERUSALEM and to an innumerable company of angels, To the general assembly and the CHURCH OF THE FIRST BORN, which are written in heaven, and to the God the Judge of all, and to the spirits of just men made perfect, and to JESUS THE MEDIATOR OF THE NEW COVENANT. And to the blood of the sprinkling, that speaketh better things than that of Abel."{Hebrews 12:22-14}*

I have taken the liberty of capitalizing to emphasize the meat of the Word that this was and is the heritage that God has given to ALL people who will come to Him through the blood of the everlasting covenant. "It is finished" the great transaction is done!

## The Literal Israel exists no more...

God has made a New Covenant and now has established a "Spiritual Israel" It is written: *"For this is the covenant that I will make with the house of Israel AFTER those days, saith the Lord; I will put my laws into their minds, and write them in their hearts; and I will be to them a God, and they shall be to me a people: And they shall not teach every on his neighbor, and every man his brother, saying, Know the Lord: for ALL shall know me from the least to the greatest. For I will be merciful to their unrighteousness, and their sins and their iniquities will I remember no more. In that he saith, A NEW COVENANT, he hath made the first old. Now that which decayeth and waxeth old is ready to vanish away." {Hebrews 8:10-13}*

Vanish away it did! The entire book of Hebrews deals with the transition from the Old Testament literal Israel worship to the New Testament Spiritual Israel worship. I have highlighted the word AFTER to draw your attention to that which happened at Calvary. AFTER those days, saith the Lord. It was AFTER the sacrifice of the Lamb of God rather than the sacrifice of sheep and goats that God could enter into this New Covenant with mankind. He can now dwell within His true temple of man, rather than an earthly tabernacle. This was the message of truth and deliverance that these, *"kings of the east"* brought to God's Spiritual Israel. We have related how they, like the literal Israelites of ancient days had been held captive in the false traditional religions, which God calls Spiritual Babylon.

Before we move on into this continuing subject, we need to ask these questions...

- **Did ALL** of these captive people choose to leave Spiritual Babylon with its ecclesiastical systems of man's bondage and return to the Biblical pattern of the city of the Living God and to the heavenly Jerusalem?
- **Did ALL**... of these captive people choose to enter into the general assembly and church of the first born {born-again} which are written in heaven?
- **Did ALL**... of these captive people choose to come to Jesus the mediator of the new covenant, and to the blood of sprinkling?
- **Did ALL**... of these captive people seek to establish the New Testament Church in the earth?

No! Sad to say, like the literal Israelites of ancient days many choose to remain in Spiritual Babylon. They remained for the same reasons, only in the "Spiritual realm." Their loyalty was to their Denominational affiliation. They had become established in their social strata and standing. All their friends were there. They had invested financially in the building programs. They were "board members" who were in control! Many people had purchased artifacts like, stain glass windows, family name pews, the purchase of a $1,000 brick in memorial of a loved one.

Their families had been raised within this Great City of religion. Their beautiful wedding ceremonies had been performed there. The children had been christened or baptized there. Memorable funerals had been held there for their loved ones. They belonged! They stayed! Their fate was the same in the Spiritual realm as it was in the literal realm of ancient Israel. They lost out with the only true and Living God!

This clear warning was given as John wrote... *"Behold, I come as a thief. "Blessed is he that watcheth, and keepeth his garments, lest he walk naked, and they see his shame." {Revelation 16:15}* There is a need to understand this "gathering" into the place called Armageddon.

**John wrote...**
**"And he gathered them together into a place called**
**in the Hebrew tongue Armageddon."**
***{Revelation 16:16}***

As I have reminded my readers throughout this writing, we must always keep focused on symbolism based on analogy, if we are to receive this true prophetic message from Christ. We are looking for that which is analogous concerning this "battle field" called Armageddon. Yes, Armageddon was and still is a literal plan in Megiddo. The plan of Megiddo {Armageddon} is approximately ten miles form Nazareth. Will this great battle be fought there? NO! As we have continually stressed, the battles that Christians fight are "Spiritual" battles! We are looking at the Spiritual conflict that ALL true Christians will be engaged in through these Three Unclean Spirits.

Now, let us examine the analogy as it is used in this particular scripture in our Revelation prophecy. According to the history of ancient Israel, Megiddo is the plan where the Israelites gathered to fight all their literal battles. The fourth and fifth chapters of Judges record two great victories that were won there by the Israelites. This is also where Gideon overcame the Midianites, according to the seventh chapter of Judges. The fifth chapter of Judges records that Deborah sang her song of victory on this plan of Armageddon. Armageddon is also noted for the two great tragedies of the death of Saul and the death of Josiah.

With this background of understanding, we can readily see why the word Armageddon is used symbolically in the Revelation prophecy. Literal Armageddon a place of war, slaughter and overthrow. As the literal Israel of God in ancient time fought her battles there, so, God has used this terminology symbolically to portray the same conflicts only in the Spiritual realm. Armageddon is an analogous term symbolizing a place of Spiritual war; Spiritual slaughter; and Spiritual overthrow! I trust that the reader will compare Spiritual things with Spiritual things, rather than nullifying God's truth with a supposed literal battle of Armageddon. According to the *"more sure word of prophecy,"* there will never be a literal battle fought by our Lord and His church!

## This Spiritual war is a war of the false ideologies of men against the Word of God...

• This war is fought on the annalogis "Spiritual" plain of Megiddo.

• This war is a war to capture the mind, because what we believe is what motivates us. What we believe determines our course of actions and reactions.

• This is a war against the inerrant Word of the Living God by the religious traditions of men.

• This war is being fought by Christians who are standing upon the *"sea of glass"* proclaiming the pure unadulterated Word of God without fear or favor of man.

• This war is being fought by those who have gotten victory over the Beast, and over his Image, and over his Mark, and over the Number of his name. {Revelation 15:2-3}

• This war is being fought by Christians who are *"contending for the faith once delivered to the saints."*

• This war is being fought by Christians who will, *"reprove, rebuke and correct"* error whenever and wherever it rises up against the truth of Christ.

## Continuing with the...

## Three Unclean Spirits

Now that we have established this bridge of understanding, let us return to our present prophetic subject. John proceeds to tell us the origin of these three unclean spirits.

• **The first** came out of the mouth of the Dragon.
• **The second** came out of the mouth of the Beast.
• **The third** came out of the mouth of the False Prophet.

At this point in time, we should be able, to fully recognize the Dragon as Paganism, the Beast as Catholicism and the False Prophet as Protestantism. God's Word is very graphic when it needs to be. God does not desire that any of His TRUE children be deceived! In these following verses, He lets us know in very plain language that these unclean spirits are "devils" working miracles, which go forth unto the kings of the earth and to the whole world. What is their mission? They are gathering themselves together to the *"battle of that great day of God Almighty."*

**True Christianity has fought and been victorious over all Her Spiritual battles...**
1. **The conflict against the "Great Red Dragon" {Paganism}**
2. **The conflict against "The Beast" {Catholicism}**
3. **The present conflict against "The False Prophet" {Protestantism}**

Satan likes to remain incognito in this realm and this is why many true Christians are unaware of this present battle. However, some of God's true people are exiting the institutional churches and beginning "Home churches" or "Cell groups" as they have become aware of the Apostate condition. Although all three of these forces of evil will keep their identity, all will unite together with one evil intent against the TRUE people of God! These Three Unclean Spirits will have one common goal in mind. It will be a combined effort to discredit, distort, undermine and adulterate the infallible Word of God... the Bible! This will be the battle to end all battles! It is the last battle that will be fought before Christ returns! It is called...

*"The Battle of Armageddon."*
*This is an intense SPIRITUAL battle!*
*TRUTH against ERROR!*

We cannot deny the profound verification of the prophetic word concerning this "Trinity of evil." Let us make these comparisons from chapters sixteen and twenty in the book of Revelation...

- **The agents used by Satan are the same in Revelation chapter sixteen...**
It is the Dragon {Paganism}
The Beast {Catholicism}
The False Prophet {Protestantism}

- **The agents used by Satan are the same in Revelation chapter twenty...**It is Satan {Paganism} Gog {Catholicism} Magog {Protestantism}

- **The field of operation is the same in Revelation twenty...**"The breadth of the earth"
The field of operation is the same in Revelation sixteen... "The whole earth"

- **The prophetic time period is the same in Revelation twenty...**"*When the thousand years* **are** *expired Satan shall be loosed.*" In Revelation sixteen...Speaking of the time of the gathering together for the Battle of that great Day of God Almighty.

## The First Unclean Spirit

We need to examine each of these unclean spirits individually in order to have a clear understanding of their activities in these final days. We will examine the first Unclean Spirit, which is said to have come out of the mouth of the Dragon. The Dragon regurgitated this frog like spirit. Perhaps an uncouth terminology, but it will get our point across. To regurgitate meant to bring it up again. In other words, this is a repeat of something that was already consumed. The original Dragon represented the Roman Empire, which was filled with Pagan ideologies, idol worship, and deities of other strange gods and goddesses. They knew not the True and Living God. Through the analogy of this first Unclean Spirit, a revival of Paganism is predicted. Yes! A revival of Pagan ideologies, idol worship, and the revival of strange gods are predicted in this closing age before the return of Christ.

In our pluralistic culture and society of today, we are taught "religious tolerance." In "Christian" America, Paganism in all its various forms has gained acceptance in the minds of many politically correct groups. Pagan ideologies have infiltrated into our society and have influenced our culture in every area! Most of society is unconcerned and does not really feel threatened by these changes. As America has become more materialistically minded, and less God-minded, She has become more accustomed to the acceptance of these Pagan ideologies. We even call these Pagan ideologies "other religions," or "other faiths." God's Word calls them *"abominations; idolatry and strange gods."* As predicted through this first Unclean Spirit, a part of this great revival or regurgitation of Paganism is the surge of eastern cults that have once again filled the world! These strange gods are fast invading America NOW!

In this year of our Lord 2002 AD, most of our citizens are comprised of the descendents of Immigrants. In the preceding generations, these immigrants came from all over the world seeking a better way of life in this place we call, "America." At their arrival into the United States of America, they gathered together by choice at one specified time and pledged their allegiance to America. They became American citizens. They began a new life as "Americans."

In recent years however, this idea seems to be changing as new immigrants enter our teeming shores. These changes reflect just what this prophetic message speaks about. The revival of Pagan cults are subtly but surely influencing our culture. The idea of a "multi cultural community" is fast replacing our American heritage. If this comes to pass, it will dilute our identity and sovereignty as one nation under God with liberty and justice for all. As Americans, we have established our own national identity, our own culture, our own lifestyle, and our own language. This Christian heritage has come from the one true and Living God of the Bible.

Our nation began under the direction and sanction of this TRUE God. In America, we all speak English, not Arabic, Muslim, Hindu, Japanese, Spanish, Chinese, Russian or one of the hundreds of other languages of the world. If others desire to become Americans and become a part of our culture, it should be their desire to learn the English language! It should be their desire to adopt to the American culture. America's national motto is printed on our money also... "In God we trust." Our God is NOT a "pluralistic" God! The God of our Fathers through His true believers founded our country! He is the only true and Living God and the Father of our Lord Jesus Christ. As Americans, we should have the prerogative and privilege of posting the Ten Commandments in our schools and public offices. Our first Amendment does allow each citizen to express his or her opinion. Others may voice their opinion if they are offended by our one true faith that began America and has been blest of this true God; others may voice their disapproval of our pledge of allegiance to the flag and all that it entails. If others have a problem with our American heritage, I offer this solution…If you are among those who find fault with America, our God, our principles, our culture, please take advantage of another great America freedom…You have a right to leave immediately and return to where you came from.

I hope I have expressed the ideology of all true Americans when I say…This is America! One nation under the true and Living God. We have an identity that reflects our faith in this one true God. As an American, I am very well pleased and satisfied with our culture and have no desire or plan to change into a "multi cultural community." We cannot place our God on stage with those who pray to Allah, Buddha or any other Pagan gods and expect to continue singing, "God bless America" for very long. According to His Word of truth, our God is a jealous God!

The "politically correct crowd" may desire to recognize these Pagan gods of antiquity, but the TRUE God does not recognize these strange gods. He has already forewarned us…*"Thou shalt have no other God before me."* Praying to unknown Pagan gods is an abomination to Him. We had better rethink these things that we are permitting to happen, lest we loose the blessing of freedom that has come directly from God.

I would be remiss in the presentation of this prophecy, if I did not begin with the greatest tragedy that America has ever experienced! It is difficult for any American to find words that we can use to even describe the holocaust to humanity that happened at the World Trade Center! Now come to be recognized as the tragedy of 9/11. I speak candidly here for the Revelation prophecy has already forewarned us that *"Satan would be loosed for a season through this first "Unclean Spirit"* which represents the REVIVAL of PAGANISM. Paganism in any form has always been the GODLESS philosophy of mankind! Paganism is derived from the DARKNESS of Satan's innermost being! Paganism denies the ONLY TRUE AND LIVING GOD and replaces Him with some form of Idolatry or strange gods.

## A cunningly devised bazaar act...

was carried out by demon possessed men on the innocent who were in the Twin Towers on 9/11, 2001. These Muslims were schooled from their infancy in their GODLESS philosophy and they acted upon their belief! They were "worshippers" of Allah! They were TRUE believers! Their devious acts that they carried out confirmed what they believed! Satan was loosed in the twisted minds of these people who have been taught that no one has a right to live unless they worship Allah! They had been promised an entrance into a utopian ecstatic eternal existence with sensual pleasures untold if they die for their dead prophet Mohammed.

This Pagan cult of the Muslims has been cultivated and prepared for Satan's use! These people have been led to believe that their leader Allah was chosen of the true God! A self-designed prophet called Mohammed said that he had received the Holy Scriptures of Islam, the Koran, from Allah. This cult began in AD 610 and claims that Mohammed was the last long line of holy prophets that proceeded from Adam, Abraham, Mosses and Jesus. These are ALL LIES from the pit of hell itself! Jesus Christ is the ONLY Prophet, Priest and King of the Universe! The Muslim cult has even copied the Holy Scriptures as a part of their Koran. WHAT A DECEPTION! What a LIE from the dark abyss! Remember! Satan must have human agents {people} to carry out his dastardly deeds!

I share what I believe to be alarming facts...According to the U.S. Dept. of State International Information Programs concerning Islam's in the United States...Islam is one of the fastest-growing religions in the U.S. By the year 2010, the Muslim population is expected to surpass the Jewish population, making it the second-largest faith after Christianity. The American Muslim community is a mosaic of cultures, its members have come from all five major continents. In fact, a recent survey showed that Muslim immigrants comprise 77.6% verses 22.4% U.S. born. Experts estimate that there are approximately six to eight million Muslims in the Unites States. The Britannica Book of the year reports that there is an average of 17,500 African Americans converted to Islam each year since 1995. There are 2,000 mosques nationwide as well as numerous Islamic Sunday and weekend schools. The exact number of businesses owned and operated by Muslims is estimated in the thousands. **Worshippers of Allah now number 840 million worldwide!**

# CHRISTIANS AWAKE!
## A brief summary of "Strange gods"

**Hinduism**...Hinduism is a term used to describe a vast array of sects to which most Indians belong. It developed from the indigenous religions of India in combination with Aryan religions brought to India in the 15th century B. C. and codified in the Veda and the Upanishads, the so-called sacred scriptures of Hinduism. The goals of Hindus are release from repeated reincarnation through the practice of yoga, adherence to Vedic scriptures, and devotion to a personal guru. {yoga is a fast growing so-called exercise in America}Various deities are worshipped at shrines; the divine trinity, representing the cyclical nature of the universe, are Brahma the creator, Vishnu the preserver, and Shiva the destroyer.
**This cult now numbers 649 million worldwide!**

**Buddhism**...This idol worshipping cult began in the 6th century B.C. by a man called Siddharta Gautama, known as Buddha or the "enlightened one." Before reaching this enlightened state which is called a Nirvana, one is subject to repeated lifetimes that are good or bad depending on ones actions or "karma."
**Buddhism now has 307 million followers worldwide!**

**Shinto…**Is the ancient native cult of Japan, established in the 5th century A.D. Shintoism stresses the belief in a great many spiritual beings and gods, known as "kami."
**There are now 3.5 million followers in the United Sates!**

**Sikhism…**Sikhism is open to all through the teachings of its 10 Gurus enshrined in the Sikh so called holy book and living Guru, Sri Guru Granth Sahib. This cult is ranked as the worlds 5th largest "religion" and has…
**a following of 20 million people!**

**Baha'i…**Bahaism was founded by Mirza Husayn- 'Ali Nuri, who took the name of Baha'u'llah while in exile in Baghdad. His coming was supposedly foretold by Mirza Ali Mohammed, known as al-Bab, in the year 1844.

**Baha'i now has more than 5 million followers!**

**Confucianism; Rosicrucianism;** Taoism and a multitude of other Pagan philosophies that flourish in our diversified culture. I have only touched the tip of the iceberg in this brief summary of the revival Pagan idolatry. America opens a "Pandora's box" when she places no guidelines upon the influx of millions who enter our freedom loving county! It will only be a matter of time until the America that our forefathers established as one nation UNDER GOD will be encompassed by Pagan ideologies. As believers in the ONE TRUE and LIVING GOD, we are already engaged in this conflict! Will we rise up to meet the challenge?

As we have heard repeatedly, the A.C.L.U. is on the side of the "Godless." Whether we realize it our not, we are in a Cultural Revolution in America! Few of God's people seem to be aware of this revival of Paganism that is affecting the whole society! If there is any "discrimination" going on, it is against CHRISTIANS practicing their religion in Christian America! Awake, Awake, O Zion, put on your strength!

The Ten Commandments cannot be posted in our schools or on public domain; Prayer and Bible reading is forbidden in the schools; Christmas carols once sung in the school plays has been outlawed; the

Christmas Nativity scenes have all been removed from the public domain; few Department stores even play Christmas carols anymore lest they offend the general atheistic and cultish customers. The clerks no longer greet you with, "Merry Christmas." They have been instructed to say, "Happy Holidays." Very few public advertisements posted here and there say, "Merry Christmas" but "Seasons Greetings." Even the Christmas cards have all been printed up with Santa, snow men or Rudolph the red nosed reindeer as the main star. What is the source of all this deception? It has been regurgitated from the mouth of this First Unclean Spirit through this slimy Satanic frog that we are considering in Revelation 16:13. Always remember! When the Light of God fades, darkness invades and prevails.

Paganistic philosophies have also gained a tremendous foothold in our society through the vast entertainment industry. Every sin and evil that was done when Paganism was prevalent in ancient times is now being propagated through the movie industry. All who participate in viewing this darkness become partakers of the deeds of darkness by proxy! Our "fun loving" society is a breeding field for Satan to again make his comeback through this Unclean Spirit! I have observed that his prize targets are our youth! Although I must say right up front that they have become vulnerable because of the desperate lack of parental guidance. The past two generations have seemingly forgotten about their reason for existence. In the beginning God created man in His own image. He wanted a human family to love and care for. Isn't that an amazing fact! However! It has become "party-time" for the majority of this present age. Paganism or Godlessness is only a natural outcome when the true and Living God is excluded from life in general. If there is a scarcity of Light, darkness is inevitable.

Are we so naïve to think that these changing circumstances have just come to be without a power source behind them? There is always a cause factor for every changing circumstance. According to the prophecy, the cause of these changes we are experiencing in our society have come from the power of Satan through these Three Unclean Spirits. They have, *"gathered themselves together for that great day of God Almighty."* There will be more radical and unwelcome changes to come UNLESS Christians...I mean REAL Christian believers are awakened and begin to get involved in this battle called, *"The battle of that great day of God Almighty,"* which is also called, *"The battle of Armageddon."*

Satan has always been effective by using "diversionary" tactics to accomplish his deceptions! Dispensationalists have played right into his hands by projecting this battle of Armageddon as a literal earthly battle. They claim it will be fought on the plan of Megiddo in Jerusalem in a supposed age to come. The Bible declares this battle of Armageddon to be a "SPIRITUAL" battle. We have previously related this is a battle of "TRUTH against ERROR."

As we continue to review the activities of this First Unclean Spirit, there is another foundational scripture that affirms the revival of Paganism. Turning to Revelation 20:7-9, we read... *"And when the thousand years are expired, Satan shall be loosed out of his prison, And shall go out to deceive the nations which are in the four quarters of the earth."* What "thousand years" is he speaking of here? We must keep this 1,000-year period in its proper context or we will loose the continuity of the message. The first three verses of this chapter are a recapping of that which has already taken place. These scriptures are rehearsing the events, which took place in our previous message within chapter twelve of Revelation. These present scriptures are also connected to that Apostolic period.

What happened during that first century? Let us make these comparisons. Under the Apostolic period, we related that the church laid hold on that old Dragon which represented Paganism and cast him down from his power. They did this by using the *"keys of the kingdom."* What are the keys to the Kingdom? The "keys" are the promises of God. Satan can only be bound or chained by the Word. He is not a physical being that he can be chained; laid hold of; bound or shut up and sealed! He is not a physical being that can be cast into a bottomless pit! He is a "spiritual being" and must be dealt with under spiritual guidelines. Amen? Isn't that understandable?

In this present chapter under consideration, these scriptures are telling us that Satan's deception through Paganism was sealed, shut up by the everlasting gospel. When you "seal" something, it renders it useless. This means that Satan's deception through Paganism was rendered useless by the truths of Christianity. In our past messages we have explained that the 1,000-year period is used symbolically or figuratively to refer to an indefinite period of time. This expression is used in Peter's writings. *"One day is with the Lord as a thousand years, and a thousand years as one day."* {2 Peter 3:8} We may safely adopt this symbolic phraseology throughout the book of Revelation.

During this indefinite period of time, which incorporates the "Dark Ages," we learned that Satan used a NEW deception. This deception came forth through the Apostate Church, which clothed itself in the garb of Christianity. At the ending of this deception, or *"when the thousand years are expired, Satan shall be loosed out of his prison etc."{Rev. 20:7}* This means that Satan would be free {loosed} to again use PAGANISM or the pagan ideologies as a means of deception in the *"four quarters of the earth."* As we have previously related, we have seen and are seeing the revival of Paganism worldwide, even the length and breadth of the earth!

### That is...IF...we have our eyes opened through the Word of God!

What is Paganism? It is Satan's Godless philosophies which he projects through men's corrupt minds. We have had some grim reminders of Satanic actions in our present society! Multitudes of "cults" have come forth from this First Unclean Spirit.

• **In 1969, the Charles Manson** "family" savagely murdered the actress Sharon Tate and four others, and then used the pregnant actresses' own blood to scrawl the word "Pig" on the front door of their home! The very next day Manson sent his demon cult members out to stab to death a wealthy business man Leno LaBianca and his wife Rosemary in their own home. At age 65, this demon possessed man and his cult followers still cling together as a "family." Several Web Sites are dedicated to him by his followers and propagate his Satanic philosophy. They suggest that Manson and Jesus Christ are one and the same! Many young people who have embraced the cult wear a tea-shirt with his face printed on it!

• **Jim Jones, with his "People's Temple"** appeared on the scene of society in the mid-1970s. Jones was an ordained minister with the Disciples of Christ. He began to condemn capitalism in America and amid a mounting government probe, he and his fanatical army of devotees fled to the isolated and impoverished South American country of Guyana. In 1978, more than 900 people were lead into a macabre Satanic ritual of mass murder and suicide! Many "members" willingly drank cyanide-laced "Flavor-Aid." Some who were not so willing had it poured down their throats and others were shot to death! This atrocious act was all done in the name of God! Jones tape-recorded the horror of that "White Night" suicide ritual in his jungle compound called, "Jonestown." Amid the screaming cries of infants and Mothers killing their own babies, Jones speaks these words from his twisted demon possessed mind…"Look children, its just something to put you to rest. Death is a million times as preferable to 10 more days of this life." His final words on the Jonestown tape of the "White Night" are these… "We didn't commit suicide, we committed an act of revolutionary suicide protesting the conditions of an inhumane world."

## There have been many more "Jonestowns" during this past decade

• Seventy two of the so-called Christian sect of the Branch Davidians lost their lives in a hellish inferno at their compound in Waco, Texas.

• Timothy McVeigh, an ex- Marine was so emotionally moved by this event which he blamed the government for, that he blew up the Murrah Federal building in Oklahoma City in 1995 killing 168 people! McVeigh planned and carried out this dastardly Satanic deed on the second anniversary of the Waco raid on the Branch Davidians.

• In 1997, thirty nine members of a Satanic cult called "Heaven's Gate" killed themselves in a mass suicide believing that they would have a rendezvou with a spaceship trailing the Hale-Bopp comet. The cult members referred to themselves as "angels" and all dressed alike in androgynous black cloths and buzz haircuts. The cult mixed Bible prophecy with spiritualism and the UFO lore. The dead were found scattered on their backs with purple cloths folded in a triangle over their heads and shoulders like shrouds.

• In Canada and Europe, 75 members of the Order of the Solar Temple killed themselves in search of a new life in a place they called Sirius.

- In Japan, the Aum Shinri Kyo cult unleashed a nerve gas attack on Tokyo subway riders killing 12 and bringing sickness upon thousands!

Who could conceive the era that we are living in 2002! Who could have conceived the ultimate Satanic thrust and attack that we as Americans have experienced through 9/11. This is the fulfillment of the "more sure word of prophecy" that we are experiencing! FEW are aware of this attack and how to fight against these unclean spirits! This is the reason I have been zealous to perform that which the true and Living God has placed upon my mind to write!

### *"Satan has been loosed for a little season"*...
through the revival of Pagan philosophies that we call, "other religions, cults and occults!" According to the authorities on cult movements and religious fanaticism, they remind us that those who are BELIEVERS in their ideologies intend to carry out their dastardly acts! They assure us that they are NOT mindless zombies. They tell us that they see themselves as engaged in a cosmic war acting out real-life battles of "performance violence."

As we all watched on television in disbelief those two plans fly right into the twin towers, we can now believe their statement! We continue to stagger in unbelief as we see via television the Satanic influence of human bombs being used to accomplish their purpose! The strange Eastern gods of Paganism have been revived before our eyes...even as it has been foretold by the Living God of the Bible! These "strange gods" are invading what we have deemed to be... "One Nation Under God."

**We are NOW engaged in the**
*"battle of that great day of God Almighty,"*
*called...*
# Armageddon.

In our new millennium, this First Unclean Spirit has also been brazen enough to openly declare the acceptance of...

# Satanism

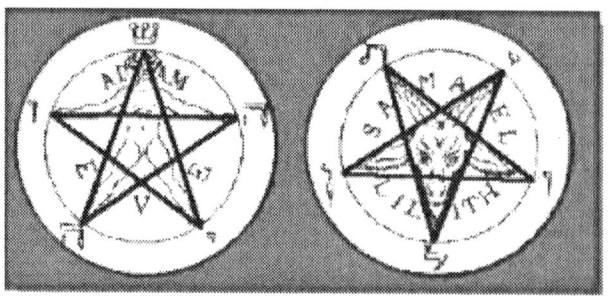

**Satanism...**as it appears in our society in this twenty first century is as diversified as the sands of the sea. The author of all its diversity is of course the living spiritual being which the Bible has identified as "Satan." Our prophetic focus is on the "revival" of or the acceptance of Paganism in all it's devious forms and rituals before the soon coming of Christ. This resurgence is predicted through the first unclean spirit that we are exposing through Christ's Revelation prophecy.

**The Church of Satan...**Would be one of the more familiar and widespread branches of revived Paganism. Anton Szander LaVey began this movement in 1966. He assumed the tittle of "High Priest" as their leader, and is credited with writing what is called, "The Satanic Bible." He died in 1998, however the followers he gathered have continued to propagate his godless philosophy. Peter Gilmore is their present High Priest. I will not use God's good time and space on these pages to relate this man's deceptions, for they are as ancient as Satan himself. Said in few words... All Satanists, regardless of what name they choose to call themselves proclaim the same "creed." Their creed is a denial of the true and Living God of the Bible, and all that He has revealed Himself to be. They consider THEMSELVES to be god.

The potpourri of Satanism goes under various labels. Many groups do actual worship Satan through their ritual of the Satanic Mass. Their Satanic Mass is even available on CD. Some go by various names such as Druiods, Demon and Voodoo worshippers, etc. etc. who learn spell casting and witchcraft. Satanism is not a vain philosophy! Their adherents continue to have a great influence upon our society!

## Enlightening statistics...

There are at present 4 BILLION professed adherents to some form of Satanism in the United States of America. Satan's followers have availed themselves to the WWW also. Their Satanic Web Sites or "Home Pages" number into 50 MILLION at present! Viewers can be connected with what is called, "The Dark Side of the Web" which links you immediately with 10,000 hand picked links exploiting Satan's realm of darkness for you to explore!

**Satanism** in one form or another is having a traumatic effect upon the whole of our present day society! Inroads into the mass media have escalated in recent years through the movie industry. Sadistic movies and demon thrillers are now among those most popular today. Thousands of videos and CDs have been made that depict the gore and horror of the demon's dark spiritual underworld. Movies! Videos! Games! Books! Music! Satan has covered the field that is ripe to harvest! Who is targeted? Satan's choice targets are CHILDREN and young people! Games such as Dungeons and Dragons and a host of others too numerous to mention, lead children into the land of demons. Their thinking is being shaped by what they are placing into their minds! It is inevitable that what they place into their minds will soon be played out in real life!

We have seen terrible atrocities of the reenactments of these sadistic actions come to pass in our present society! Books, such as the popular Harry Potter series have lead thousands of children into this familiar spirit of devil worship! So-called "concert artists" come forth with Satanic lyrics that glorify EVERYTHING that comes from the pits of hell and the lake of fire! Satan has always presented himself as the god of this world. He uses the five senses of humanity to distort and destroy all that God intended for humanity to be! Whatever a person places in the mind will ultimately control him. The BIBLE speaks this truth... *"As a man thinketh in his heart, so is he."*

**Satan** has something to offer for every age group in our society. People of all ages are now being swept into the so called, "Aquarius Age." Psychics, channeling, tarot cards, astrology, crystals etc. etc.

177

are all age-old Pagan deceptions! The Lord still calls these deceptions "familiar spirits" and has warned all humanity to have nothing to do with them.

It was disturbing to say the least and hard to believe when I learned via the "Information Highway" that 15% of the population of New Orleans still practices Voodoo TODAY and has a public Voodoo historical museum there. Christian America's moral fiber is being attacked through this unclean spirit of Paganism in its many forms! The sleeping giant called the church remains silent on the issues that are shaping our future generations!

**Sexual perversion** is promoted through the advertising media constantly. Sexual innovations are used to advertise and market just about everything! Ancient Pagans had their temples of Prostitution, this society has its brothels! Nudity and vulgarity has encompassed this generation! Pornography has escalated to the point of no return, even now incorporating child pornography! Pornography has prepared the way for lust to take action upon the innocent in untold rapes and murders! It appears that nothing is sacred anymore! Our clothing and fashion industry follows these Paganistic trends. Models present the "Jezebel" look and the fashion trend continues! A great majority of women think it is fashionable to have the look of Jezebel or a harlot, if they are to be numbered among the glamorous. Innocent youth are being clothed {or un-clothed} in indecent and even lewd apparel because it is advertised a "fashionable."

**The Pagan practice of piercing parts of the body** that existed in ancient time has been revived. The mention of this practice may seem immaterial to many, however it is another proof of the Paganistic influence that has been revived through this First Unclean Spirit. This practice began in a very subtle way some years ago, as the "pierced ear ring" was introduced. This ungodly practice is even permitted on infants and children in our present day society! The true God of the Bible speaks clearly against "mutilating" the body, which was made to be His temple. This mutilation also includes the popular practice of tattooing the body. Yes! Paganism is becoming an accepted part of our overall culture!

**The "blood-thirsty" spirit of Paganism** is revived through the so-called sports arena of our society today. Our society has received the "blood-thirty" spirit of the gladiator crowd of ancient Rome!

Millions of boxing fans pack the "sports" arena to SEE blood! The only difference in the two bloodthirsty crowds is this…Today the referee has to give a count down just before the opponent is bulgeded to death to stop the fight. In ancient days, it was the King that gave the crowd the choice between a "thumbs up" or a "thumbs down" for life or death!

## As an ambassador of Christ

in this present world, I can do no other than rise to the occasion of speaking in defense of the gospel in this area! If any choose to be in the arena of boxing, a free country offers this opportunity…However! When these people embrace this ungodly activity and then link it with the true and Living God of the Bible, it involves me! I speak specifically of Evander Holyfield, the well-known popular boxer of this era. As in ancient Pagan days, the blood thirty crowds lauded their gladiators that fought to the death, so he has been lauded as a god of the sport's world. This "pugilistic great" professes to be a believer in Jesus Christ! Yes! He even prays before he begins to beat his opponent into a semi-conscious state! He defames Christ even more by his profession on his Web Site!

He has the brazenness to use this scripture on his home page of that Web Site! *"Be strong and of good courage, fear not, nor be afraid of them: for the Lord thy God, he it is that doth go with thee; he will not fail thee, nor forsake thee." {Deuteronomy 31:6}*

Evander Holyfield has distorted the true meaning of this scripture by using the Word of God out of its proper context! This promise from God is to HIS obedient children, not to the disobedient who keep not His commandments! What blasphemy! This stirs my righteous indignation! What a reproach and a misrepresentation of the Loving creator! If Evander Holyfield wishes to be a "humanitarian" that is his business, However! When he evolves MY God, now he has involved me! I would hope that this pugilistic great would be honest enough to retract his profession as a "Christian" and make a public apology before God. He is deceiving many of our youth when he connects pugilism with the true God of the Bible!

**The racing arena** is another deception, claiming itself to be a "sport." We view this bloodthirsty spirit in the "fans" at all the racetracks! The daredevil race car drivers sense of reason has been

179

perverted. He is consumed with the glory, popularity and money that comes with being THE winner! His mind cannot conceive that he may be killed and enter into a Christless eternity in Hell, or be injured for the rest of his life. He is *"tempting the Lord"* by his very own actions. What a deception to actually see a so-called Chaplain at the racetrack! He is there supposedly to pray for God's protection over the drivers at these daredevil escapades! God's great heart of Love is grieved by the so-called sport of racing! God is even more grieved when He is misrepresented by an act of prayer at such an occasion.

**There are many other so-called sports** that are surfacing and becoming accepted in this thrill crazed society of the twenty-first century! Children now have their own racetracks! In our pleasure seeking society, daredevil thrills have become the IN thing! Something new is invented continually...There is sky diving, bungie jumping, riding the rapids. Anything to start the adrenaline flow! All the glorified theme parks are outdoing themselves with extremely dangerous rides that promise the crowds the ultimate adrenaline high! Many have even been killed on these thrill rides! The more dangerous, the more thrill! The more money into the theme park's coiffures! Where does this mindset of extreme danger and flirting with death come from? It comes from a mind that is void of the Divine purpose for which God created us. The thrill seeking is proof of the emptiness of God in the human Spirit. Life in general is presented as a fantasy to our affluent society of today.

I would be remiss, if I did not mention the ultimate sin of our nation that has been accepted by a Godless judicial system. The United States Supreme Court has sanctioned the extinction of a part of the human race! They term it a woman's choice. This misguided group of individuals have lost any concept of a God who programmed every sperm of life to be a human being created in His image. Abortion is still MURDER in God's mind! All who participate in this ongoing program of murdering babies in the womb will stand before the Great Judge and answer to His supreme justice! Over five million murders of babies take place every day in our so-called "Christian" nation under the American Supreme Courts approval! Where is the outcry from the Christian community? The answer...Too little too late! When Paganism is summed up into one word it can be identified as "ungodliness."

As we have discovered through this context, a Godless philosophy has perverted the five senses. This is Paganism! All these social changes can be attributed to the revival coming from this First Unclean Spirit. God's more sure word of prophecy has forewarned us that these Pagan ideologies would again be revived! I hope what I have shared will bring an awareness of what is happening through this Unclean Spirit in this end time. I also hope that there will be an outcry against these things that destroy, rather than build up humanity! Some are even calling this the "Satanic Millennium!" The Bible tells it this way... *"Satan shall be loosed from his prison, and shall go out to deceive the nations which are in the four quarters of the earth.* *{Rev. 20:7b-8}*

Perhaps it would be well to question just why this darkness and deception has been able to gain such a foothold in our society. The Lord has given us the answer... *"The light of the body is the eye: if therefore thine eye be single, thy whole body shall be full of light. But if thine eye be evil, thy whole body shall be full of darkness. If therefore the light that is in thee be darkness, how great is that darkness." {Matthew 6:22-23}*

It is the Light of the glorious gospel of Jesus Christ that brings the singleness to the eye, which brings Light to the whole body. The great "sleeping giant" of churchanity has for the most part lost that Light and replaced it with their forms, rituals and entertainment programs. "Darkness" is the end result.

## The time is here when society is calling
## "Evil Good and Good Evil"

"And as it was in the days of Noah, so shall it be also in the days of the Son God." {Luke 17:26} How was it in the days of Noah? The account given in Genesis tells it best... *"And God saw that the wickedness of man was great in the earth, and that every imagination of the thoughts of his heart was only evil continually. And it repented the Lord that he had made man on the earth and it grieved him at his heart. And the Lord said, I will destroy man whom I have created from the face of the earth; both man, and beast, and the creeping thing, and the fowls of the air; for it repenteth me that I have made them." {Genesis 6:5-7}*

This 21$^{st}$ Generation has become a fulfillment of that 7$^{th}$ generation! Every imagination of the thoughts of men's hearts have become increasingly evil! The movie industry is a refection of what our society desires to see or Hollywood producers would not be promoting such sadism! This 21$^{st}$ Generation is living by proxy what they are putting into their minds through the media. As a man thinketh in his heart, so is he. It is not just fiction or fantasy. God's Word tells us that we become what we think! Surely the Lord is grieved in His heart for the condition of fallen mankind! This is the reason I am compelled to write as I do. It is not God's will that one should perish, but that all should come to repentance and faith. He has no pleasure in the death of the wicked. He would have all men to be saved! God has placed that same desire in my heart.

## The Second Unclean Spirit...

Regurgitates from the mouth of the "Diverse Beast." We recall that this particular Beast represents the Apostate Church which developed during the "Dark-Age Period." According to the more sure word of prophecy, we have learned that the *"little horn"* representing the Papacy in Daniel's prophecy rose to power with the kings of the earth, or the Emperors.

It is stated that...

*"the same horn made war with*
*the saints, against them."*
*{Dan.7:20-21}*

# Man of Sin Whose Number is 666

"Let no man deceive you by any means, for that day shall not come,
except there come a falling away first, and that man of sin be revealed,
the son of perdition; who opposeth and exalteth himself above all
that is called God, or is worshipped; so that he as God
sitteth in the temple of God, shewing himself that he is God."
{2 Thessalonians 2: 3-4}

Through this Second Unclean Spirit, Satan, the arch deceiver of all mankind is once again reviving the exaltation of the Papacy. However! The Pope's exaltation and purpose will be a covert action in these final days before the return of Christ. During the tyranny of the Dark Ages, he aligned himself with the Emperors to do his dastardly deeds against all who would not bow the knee to his supreme authority! Today, he is aligning himself with the religious kings of the earth and presenting himself as a great humanitarian. He projects himself as a "loving Father" who is now concerned about ALL peoples of ALL religions. Since John Paul has assumed his position as the "Head" of the Roman Catholic Church, he has become a world traveler! The "red carpet" has been repeatedly rolled out wherever he appears with his kingly entourage of prelates in their robed elegance.

He is now heralded as a GREAT Potentate the world over! Presidents of nations go to him for an audience, including our own Presidents! Millions of Catholic adherents pack St. Peter's Square in Vatican City to hear him say a Mass. They bow down before him and pay homage to him as if he were God Himself. As we have previously related during the Medieval Period, the Apostle Paul gave a complete description of these Popes' as the "man of sin" in 2 Thessalonians 2:1-4. Has the Pope changed? No! His purpose is still the same as it was during the time of his temporal power and authority. "Deception" is still the supreme purpose for his actions.

The "outward" show of kingly pomp and ceremony has always appealed to the "fleshly mind" and impressed the religious. The more extreme and august, the more "awesome" it appears, the more the fleshly mind wants to identify it in their concept of God. The Bible does not reflect our Lord Jesus Christ who was and is the *express image of God"* in this paganistic setting! Read all four gospels...Christ walked among men almost unnoticed as he traveled from city to city in a quiet manner, preaching the gospel of the Kingdom, healing the sick, offering forgiveness. He did not present Himself as a "kingly dignitary" parading from city to city with a great entourage escorting him as the great "I Am" although He was! He dressed in the same manner as his disciples in the common robe of the day. He did not clothe Himself in the elegance of the velvet and embroidered robes of Paganism. He refused those who tried to make Him an earthly king!

May I remind my readers that we are speaking about the Great Apostate Church, which has been revealed through the Revelation prophecy! The MOTHER OF HARLOTS AND THE ABOMINATION OF THE EARTH. {Revelation 17:5b} It is this same church that is at present enjoying a revival of interest and acceptance world wide as representing Christianity! The second deception is worse that the first!

As we have related throughout these messages, the prophecies declare that *"AFTER all these things come to pass,"* we would arrive at the *"end time."* John Paul II has simply taken his place in the vast history of prelates that have gone before him as reigning "Infallible Head" over the Roman Catholic Church. {Please refer back to the complete detailed heresies of Rome that were previously related} These heresies are still in effect today! The false dogmas of the Popes and the Pagan ceremonies are still being used to deceive multitudes of unsuspecting loyal Catholic adherents!

## A Brief Recapping of these heresies...

• Contrary to the Word of God...The Pope still holds to the blasphemous tittle "Vicarius Filli Dei" claiming to be the "Vicar of the Son of God" on the earth!

• Contrary to the Word of God...The "Papacy" continues to claim a direct lineage to Peter as their first Pope.

• Contrary to the Word of God..."Papal Infallibility" is still proclaimed! God still calls this Blasphemy.

- Contrary to the Word of God...The "Bloody Mass" is still crucifying the Son of God afresh!
- Contrary to the Word of God...The "Worship and Adoration" of Mary continues to be blasphemy as she is called the "Mother of God!"
- Contrary to the Word of God...The dogma of "purgatory" gives a false hope of heaven after a sinful life!
- Contrary to the Word of God...Praying to DEAD people who have been canonized calling them patron saints continues!
- Contrary to the Word of God...The "Rosary" continues as a vain repetition on Pagan prayer beads!
- Contrary to the Word of God...the "Auricular confession" to a man called a priest is still in effect!
- Contrary to the Word of God...the dogma of the transubstantiation and the adoration of the wafer continue as Idol worship!
- Contrary to the Word of God...The cup is still forbidden to the laity calling it the cup of one kind!
- Contrary to the Word of God...The Bible is a closed Book to the Catholic adherents!
- Contrary to the Word of God...The false doctrines of the so-called "Seven Sacraments" continue to deceive! {The Bible tells us that we are COMPLETE in Christ}

The Catholic religion is NOT Biblical Christianity! According to the Revelation prophecy, God has Her pictured in chapter 17 as...
### *"MYSTERY BABYLON THE GREAT, THE MOTHER OF HARLOTS AND ABOMINATIONS OF THE EARTH."*
John wrote this description of what God calls the Harlot Church... *"And the woman was arrayed in purple and scarlet colour, and decked with gold and precious stones and pearls, having a golden cup in her hand full of abominations and the filthiness of her fornication." {Rev. 17:4}*

During the Dark Age period, this great Harlot Church became wealthy through confiscating houses and lands. She has never ceased to add to her wealth...

# For your information:

The Vatican's treasure of solid gold had been estimated by the United Nations World Magazine to amount to several BILLION dollars. A large bulk of this is stored in gold ingots with the U.S. Federal Reserve Bank, while banks in England and Switzerland hold the rest. But this is only a small portion of the wealth of the Vatican, which is in the U.S. When to this is added all the real estate, property, stocks and shares abroad, then the staggering accumulation of the wealth of the Catholic Church becomes so formidable as to defy any rational assessment.

The Vatican's wealth is greater than that of the five wealthiest giant corporations of the country. The Catholic Church is the largest financial power, wealth accumulator and property owner in existence. She has greater possessions and material riches than any other single institution, corporation, bank, giant trust, government or state within the whole globe. The Pope, as the visible ruler of this immense wealth, is consequently the richest individual of the twentieth century.

The Vatican also has billions of shares in the most powerful international corporations such as Gulf Oil, Shell, General Motors, Bethlehem Steel, General Electric, International Business Machines, T.W.A. Pan American Airlines etc. etc. The Vatican wealth is conservatively estimated at more than 500 million dollars in the U.S.A. alone.

In a statement published in connection with a bond prospectus, the Boston archdiocese listed its assets at Six Hundred and Thirty Five Million {$635,892,004} that is 9.9 times its liabilities. This leaves a net worth of Five Hundred and Seventy-one million dollars {$571,704,953} It is not difficult to discover the truly astonishing wealth of the Catholic Church, once we add the riches of the twenty-eight archdioceses and 122 dioceses of the U.S.A. Source: Cry of the People by Penny Lernoux

**www.vaticancityrome.com**

This Symbol of the Paganistic Egyptian trinity is openly carried by this supposed kingly dignitary, misrepresenting our Lord Jesus Christ. This emblem is also engraved on every gold cross placed on the Protestant communion tables in their sanctuaries. *"And they made an image to the Beast."*

As predicted, the Pope's deception clothed in the cloak of Christianity is more effective in this age than it was during the Dark Age period! Why is that? According to the prophecy, it is because so few people {even those who consider themselves Christians} are awakened to Satan's subtle way of deception! Why is that? It is because most of the "Christian world" has been taught their religious beliefs from traditional religions rather than the BIBLE! They have for the most part, been taught by the "False Prophet" who represents Protestantism. All believers are admonished to *"search the scriptures"* to compare what they have been taught by the Word of God. Jesus Christ is the ONLY truth! He said,

## *"Ye shall know the truth, and the truth shall make you free." {John 8:32}*

**This brings us to our next individual examination of...**

## The Third Unclean Spirit.

John saw this Third Unclean Spirit regurgitated from the mouth of the *"False Prophet."* We have previously related the full description of this self-styled False Prophet in our discourse on, "The Two Horned Beast." This present scene identifies the Two Horned Beast to be one and the same as the "False Prophet." We recall in Revelation 13:11-18, that John beheld, *"another beast coming up out of the earth; and he had two horns like a lamb, and spake as a dragon."* This self-styled False Prophet spake as the Dragon! Remember! The "Dragon" represented Pagan ideologies. Yes! Pagan ideologies are being revived through the False Prophet under the umbrella of Protestantism today! Yes! In the year 2002!

# Gog and Magog

Let us continue in our understanding of this deception of Paganism coming forth in the earth through this third Unclean Spirit...John confirms these end time events in Revelation 20:7-9. *"And when the thousand years are expired, Satan shall be loosed out of his prison, And shall go out to deceive the nations which are in the four Quarters of the earth, Gog and Magog, to gather them together to battle: the number of whom is as the sand of he sea. And they went up on the breadth of the earth, and compassed the camp of the saints about, and the beloved city: and fire came down from God out of heaven, and devoured them."*

Remember, we are not speaking of a literal one thousand years here. As we have previously related, this term is used in the same context that Peter used when he wrote, *"one day with the Lord is as a thousand years and a thousand years as a day."* We must always consider this as a symbolic time or an indefinite period known unto the Lord. The *"seal of God's Word"* was set upon Satan's activities as the church was birthed into the first century. John wrote, *"that he {Satan} should deceive the nations no more, till the thousand years should be fulfilled"* and after that he must be loosed a little season." *{Revelation 20:3b}*

This meant that Satan could no longer deceive mankind through Paganism for the future years ahead of this indefinite symbolic period until the thousand years were fulfilled. We know that Satan did come forth to use another deception through the Apostate church that clothed itself in Christian garb However...this symbolic period of time is incorporated within this chronological time frame. John tells us that *"after that he must be loosed for a season."* This season has now come through the third Unclean Spirit. Satan is now "loosed" or has the freedom to once again introduce Pagan ideologies throughout all nations! How is he doing this?

The scriptures tell us that Satan would gather, *"Gog and Magog"* to the *"battle of the great day of God Almighty."* John writes that their number is as the sands of the sea! I would say that this would incorporate MILLIONS of adherents! But...Who and what does Gog and Magog represent here in the prophecy? Again, we refer to the line upon line, precept upon precept principle, that our Lord God has placed in His writings to receive greater understanding. As always, we keep in mind that the book of Revelation is written in symbolic language, which is based on analogy. Let us pursue the identity of Gog and Magog through these guidelines.

Ezekiel, God's prophet of old is given this message... *"And the word of the Lord came unto me, saying, Son of man, set thy face against Gog, the land of Magog, the chief prince of Meshech and Tubal, and prophecy against him. And say, Thus saith the Lord God; Behold I am against thee, O Gog, the chief prince of Meshech and Tubal."* {*Ezekiel 38:1-3*} Chapters 38 and 39 of Ezekiel speaks of many things concerning Gog who by all the details given was an enemy of God and His people Israel in ancient times. I recognize that there are many Dispensationalist that want to bring Gog and the land of Magog into focus as a present day literal battle. Not so! Ezekiel's prophecy was fulfilled at the time of his writing. The Revelation presents this scene as an analogy to describe this end time SPIRITUAL battle that is taking place NOW. As Gog and his land of idolaters were the literal enemies of God's people in the ancient days, so Gog and the whole land of Magog are used in the Revelation prophecy as an analogy to identify the spiritual enemies that are now coming against God's New Testament Israel. God's New Testament Israel are ALL believers in Christ.

Now that we have established the identity of Gog and the land of Magog as the enemies of the true God, let us proceed with the enemy's intent. According to our present scripture under consideration in Revelation 20:8-9, the intent of Satan was to deceive the whole earth. We recall that this Two Horned Beast *"spake as the dragon."* {*Revelation 13:11b*} Yes! It is written that they, meaning the Pagan enemies of God's truth would be brazen enough to enter right into a "Christian Fellowship" in order to deceive the very elect of God! God says it this way...They *"compassed the camp of the saints about and the beloved city."* We will see how this first Unclean Spirit of "Paganism" comes in many forms of deception.

Let us consider just how Paganism has, *"compassed the camp of the saints about the beloved city."* This statement means that the Unclean Spirit of Paganism would try to gain entrance RIGHT IN THE MIDST OF THE TRUE CHURCH OF GOD. I am not referring to a denominational name here. I am speaking about ALL the saints that have been born again into God's TRUE church. This is what the camp of the saints refers to. I believe this Pagan infiltration to be the so-called, "New Age Movement." Remember! This Unclean Spirit is a DECEPTIVE spirit! This spirit not only appears openly, but also incognito! The "New Age Movement" is not NEW! It is Monotheistic, which in essence has its roots in Pagan philosophy. This Paganistic philosophy is capturing the minds of many in astounding measure! Thousands of New Age Web Sites have emerged to introduce this Pagan deception and gather new adherents. I have researched many of these Web Sites and found one in particular, which amazed my thinking! The counter on their Web Site registered 1.45 MILLION hits since January 1, 2002!

## A brief sketch of the basic tenants of the
# "New Age Movement"

- New Age adherents confuse the Creator with His creation. They do not consider His Divine position as being separated from it and in control of it. They have their roots in the Pagan philosophy of Monism. The belief in Monism is really Hinduistic pantheism, which means ALL is God.
- New Age adherents view God as an impersonal force, rather than a personal loving Heavenly Father. They do not believe that Jesus Christ is the TRUTH. They contend that "truth as objective." They deny the deity of Christ, claiming that Christ is a cosmic principle or an ideal and that He dwelt in Hercules, Hermes, Rama, Mithra, Krishma, Buddha etc.
- New Age adherents believe that each person is god and that they have no need of a Savior since they explain away sin. They do not believe, as the Bible tells us that man was born inherently sinful and utterly depraved. Mimicking the eastern cults, New Age adherents distort the distinction between good and evil. Since they believe that "all is One" ultimately there is no good or evil.
- New Age adherents embrace the eastern Pagan philosophies of reincarnation, which entails a long process of rebirths in which man can eventually reach perfection. They also place animals on the same plan as man and believe that animals are also reincarnated souls. They teach the Hindu principle of "karma" which means that what a person sows in this life he will reap in his next life in his reincarnated state of

being. This belief in reincarnation has produced "spirit guides" or "channels."

• New Age is simply a repeat or the revival of Paganistic deception…that there is no death; that man is god and that knowledge of self is salvation and power. New Age groups have slipped subtly into Christian circles under the umbrella of Protestantism. Why has that been so easy to do? It is because every wind of doctrine has been accepted within the False Prophets realm of religion. Remember! That the Word and the Spirit lay dead in the street of that great city. When God's truth is not present to *"reprove, instruct and correct,"* the evil one has free access into people's thinking. Once an individual receives a deceptive or a seducing spirit, it is almost impossible for them to discern the Spirit of truth. This is why it is written, that *"God hates every false way."* I would hasten to add that I do also! God doesn't want to see any of His creatures cast into the lake of fire for eternity. I do not either! This is the reason that I have dedicated my time and effort in writing this book. I am striving earnestly to relate God's Revelation prophecy to *"whosoever will hear what the Word and the Spirit saith to the churches."*

## This prophetic message is
## God's ultimatum of Love to His children.

God has exposed the devil's deception through this prophetic message! Yes! Out of the Mouth of this *"False Prophet"* has comes every wind of doctrine to deceive the very elect…IF…possible. The "IF" God has left with us. As true believers, we are admonished to *"prove ALL things to see if they are of God or man."* God has placed this responsibility of faith upon all His redeemed children. Our walk is a walk of faith. Our walk of faith is a probationary journey to fit us for our eternal home. God will have a tested and a tried people to dwell with Him throughout the ceaseless ages of eternity! This walk is called a "refining fire." Amen? This responsibility is given to help every believer to grow in grace, in knowledge and in an intimate relationship with our God. It will ultimately bring us into the promised eternal life with God.

# Another deceptive and subtle element that has *"encompassed the camp of the saints"* is...

## The Great Ecumenical Movement or WCC

Perhaps more familiarly known as World Council of Churches. I hope this brief summary about this deceptive organization will bring enlighten for true Christians. The first approach to the One World Church concept began about 1910. This organization has been largely sponsored by the liberal clergy of all denominations. They have always been captivated by presenting the Social Gospel...if there be such a thing! This organization and structure is fearfully and wondrously designed. In effect, it is actually a huge super church. A tightly controlled Central Committee of about one hundred members make all the decisions.

The Secretariat in the Geneva headquarters has immense power, and directs the whole operation of the council. All the member churches await any official announcement for all their programs until they have been approved. These programs are then filtered down and into every denomination that is affiliated with the National and World Council of Churches today. These tentacles of power reach out from the Geneva headquarters and into all the interchurch organizations at the world and national levels. Pressure has always been exerted upon any group which terms itself Christian to come under it's jurisdiction and control.

I share just the basic format and a few past activities of this Great Counterfeit calling itself the "World Council of Churches." I ask this question of true believers…

## Does the World Council of Churches speak for you?

- When one third of the delegates in the General Assembly could not affirm an unqualified belief in the reality of God, or the divinity of Jesus, or in life after death?
- When the General Board votes to raise $500,000 to meet the extortion tactics and revolutionary demands of James Forman's Pro-Marxist Black Manifesto?
- When it has published through its educational division materials for our youth groups in sanctioning free love?
- When its Department of Internal Affairs used their great influence to have the United States extend diplomatic relationship with Red China?
- When the National Council of Churches lobbies in Washington against voluntary prayer and Bible reading of the Word of God in public schools?
- When this National Council of Churches is in full cooperation and supports the world Council, which has avowed communists involved in its Central committee?
- When it sanctions any major political issue, such as abortion and homosexuality with a quorum of only twenty members needed then voices the decision as the will of forty million Protestants?

The World Council of Churches goes on with its great deception, seemingly unnoticed and accepted by the sleeping giant called Protestantism. The obedient, loyal, vulnerable and unsuspecting church member continues to support financially that which is totally foreign to the true God of the Bible!

An informative article from the Readers Digest called, "Do You know Where Your Church Offerings Go" was written by: Rael Jean Isac. Her comment in the opening of the article said this…"You'd better find out, because they may be supporting revolution instead of religion." For reprints {if still available} write: Reprint editor, Reader's Digest,

Pleasantville, N.Y. Surely all that has been published in the Reader's Digest must be credible or they would be open to a law suit!

Before we leave this subject matter, I must pick up the last statement that I have listed concerning the World Council of Churches.

• When the Council has employed identified communist fronters to translate the Revised Standard Version of the Bible?

## The battle is on!

The inerrent of Word of God is being attacked in such subtle and beguiling ways that people are actually "applauding" all the various translations that are coming forth flooding the market of Christian bookstores! We are enveloped in a potpourri of confusion! Satan has struck at the "ROOT" and gullible uninformed Christians are falling for it! If these translations were nothing more than a change in the use of the modern day vernacular, this would bring enough confusion! However! The error goes more deeply than this!

Let us examine some pertinent facts…It actually began back in the late 1800s when Wescott and Hort dethroned the Textus Receptus and the Greek manuscripts that stood behind it. I quote several paragraphs from…

"The Conspiracy Behind the New Bible Translations"
written by: Daniel B. Wallace
"The first major English translation of the Bible to appear since the King James {1611} was the Revised Version of 1881. Since then, numerous English translations have sprung up, almost all of which have used a different textual basis from the one found in the KJV. This difference is especially seen in the New Testament. Simultaneously published with the RV was the Greek text of Wescott and Hort, two Cambridge scholars. This Greek text had been in the works for 28 years, coming to light on May 12, 1881. It was accomplished by an introductory volume, which gave rationale for the choices made.

Wescott and Hort were able to convince the vast majority of New Testament scholars of the truth of their textual choices. Essentially, they argued that the Greek text behind the KJV NT was inferior and late. Of course, as is well known, the Greek text used in 1611 was for the most part based on about half a dozen very late manuscripts {none earlier than the 12th century AD} These manuscripts were used by Erasmus in 1516 when he published the first Greek NT.

But these few manuscripts {MSS} came from a much larger pool. In fact, for the most part they looked very much like the majority of Greek MSS of the medieval ages. But Wescott and Hort said that this majority text was late and inferior. They preferred the five great uncial MSS {known by their letters, Aleph, A, B, C, D} all of which dated from the forth or fifth century, as well as early versional and patristic evidence. Two MSS in particular, B and aleph, were favorites of Wescott and Hort. Both came from the fourth century." End Quote

These things may seem a little "deep' for the average person to digest! However! In spite of the attacks on the KJV of the Bible, there is ample proof it has stood the test throughout the ages and still remains in tact. In my studied opinion these "scholars," Wescott and Hort laid the wrong foundation. Others have accepted their false conclusions, and the chaos and confusion has multiplied! The so-called Unisex- version of the Bible is another abomination coming forth to bring disgrace into the Christian community! Yet! In spite of it all! God's Word is forever settled in heaven. I will stand firm on it with multitudes of others of "like faith."

For the sincere child of God, there is a wealth of substantial information from many reliable sources to reveal the sorcery behind this devious translation movement. There are literally thousands of legitimate Web Sites available containing valid information on the subject of Bible translations. If the reader has a computer available, I would highly recommend a continuing search on the Internet.

The various Bible translations are too numerous to mention, however, these are just a few of the more popular ones...Contemporary English Version; The Living Bible; New American Bible; New American Standard Bible; New International Reader's Version; New Jerusalem Bible; New King James Version; New Revised Standard Version...and the list goes on! I stated previously that...If these translations were nothing more than a change in the use of the modern day vernacular, this would bring enough confusion! However! The error goes more deeply than this! I share the following research material that I have done personally for the reader's evaluation.

The following translators, Criesbach, Lachmann, Tischendorf, Tregelles, Alford, Wordsworth and Hart, in their footnotes and translations, have changed the Greek Textus Receptus in approximately 6,000 scriptures. This is the reason why there are so many omissions in the various modern translations of the Bible. If you are using another translation that the KJV, you will find these many omissions. Check them out with the samples I have listed below. The few that I am sharing should convince you why the true believer should hold fast to the original King James Bible!

### From Matthews Gospel

1:25    The word *"firstborn"* is omitted.
5:44    The whole phrase, *"Bless them that curse you"* is omitted.
6:13    *"Kingdom, power and glory"* is omitted.
6:27    The word *"statue"* is changed to "span of life."
6:33    *"Of God"* is omitted which refers to the Kingdom.

### From Mark's Gospel

1:1     "Son of God" is omitted.
1:14    *"Of the Kingdom"* is omitted
1:31    *"Immediately"* is omitted from, *"The fever left."*
2:17    *"To repentance"* is left out from *"call sinners."*
6:11    *"More tolerable for Sodom & Gomorrah"* is omitted.

### From Luke's Gospel

1:28    *"Blessed art thou among women."* is omitted.
2:33    *"Joseph"* is changed to say *"Father."*
2:43    Joseph and his Mother is changed to say, *"parents."*
4:4     *"But by every word of God"* is omitted.
4:8     *"Get thee behind me Satan"* is omitted.

### From John's Gospel

1: 14   *"Begotten"* is omitted in 1:18, 3:16, 3:18
1:27    *"Preferred before me"* is omitted.
3:13    *"Which is in heaven"* is omitted.
3:15    *"Should not perish"* is omitted.
4:42    *"The Christ"* is omitted.

### The Book of Acts

2:30    *"According to the flesh"* is omitted.
7:30    *"Of the Lord"* is omitted concerning an angel.
7:37    *"Him shall ye hear"* is omitted.
8:37    This verse is omitted or in italics.

10:6    *"What thou oughtest to do"* is omitted.

## The Book of Romans

1:16    *"Of Christ"* in omitted or in italics.
1:29    *"Fornication"* is omitted.
5:2     *"By faith"* is omitted in Moffatt, RSV and NEB.
8:1     The last ten words are omitted or in italics.
9:28    *"In righteousness"* is omitted.

## 1 Corinthians

1:14    *"I thank God"* is omitted.
5:7     *"For us"* is omitted concerning Christ's sacrifice.
6:20    7 words are omitted concerning *"your spirit"*
7:5     *"Fasting"* is omitted.
7:39    *"By the law"* is omitted.

## 2 Corinthians

4:6     *"Jesus"* is omitted.
4:10    *"The Lord"* is omitted.
5:18    *"Jesus"* is omitted or in italics
11:31   *"Christ"* is omitted.

## Galatians

1:15    *"God"* is omitted
3:1     *"Of our Lord Jesus Christ"* is omitted.
3:17    *"In Christ"* is omitted.
4:7     *"Through Christ"* is omitted.

## Ephesians

3:9     *"By Jesus Christ"* is omitted.
3:14    *"Of our Lord Jesus Christ"* is omitted.
5:30    *"Of his flesh and bones."* Is omitted.
6:1     *"In the Lord"* is omitted.

## Philippians

3:16    *"Let this mind be in you"* is omitted.

## Colossians

1:2     *"The Lord Jesus Christ"* is omitted.
1:14    *"Through His Blood"* is omitted.
1:28    *"Jesus"* is omitted.
2:11    *"Of the sins of"* is omitted.

## 1 Thessalonians

1:1    *"From God our Father and the Lord Jesus Christ"* is omitted.

2:19   *"Christ"* is omitted.

3:11   *"Christ"* is omitted or in italics.

## 2 Thessalonians

1:8    *"Christ"* is omitted.

## 1 Timothy

1:17   *"Wise"* is omitted from *"The only wise God."*

2:7    *"In Christ"* is omitted or in italics

3:16   *"God"* is omitted from "Manifest in the flesh."

## 2 Timothy

1:11   *"Of the gentiles"* is omitted.

4:1    *"Lord"* is omitted.

4:22   *"Jesus Christ"* is omitted or in italics.

## Titus

1:11   *"The lord"* is omitted

## Philemon

1:6    *"Jesus"* is omitted.

1:12   *"Receive him"* is omitted.

## Hebrews

1:3    *"By Himself"* is omitted from "purged our sins."

2:7    *"Set him over the works of thy hands"* is omitted.

10:30 *"Saith the Lord"* is omitted

## James

5:16   *"Faults"* is changed to the word sins.
        {wrong Greek text}

## 1 peter

1:22   *"Through the Spirit"* is omitted.

4:1    *"For us"* is omitted referring to Christ suffered.

4:14   The last 15 words are omitted or in italics.

## 2 Peter

2:17   "Forever' is omitted or in italics.

3:9    "Us" is changed to "you" which destroys the meaning.

## 1 John
1:7     *"Christ"* is omitted.
2:7     *"From the beginning"* is omitted.
4:3     *"Christ is come in the flesh"* is omitted.

## Jude
1:25    *"Wise"* is omitted referring to God.

## Revelation
1:8     *"The beginning and the end"* are omitted.
1:11    10 words are omitted... *"Alpha and Omega"* etc.
5:14    *"Him that liveth forever and ever."* Is omitted.

### I would bring this scripture to remembrance...

*"For I testify unto every man that heareth the words of the prophecy of this book, If any man shall add unto these things, God shall add unto him the plagues that are written in this book. And if any man shall take away from the words of the book of prophecy, God shall take away his part out of the book of life, and out of the holy city, and from the things written in this book." {Revelation 22:18-19}*

### Another strange twist of...

"theological" thinking that perhaps many people are not aware of. There is a move on to change the use of BC {Before Christ} and AD {Anno Domini or in the year of our Lord} on our calendar. We have always used BC and AD. Only recently some great thinkers called theologians invented the idea of using BCE and CE. BCE stands for "Before Common Era." It is expected to replace BC, which means "Before Christ." CE stands for "Common Era."

It is a new term that is eventually expected to replace AD, which stands for "Anno Domini" in Latin or "in the year of our Lord" in English. These theologians introduced this notation for change because they wanted to follow the golden rule and to avoid distressing the non-Christians of the world. Forcing a Hindu, for example to use AD and BC might be seen by some as coercing them to acknowledge the supremacy of the Christian God and of Jesus Christ. It was they're feeling that the use of a neutral religious term like CE and BCE would cause less pain to non-Christians than would AD and BC. Religious tolerance is their thought.

This is their "reasoning"…The world is becoming more integrated financially, politically, socially and religiously. A universal calendar is needed. Only one out of every three people are Christians in the world today. References to Christ may offend those who are non-Christian. A universal calendar should be religiously neutral in order to be generally accepted. Ce and BCE meet these requirements. I Ask…What about offending the TRUE and LIVING GOD and the Father of our Lord Jesus Christ!

**Truth against Error**
**This is the…**

*"Battle of Armageddon"*

# The Two Suppers
## "The Supper of the Great God"

*"And I saw an angel standing in the sun; and he cried with a loud voice, saying to all the fowls that fly in the midst of heaven, Come gather yourselves together unto the supper of the great God. That ye may eat the flesh of kings, and the flesh of captains, and the flesh of mighty men, and the flesh of horses, and of them that sit on them, and the flesh of all men, both free and bond, both small and great."*
*{Rev. 19:17-18}*

The Revelation prophecy declares that there are two suppers being prepared here at the end of Christian dispensation. Let us consider first the, *"The Supper of the Great God."* Then, we will consider the *"The Wedding Supper of the Lamb"* which is spoken of in this same chapter, verses seven through nine. We will find one to be a deception. As we examine the symbols, we will be able to discern which of these suppers is the deception and which one is the true supper. We are viewing another scene that is placed *"in the midst of heaven,"* with an angelic messenger.

Keep in prospective, this expression symbolizes events pertaining to the church realm on earth. Angels may in some instances symbolize "human messengers" who are called to accomplish their purpose in the religious world. We have previously established that these angels can be good messengers sent by God or they may be evil angels sent from Satan. The angel heralding this invitation was a messenger from the evil one. We can discern this by the content of the message and also to whom the message is addressed. This invitation was given to *"all the fowls that fly in the midst of heaven."* This word "fowl" has a significant meaning, and we find it in the book of psalms. Psalm seventy-eight relates the historical account of the Lord's Covenant with His people Israel. This narrative relates the mighty acts of God and also speaks of the mighty rebellion of His people! It is written that the Lord rained manna from heaven to feed that great host of people as they journeyed in the wilderness and yet they were not satisfied! According to the further record, God dealt with them in another way. It is written in verse twenty-seven that the

Lord *"rained flesh also upon them like dust, and feathered FOWLS like the sand of the sea."* Verse twenty-nine tells us that *"he gave them their own desire."* The story continues in verses thirty and thirty one and lets us know that, *"while their meat was yet in their mouths, The wrath of God came upon them...and smote down the chosen men of Israel."*

We learn from these scriptures that the fowls symbolize the rebellion that took place among the chosen men of Israel. It is written... *"He gave them their own desires."* In our present chapter of Revelation, these fowls represent the "foul spirits" of the leadership who are in rebellion against God's Word and His Spirit. This is an analogy of the great city of religion that was not content to be fed upon God's true manna. As we have learned previously, the institutionalized church world has chosen it's own traditional ways. Since this great city of religion has desired their own way, God has given it to them.

## *"He gave them their own desires."*

In our present chapter of Revelation, the invitation was given, *"Come and gather yourselves together unto the supper of the great God."* It is true that men gather themselves together to fulfill their own desires. However! God draws men by His Spirit and His Word to fulfill His purpose. Let us take particular notice of what these guests are eating at this supper. It is written that they are eating the, *"flesh of kings and captains; the flesh of mighty men and the flesh of horses; them that sit on them; and the flesh of all men both bond and free."* The whole gauntlet seems to be covered in this scripture! The kings, captains and mighty men represent the hierarchies of the great apostate church. They control their adherents through their membership. The flesh of horses represents all the denominational systems, which support this great corporate church extravaganza. The "flesh" of all men, free, bond, small or great represent every wind of doctrine within all sectarianism. Remember! We are considering things in the Spiritual realm. The flesh that these guests are eating at this supper symbolize the doctrines, dogmas, traditions, rituals and forms of Babylon's religious system. They are eating or rather feeding their spirit man on the false food of men's religious dogmas and traditional teachings....Yes! Leadership and laity alike.

We will gain perfect understanding of this analogy as we hear Christ speak on this subject... *"I am the bread of life. Your fathers did eat manna in the wilderness and are dead. This is that bread which comes down from heaven, that a man may eat thereof, and not die. I am the living bread which cometh down from heaven: if any man eat of this bread, he shall live forever: and the bread that I will give is my flesh, which I will give for the life of the world. The Jews therefore strove among themselves, saying, How can this man give us his flesh to eat? Then Jesus said unto them, Verily, verily, I say unto you, Except ye eat the flesh of the Son of man, and drink his blood, ye have no life in you. Whosoever eateth my flesh, and drinketh my blood, hath eternal life; and I will raise him up at the last day."* *{John 6: 48-54}*

How clear this insight is given through Christ's own words. Christ was speaking of His Word, His doctrines and teachings that are written. He is the LIVING Word. As true believers, we feed upon Christ's Word. When we believe it and act upon it, we are eating of Christ's flesh. The Word gives us Life to begin with as we are born again, however, we continue this Life as we continue to eat or partake of the Word. As believers, we must renew our minds daily on Christ's Word. We must, *"meditate on these things, for in doing so we shall both save ourselves and them that hear us."*

## The Conditional Promise...

Whosoever will endure to the end shall be saved. Jesus said... *"IF ye continue in my Word then are ye my disciples indeed."* The *"eating"* of the Word continues to give us Spiritual Life. Praise God! As true believers, we may eat of the Living Bread and drink of the Water of Life freely. Now, we may better understand the analogy given in the prophecy. Although this gathering is being called, *"The Supper of the Great God,"* we notice that the true *"Bread of Life"* is not on the menu. These people were feeding their spirits on the fleshly doctrines, dogmas and traditional religion of this *"Earth Born Beast."* Jesus said, The words that I speak unto you are Spirit and Life and the flesh proffiteth nothing. There was no LIFE being served at this false supper!

We have mentioned that this self-styled False Prophet who is serving this "Supper of the Great God" has the power to deceive, or use a counterfeit to represent God. The counterfeit that has been used by this False Prophet is a form of religion denying the power thereof. A one hour pre-programmed church service is served, rather than preaching and teaching the doctrines of Christ and the Word of God. God has already forewarned us that people would be perishing for lack of knowledge concerning His Word in these end times! The past two generations of religion have brought forth a people who are Bible illiterates! I do not intend to be unkind as I make this statement. I am only considering the available statistics which tell us that few church members even read their Bible, let alone *"study to shew themselves approved unto God."* The acceptance of *"every wind of doctrine"* is prevalent in this extremely religious society.

The apostle Paul penned these stirring words of warning and admonition to All believers of every age. It is written…*"I marvel that ye are so soon removed from him that called you into the grace of Christ unto another gospel: Which is not another; but there be some that trouble you, and would pervert the gospel of Christ. But though we, or an angel from heaven, preach any other gospel unto you than that which we have preached unto you, let him be accused."*

{Galatians 1:6-8}.

This is a stirring admonition! Even if an "angel" appears to present some great revelation…IF…it is not written in the Word…LET HIM BE ACCUSED! All things that we believe MUST be proven by the Word of God. I have accepted this scripture as my one and only guide to determine the difference between the genuine and the counterfeit of any seducing spirit. The Apostle Paul continues to reprove the Galatians for other abuses, as he enters into the third chapter of his epistle. Evidently there was a turning to the "flesh" rather than continuing in the Spirit and faith realm. Although these scriptures are referring primarily to the things of the law, they are also relevant in distinguishing any work of the flesh that would seek to exalt itself above the Spirit. God has given to all believers a "fail safe" method in which we may check for the seducing counterfeit spirits. It is the AGREEMENT that the Word and the Spirit must have in order to claim any experience as the genuine gift from God!

I have endeavored to lay a scriptural foundation in order to examine another deception of the "flesh" that is being served at this false *"Supper of the Great God."* The terminology "speaking in tongues" has been used to describe two very different types of verbal abnormalities...

- **Glossolalia:** This is the most common meaning of "speaking in tongues." The term is derived from two Greek words: glossai, which means "tongues" or "languages," and lalien, which means to "speak."

The Interpreter's One Volume commentary on the Bible defines glossolalia as: "The ecstatic utterance of emotionally agitated religious persons, consisting of a jumble of disjointed and largely unintelligible sounds. Those who speak in this way believe that they are moved directly by a divine spirit and their utterance is therefore quite spontaneous and unpremeditated."

The record of this phenomenon has always been prevalent among heathen tribal religions throughout the past ages of time. Many others who claim this experience are avowed Atheists and Agnostics. This unusual phenomenon had little if any mention in the history of true Christianity until the 20th century. Glossolalia is also practiced by a large number of non-Christian religions around the world...Malaysia, Indonesia, Siberia, Artic regions, China, Japan, Korea, Arabic, and Burma. It is also present extensively in all the African tribal religions. Glossolalia is found among the Inuit {Eskimos} The Saami {Lapps} in Japanese seances in Hokkaido, in a cult led by Genji Yanagide of Moji City, the Shamans in Ethiopia in the zar cult and various spirits in Haitian Voodoo. Does this phenomenon originate with the true God of the Bible? We shall present the truth as we pursue this very vital subject matter.

**Source of information from:**
**www.Religious Tolerance.org**

"So-called "tongues" have reappeared since the Renaissance. In the late 17th century in southern France during the attempted extermination of Protestants by the Roman Catholic church, many victims who exhibited this so-called "gift" were French Calvinists, called Huguenots. In the 18th century: among the British Quakers and American Methodists. In the 19th century: In England among the members of the Catholic Apostolic church and in the United States among the members of the Mormon churches. Later in the 19th century, it became common within the Holiness churches. Early in the 20th century, it was an important factor...perhaps the defining characteristic...at the founding of the Pentecostal movement. In 1900, Charles Parham and a small Bible study group in Kansas began to study Bible passages about the gift of tongues. They began to speak in tongues. In 1906, Parham went to Los Angeles and spoke at the Azusa Street Mission Revival. The movement quickly spread from there. In the 1960s' Believers who spoke in tongues began to form Charismatic groups with existing denominations, both Protestant and Catholic. The "Toronto Blessing" Vineyard church split came. Next, the Pensacola Blessing. Such things as being "slain in the spirit", fainting and remaining motionless for several hours on the floor, uncontrollable waves of laughter, getting "drunk in the spirit," weeping in the spirit, barking like a dog, or other paranormal activities." End quote

We are viewing a revival of the *"works of the flesh"* in these unseemly fleshly activities. Remember...we are still within the boundaries of understanding the, *"Supper of the Great God."* Remember...the *"fowls that fly in the midst of heaven."* Remember...what these kings of the earth were feeding on! FLESH! Even the fleshly seducing doctrines and traditions of men. Remember...It was also written in the previous scriptures that, *"God gave them the desires of their hearts"* when they refused His manna. God will not change His Word to fit or agree with "YOUR" experience. Your experience MUST agree with His Word! Jesus spoke very clearly on the subject of, "signs and wonders," as He walked among us...He said that a, *"Wicked and an untoward generation seeketh after a sign."* He also reminded us that NO sign would be given other than His death, His resurrection and His ascension to the Meditorial Throne of Heaven. It is written that the *"Just shall live by faith."* "Signs and wonders" are supposed to follow believers, not believers following signs and wonders! Even then, the signs and wonders MUST agree with what is already written. The individual's "experience" is NOT the evidence of the genuine gift, unless it is confirmed through the written Word of God! If the experience is not recorded within the pages of Genesis through Revelation, then we must apply the Apostle Paul's admonition... *"But though we, or an angel from heaven, preach any other gospel unto you than that which we have preached unto you, let him be accursed." {Galatians 1:8}*

Granted, there has been great controversy concerning the scriptural accounts as they are written in the book of Acts and in the

Corinthian letter. However, if we would apply the "fail safe" method of proving the experience by the Word, I am convinced that the controversy would soon be eliminated! We will strive to do this after we present this next examination of phenomena called...

• **Xenoglossia:** This is the ability to spontaneously speak a foreign language without having first learned it, or even been exposed to it. This term is also derived from two Greek words: Xenos, which means "foreign" or "foreigner," and glossai, which means "tongues" or "languages." This is an event in which the individual who knows only English, has never been exposed to any other language, and who suddenly starts to speak fluent Swahili. This would be an example of Xenoglossia. Stories of Exenoglossia are well known, particularly within the Pentecostal movement and also psychic research. However! Psychic research has found, *"No scientifically attested case of Zenolalia that has come to light."*

In a massive study of Glossolalia from a linguistic prospective by Professor William J. Samarin of the University of Toronto's Department of Linguistics published after more than a decade of careful research, he rejected the view that glossolalia is Xenoglossia i.e. some foreign language that could be understood by another person who knows that language. Samarin concluded that glossolalia is a *"pseudo-language."* He defined glossolalia as, *"unintelligible babbling speech that exhibits superficial phonological similarity to language, without having consistent syntagmatic structure and that is not systematically derived from or related to known language."* Source: William J. Samarain, "Variation and Variables in Religious Glossolalia." Language in Society, ed. Dell Haymes, Cambridge: Cambridge University Press, 1972 pgs. 121-130

Felicitas D. Goodman, a psychological anthropologist and linguist, engaged in a study of various English – Spanish – and Mayan – speaking Pentecostal communities in the United States and Mexico. She compared tape recording of non-Christian rituals from Africa, Borneo, Indonesia and Japan as well. She published her results in 1972 in an extensive monograph {Speaking in Tongues: A Cross-Cultural Study in Glossolalia by Felecitas D. Goodman, University of Chicago Press, 1972} Goodman concludes that *"when all features of Glosolalia were taken into consideration – that is, the segment structure {such as sounds, syllables, phrases} and its suprasegental elements {namely rhythm, accent, and especially overall intonation} –she concluded that there is no distinction in glossolalia between Christians and the followers of non-Christian {pagan} religions. The "association between trance and glossolalia is now accepted by many researchers as a correct assumption."* Goodman also concludes that Glossolalia *"is actually, a learned behavior. Learned either unawarely or, sometimes consciously.* Others have previously pointed out that direct instruction is given on how to "speak in tongues," ie. How to engage in glossolalia. In fact, it has been found that the "speaking in tongues" practiced in Christian churches and by individuals is identical to the chanting language of those who practice voodoo on the darkest continents of this world." End quote.

Those who engage in this Glossolalia activity are also seduced into the so-called, holy uncontrollable laughter; having seizure like activity, being struck down as dumb or the so-called slain in the spirit. Most every Pentecostal or Charismatic denomination uses the same format of, "worked up" emotions to begin a worship service. "Praise Teams" control and monopolize the music program with vain repetitious choruses. Compare these instructions our Lord gave as recorded in Matthews gospel…*"But when you pray, use not vain repetitions, as the heathen do; for they think that they shall be heard for their much speaking." {Matthew 6:7}*

Many Pentecostal people exhibit another strange fleshly phenomenon. Benny Hinn, Television Star of the T. B. N. is famous for his "blowing" on hundreds of people in succession, whereby they all fall in one massive faint! Secular marvels of mass hypnosis have been doing this act for many years, yet he avows it to be a "move of the Holy Ghost." Evidently, he has convinced his vast audiences that this is the case, for they all fall for it or rather fall at his command.

PLEASE…know that I am sharing God's truth in Love for the multitudes who do desire to know the truth. Jesus was always honest with all to whom He corrected. It is thus written… *"Whom the Lord loveth, He chasteneth betimes."* It is my desire to use the chastening Word of God to help those who have received this deception. The answer…Search the scriptures! Examine "your" experience in the Light of God's Word! Renounce these seducing fleshly spirits, and receive from God the genuine walk of FAITH. Let us look into the Word…You will never find Christ or any of the disciples behaving in the unseemly mannerism previously mentioned. In fact, these various incantations which we have been mentioning that accompany

Pentecostal and Charismatic groups, were the very reason Jesus came into this earth. He came to deliver us from those seducing fleshly and unseemly activities. It was the "demonical" that were out of control of their minds, writhing upon the ground that Christ came to deliver! NOT the believers!

Luke's gospel gives us the account of the demon possessed man who lived in the tombs at Gadaria. AFTER Jesus cast out the "Legion" of devils, the man is seen sitting quietly at the feet of our Lord, clothed in his right mind. He no longer wallows upon the ground in an unseeming manner! {Luke 8:26-39} The Bible mentions only one incident of falling backward under the power of Jesus. This happened when Judas brought the company of armed men to betray our Lord in the garden on that fateful night. This power was not used to "bless believers" with a sensational feeling of exuberance! It was directed upon the enemies of Christ! {John 18:6}

The love of Christ constrains me to address this particular subject matter of speaking in tongues in depth, because it has effected so many sincere people. We are considering an estimated 140 to 370 million people professing Christianity that engage in this verbal abnormality! These statistics reveal then that up to 20% of people who profess Christianity engage in Glossolalia, and the number is growing dramatically! Charismatics usually consider "speaking in tongues' as the fulfillment of the Latter Rain promised in Joel 2:28-29. They believe that Glossolalia is a final manifestation of the Holy Spirit in the end time before the Second Coming of Christ. There is a desperate need in this area to…

> *"examine ourselves to see if we be*
> *in the faith or if we be reprobates."*

Now that we have looked "scientifically" at this phenomenon, let us examine it in the realm and Light of the "Spirit." We are instructed by God to compare… *"Spiritual things with Spiritual things."* Let us look at God's "fail safe" method, which alone is able to reveal and eliminate all seducing spirits and doctrines of devils. Every experience must be in agreement with the Word of God. We are instructed to *"test or try"* the spirits. We can only do this by what the Word says.

## Questions that need Biblical answers...

- What is the origin of Glossolalia?
- Is it from the true God and the Father of our Lord Jesus Christ as He has revealed Himself to be through the Bible?
- Is it a supernatural phenomenon or is it a trance-state, a form of self-hypnosis?
- Is Glossolalia identical with the outpouring of the Holy Spirit at Pentecost as described in the second chapter of Acts?
- Is it identical with Paul's descriptions of the spiritual gifts in 1 Corinthians 12: 14

With the express purpose of analyzing and evaluating the aforementioned questions, we will enter into a systematic study of what the Bible has to say on this subject of "speaking in tongues."

## Let us first consider The Promise From Jesus

*"And behold I send the promise of my Father upon you, but tarry ye in the city of Jerusalem until ye be endued with power from on high."* *{Luke 24:49}* Luke takes this subject up as he writes concerning the promise of our Lord in Acts 1:8...*"But ye shall receive power, after that the Holy Ghost is come upon you; and ye shall be witnesses unto me both in Jerusalem, and in all Judea, and in Samaria, and unto the uttermost part of the earth."* The coming of the Holy Spirit was confirmed and manifested to those who were waiting even as it is written in Acts 2: 1-21. I admonish the reader to redeem the time to read the entire account. We must consider just what this manifestation and confirmation was in order to keep everything in proper prospective.

## Let us evaluate the things that happened in this event.

• *Suddenly there came a sound from heaven as of a rushing mighty wind and there appeared unto them cloven tongues like as of fire; and it sat upon each of them; and they were all filled with the Holy Ghost; and began to speak with other tongues as the Spirit gave them utterance.*

The "wind" is a Biblical symbol, which conveys the idea of an independent power. The wind also implies reviving or refreshing. The "cloven" tongues like as of fire which sat upon each of them symbolizing the two phases of the work of the Holy Spirit, namely cleansing and empowering elements. These disciples all had an individual personal experience. Next it is written that they, *"began to speak with other tongues, as the Spirit gave them utterance."* Notice that this scripture says, "other" denoting that this utterance from the Holy Spirit was a known language that was intelligible and understandable.

- Next, let us analyze the "reason' why these believers received this manifestation of speaking in various languages. Understanding the setting of this occasion will help us to keep all things in proper prospective. During this Apostolic time, there was a different language or dialect spoken about every twenty miles. Many people had gathered in Palestine for the Feast of Pentecost. There were eighteen different dialects or nationalities assembled here on the Day of Pentecost. These are all mentioned in Acts 2:9-11. It is written that, there were devout men out of every nation under heaven gathered together there at Jerusalem.

What an opportunity God had to present to EVERY MAN the message of Christ's resurrection! This is why Jesus said for the disciples to wait...He knew the exact time that the Holy Spirit would descend and for what purpose. We see that there was a problem presented here. The apostles were all Galileans. How could they convey this glorious message to every man? Thus, we find the express purpose and reason for this unusual manifestation of the Holy Spirit. Without this miraculous moving of the Holy Spirit, only a small minority would have heard the Gospel message! The miracle was NOT that of speaking in an incoherent unintelligible manner as Glossolalia is performed today, but the miracle was that... *"Every man heard them speak in his own language."{Acts 2:6}* At NO time did they need an interpreter. Verse seven relates this... *"And they marveled, saying one to another, Behold, are not all these Galileans? And how hear we every man in our own tongue, wherein we were born."* These scriptures confirm beyond a shadow of a doubt that what was said and done was intelligent and understandable with the Divine purpose fulfilled.

## The scriptures present three languages
## to reckon with...

**1. The language of the soul:** The scripture makes this distinction. *"Likewise the Spirit also helpeth our infirmities, for we know not what we should pray for as we ought; but the Spirit itself maketh intercession for us with groaning which cannot be uttered."* *{Romans 8:26}* The language of the soul is NOT a verbal abnormality of unintelligible babbling, but it is rather an unuttered, inexpressible burden of the soul. It is written that the Holy Spirit helps this infirmity by making intercession for us with HIS groanings, which cannot be uttered.

**2. The supernatural gift of languages:** The supernatural gift of languages is recorded in the second chapter of the book of acts. We have already given considerable attention to this portion of scripture, but will make this brief summation. The supernatural gift of languages would be the empowering of the Holy Spirit that enables the human voice to speak a language that was not learned, yet is understandable to the listener.

**3. The natural language:** Is that language that we have learned progressively from infancy. It is known as our mother tongue or native tongue. A child will learn to speak any language that it is nurtured in.

The fourteenth chapter of first Corinthians appears to be that which brings the most controversy concerning this subject of "speaking in tongues." I ask the reader to redeem the time to read the entire fourteenth chapter of first Corinthians, as we will be touching on only the key scriptures in this discourse. Paul's letter to the Corinthian church is actually a letter of reproof or correction. It will help us to know the proper setting or background for this church situation...

## The proper setting or background

Corinth, the ancient city of Greece was a commercial city of great wealth, filled with lewd practices and vice. Their commercial enterprises drew many people from the surrounding areas. These various nationalities gathering together into one locality brought a certain amount of confusion and trouble. There was a tremendous language barrier within the city. This language barrier had evidently become a problem in the established Christian church, which the Apostle Paul had founded there in A.D.52. In the Corinthian letter, we hear Paul trying to correct some of these abuses. The cause of the confusion within the congregation was NOT one of false tongues. The confusion came from a lack of the proper use and place for the language of the soul, the proper use and place for the supernatural gift of language along with their various native tongues. How to put these things in order is the focus of Paul's letter designed to correct this situation.

We will follow his format...Paul had already outlined God's design for the church to operate in these Spiritual gifts in the twelfth chapter of this same Epistle. It would again be profitable for the reader to read the entire chapter for understanding the overall picture. The summation of this process is related in verses seven through eleven. *"But all these worketh that one and self same Spirit, dividing to every man severally as he wills. {1 Cor. 12:11}* Paul then begins the admonishment in the first verse of chapter 14, to *"Follow after charity, and desire spiritual gifts, but rather that ye may prophesy."* The priority is preaching the Word! It is the Word of God that brings salvation! It has pleased the Lord through the foolishness of preaching that all men might be saved. Faith comes by HEARING the Word. This is why Paul begins his reproof about speaking in an *"unknown"* tongue. He tells us that the man who does this is only edifying himself. In other words it is a mystery what the person is saying if you do not understand the language he is speaking. What actually is this *"unknown"* tongue Paul is referring to? Well, first of all many conjecture that this word was placed there by the translators and was not in the original. This perhaps may be the case, however I do not believe that it is relevant to bring proper understanding. With or without the word "unknown" we may still receive the understanding...if...we just use good common sense.

Remember! Paul is referring to a language. He is referring to one of the many diversified native tongues that were spoken within this mixed congregation of Christians. In order for Paul to rightfully call this a "tongue" it would have to be known by someone, or it would be gibberish. When this person is praying or speaking a testimony, those who do not know the language cannot understand him. It is a mystery to them as to what the man is saying. It is as simple as that!

This is why Paul admonishes the people to have an interpreter so that all may be edified. He goes to great length in the continuing verses {7-14} to explain through the natural laws how confusing it would be to discern what was being said or done, except the trumpet give a distinctive sound. He even reemphasizes this in asking this question..."*Else when thou shalt bless with the spirit, how shall he that occupieth the room of the unlearned say Amen at thy giving thanks, seeing he understandeth not what thou sayest?*" He even gives further instructions about interpretation in verses 26-33. He instructs the people to *"keep silent"* in the church if there is no one to interpret the foreign language. He concludes with this statement... *"God is not the author of confusion."*

Many people become confused at Paul's statement that he himself spoke with more tongues than all. If the circumstances are known, there is no confusion. Paul was a highly educated man. He had learned the various languages of that day. It is said that he could speak in nine different languages. Paul was able to communicate the gospel to the many people living within Corinth who had diversified languages. This would have attributed to his success in the foundation work of the Corinthian church. Paul was NOT operating in the supernatural gift that is spoken of in the book of Acts. It is very important to keep all these scriptures in their proper context, if we would rightly divide the Word of truth. Paul relates the express purpose for the genuine supernatural gift in verse twenty-two. Let us consider what he is saying... *"Wherefore tongues are for a sign, not to them that believe, but to them that believe not:..."*Paul uses a synerio to explain this further. *"If therefore the whole church come together into one place, and all speak with tongues, and there come in those that are unlearned, or unbelievers, will they not say that ye are mad?"*

May I use this simple modern synerio of my own... If I am a believer, and I desire as did the disciples on the day of Pentecost wish to convey the message of Christ to a person who is an unbeliever, I have the same right to expect God to impart to me a "supernatural" ability to speak their language. They will have the same response as

216

did those who, *"heard in their own language"* which is recorded in the Bible. They will consider this a miracle, since I did not learn their language. If I may interject this thought here...I do believe that the gifts of God are still operable in the Body of Christ...IF...they are needed. God's supernatural gift of speaking in a language, which was not learned, would be of great benefit to those who would be called into various mission fields. They would not need a sentence by sentence interpretation by another person about what they were preaching. The preaching of the gospel would surely be more effective in this manner.

The whole objective of any public gathering of the church is to edify, build up and increase the faith in God through the "hearing" of the word. Paul is drawing upon this contrast as he relates... *"Now, brethren, if I come unto you speaking with tongues, what shall it profit you, except I shall speak to you either by revelation, or by knowledge, or by prophesying, or by doctrine?"* Many of God's people have fallen prey to this counterfeit experience called *"speaking in tongues."*

The WORD of God is our only protector! If the experience does not stand the scrutiny of the Word, we should be afraid of it. Satan is the arch deceiver of mankind. If he can deliver a counterfeit experience, it will not be long until you will loose your spirit of discernment for truth. You will loose your faith ability to rebuke Satan's continuing harassments as he tries to attack you in other ways. Satan will have you "babbling in an incoherent manner" which has no power. If you do not know what you are saying to God to pull down the strong holds, you will be defeated! God is a covenant God. We must act through that covenant which incorporates His Word.

Our Lord Jesus spoke this warning to His followers concerning these last days... *"Then if any man shall say unto you, Lo, here is Christ, or there; believe it not. For there shall arise false Christs, and false prophets, and shall shew great signs and wonders; insomuch that, if it were possible, they shall deceive the very elect."* {Matthew 24; 23-24}

This is a very strong warning! Even the very elect of God are included in this warning. Notice the phrase *"insomuch that, if it were possible."* Again affirming that the *"elect of God"* must keep their faith in God's Word to prevent that possibility. These fleshly exhibitions are surely a confirmation that the true church has entered into the "Battle of Armageddon." Again, we affirm this battle to be the final SPIRITUAL battle of God's truth against Satan's error, which has come through Babylon's religions. God will separate His people as this battle rages!

## Other Diversified Deceptions

I have labored to a great extent in exposing these more profound errors, which confront our religious society. Yet… there are many other cults and groups outside of the mainline denominations which also have brought forth their deceptive heresies. This book could not contain the whole, if I were to relate all the deceptions that have come forth through this *"Supper of the Great God."* However! I am impressed of the Lord to bring an awareness of those deceptions that appear to be the most accepted in our religious culture of today. The following information is taken from the book…

## "Strange New Faiths"
### by: Kenneth E. Jones.

* **Jehovah's Witnesses**

Jehovah's Witnesses have used many names in the past to identify themselves…Millennial Dawn, Watch Tower and Tract Society, Peoples Pulpit Association, Brooklyn Tabernacle, and the International Bible Students' Association. Jehovah's Witnesses consider themselves to be the only witnesses of Jehovah on earth. Charles Taze Russell was the originator of this movement in the late 1800s. However, it was another leader that came on the scene in 1931 called J.F. Rutherford who introduced the name, "Jehovah's Witnesses." Rutherford claimed that Abel was the first Witness, and all who become Jehovah's Witnesses are a direct descendent of Abel. They stand against all other organized religion. They center their attention on a door to door visitation and literature outreach to gain new adherents. The seeming success of this movement comes from those among them that are "special" group workers. Part-time workers called "Publishers" are committed to spend sixty hours a month for literature distribution. Full-time workers are called "Pioneers." They have distributed millions of copies of Studies in the Scriptures. This book is Russell's interpretation of the Bible. The Jehovah's Witnesses must use this book to study their Bible. This cult not only denies the doctrine of the Trinity which in itself is heresy, but they also deny the divinity of Christ. They do not believe that Jesus human body was ever raised from the dead. They teach that his body was removed from the tomb, so that it would not prevent the disciples from believing in Him. They also come forth with a bazaar teaching that Christ's corpse will be on exhibition during their supposed Millennial Age. There is no assurance of salvation, because they do not believe in the full atonement that Christ provided through Calvary. According to their philosophy the work of redemption will be completed during the millennium. Jehovah's Witness doctrine teaches that there is no place called Hell. They deny that the soul of man is immortal. According to their doctrine, the resurrection will not be a resurrection of our original bodies, but a re-creation. Those who have died will be created all over again in order to have another chance at salvation. Those who refuse salvation will be annihilated. They will not suffer hell, but will just cease to exist.

{What a distortion has come forth to deceive men's souls!}

- **Mormanism**

More recently named Church of Jesus Christ of latter Day Saints, was like all other cults founded by an eccentric one-man stance. In the early 1800s' Joseph Smith claimed to have seen visions when he was fifteen years old. As he wondered about in the woods, he said he saw two people. One of them he said was God, the Father and the other he said was Jesus. Two years later, he is said to have another vision of one called, "Moroni" who told him that he had been chosen of God for this new undertaking. Later, he said he went to a place on the hill called Cumorah and found some gold plates with strange writing on them. Buried with them were two magic stones, which were to help translate the writings. Moroni was supposed to have appeared at that time and told him he could not take these plates as yet. He returned four years later to take the plates home and translate them. He says, that he did this translating in secret with the precious plates and magic stones. Separated by a curtain, he is supposed to have read the translation to this unknown "someone" sitting on the other side of the curtain. This "story" claims validation by eleven witnesses who said that they saw the golden plates. This claim is still printed in the front of each copy of the book of Mormons. The Book of Mormon tells how a group of Jews in the time of Jeremiah migrated from Jerusalem to America. Here they prospered and divided into two groups. One group developed a strong civilization and built huge cities whose ruins have been found in Central and South America. The other group degenerated, became dark skinned and forgot the worship of the Lord. These are the American Indians. The first group was eventually destroyed in a final battle, which took place near the hill of Cumorah, in New York State. But before this God had sent prophets among them, just as in Palestine. Jesus appeared to them after His ascension and taught them some of the same truths he had taught during His earthly ministry. The story of the revelations of God in the Western Hemisphere was condensed by the prophet Mormon and given to his son Moroni who added to it and buried the golden plates containing it on the hill of Cumorah. Mormonism has two other books by Joseph Smith...Doctrines and Covenants and The Pearl of Great Price. In spite of all evidence to the contrary concerning the whole structure of Mormonism based upon this alleged story, Mormon's still defend the "story" told by John Smith.

### {Their articles of faith}
Mormons believe that God Himself was once as we are now and is an exalted man. Spirits are begotten by gods and their polygamous wives and are put in human bodies to learn of nature and in turn become gods. Righteous Mormons are "sealed in celestial marriages." and will go to a third heaven and eventually be gods. Mormons are baptized for the dead and even married to those who have already died, for the salvation of the dead.

### {Salvation Issue}
After stating that men may be saved through the atonement of Christ, they further more teach that those who die in their sins are not lost. All will eventually be saved, for there is another opportunity beyond the grave. There will be no eternal punishment after death.

### {Confusion concerning the Trinity of God.}
Disagreement stems from the belief that the Holy Spirit is spirit, but that the Father and the Son have bodies. They are perfect bodies, but human nevertheless. An important teaching of the Mormon Church is that Christ will soon come again to bring in the millennium and set up His throne in the Mormon temple in Salt Lake City or in independence Missouri. The tribes of Judah will be gathered in Jerusalem, but the rest of the righteous will be gathered into the New Jerusalem in the Western Hemisphere. During the thousand years the gospel will be preached to all who have not heard it. At the end of that time, Satan will rule for a time over many. Then will come the Battle of Armageddon, the final resurrection and the judgement. The earth will pass away, and there will be a new heaven and earth. Eventually all will be saved, but some will reach higher planes than others. Some will barely make it into heaven, while others will be gods. There are now six groups of Mormons, each claiming to be the only true followers of Smith. But the Utah group is by far the largest, having more than half the total membership. It has become a large and prosperous business. Tithing is practiced and a vigorous missionary program is carried out with excellent service agencies maintained. They believe in a continuing revelation through their prophets apart from the finished work of the Bible.

**{God's warning is that if anyone add to or take away from His Holy Writ, let him be accursed}**

- **Christian Science**

  Mary Baker Eddy, was born in 1821 in New Hampshire, the youngest of six children. She was an impressionable child and often spoke of hearing voices when no one else was near. She spent much time in reading the Bible. She had joined the Congregational Church while young, although she did not agree with all their teachings. She retained her membership until she founded her own church years later. Her first husband died and she remarried. After her second husband deserted her, she established herself as a healer and teacher of the healing art. She herself had been more or less an invalid for most of her forty years. At this time she suffered from frequent attacks of a spinal affliction. She heard of a man named P. Quimby of Portland, Maine who was performing miracles of healing without medication. She went to him and was supposedly healed. He was known to be a "mesmerist healer." Mary Baker Eddy studied under this man's teachings. In 1875, Mrs. Eddy published her first book, Science and Health. She began to teach others her method of healing and sent them out to set offices up of their own. Instead of a sermon, portions of scripture are read along with selections from Science and Health.

  **{Basic statements of Christian Science}**

  God is all...This would be Hindu pantheism, which means that the Universe taken as a whole is God, yet, Christian Science denies the existence of matter. It says that God is not matter, for matter does not exist. All that is not God is unreal, nonexistent. Any apparent existence other than God is the result of ignorance and error. So sin, death and disease do not really exist, but are simply wrong thinking, an illusion and a dream. Evil is not real but only appears to be because of our wrong thoughts. Christian Science says to the sick person..."If you will believe that you are well, you will be well, because you really are well already; you only think you are sick." Yet! Christian Scientists play up their cures and make testimonials a part of their services and all their publications. They are quite illogical, in that at the same time they deny there is a sickness of which to be healed. If the disease is not real, there can be no logical cure. Christian Science healing is not related to the Christian prayer for healing. James writes..."And the prayer of faith shall save the sick, and the Lord shall raise him up; and if he hath committed sins, they shall be forgiven him. {James 5:15} Mary Baker Eddy's book, Science and Health: denies this scripture. She states: "A mere request that God will heal the sick has no power to gain more of the divine presence than is always at hand. The beneficial effect of such prayer for the sick is on the human mind...The common custom of praying for the recovery of the sick finds help in blind belief, whereas help should come from the enlightened understanding." This amounts to a flat contradiction of the teaching of the Bible. Christian Science rejects the doctrine of the Trinity. Their idea of the Trinity is this: God is called "Father-Mother." Christ is called 'the spiritual idea of sonship." The Holy Spirit is "Christian Science itself." Christian Science teaches that God did not create man, but that man is now, and forever has been, perfect, eternal child of God. This totally denies the record of Genesis 1:27. Christian Science teaches that man has never been separated from God and therefore needs no redemption or atonement. However! Isaiah writes: "But your iniquities have separated between you and your God, and your sins have hid his face from you, that he will not hear." {Isaiah 59:2} In her book, Science and Health, Mrs. Eddy writes: "The atonement is achieved by human effort and not by the vicarious sacrifice of Jesus on the cross of Calvary. The material blood of Jesus was no more efficacious to cleanse from sin when it was shed on the accursed tree than when it was flowing through his veins. Compare this with what is written in the Bible..."The blood of Jesus Christ his Son cleanseth us from all sin." {1 John 1:7} All of these false teachings and many more will be found in Mary Baker Eddy's books, Key to the Scriptures and Science and Health. These books are filled with controversial statements, half-truths and peculiar interpretations. End Quote

## Unscriptural Ideologies of Mainline Denominations

We are also confronted with a multitude of unscriptural ideologies within mainline religions professing Christianity.

• **The Presbyterian doctrine** has always propagated their "predestination" theory. This error distorts God's gracious plan of choice based on His love for every individual born into this world. Presbyterian doctrine teaches that God chooses certain people to be saved, and others He chooses to eliminate. This has always been a damnable heresy! The greatest gift of God is the freedom of choice that He has granted to ALL mankind! God's gracious invitation is..."*Whosoever will*" may come. Surely this is not that difficult to understand!

Hear God's eternal purpose for ALL who will make their choice to serve Him... "*Blessed be the God and the Father of our Lord Jesus Christ, who hath blest us with all spiritual blessings in heavenly places in Christ: According as he hath chosen us in him before the foundation of the world, that we should be holy and without blame before him in love: Having predestined us unto the adoption of children by Jesus Christ to himself, according to the good pleasure of his will. To the praise of the glory of his grace, wherein he hath made us accepted in the beloved. In whom we have redemption through his blood, the forgiveness of sins, according to the riches of his grace."* {*Ephesians 1:3-7*} God has predestined ALL who will accept His gracious offer of salvation through the atonement of Christ.

• **The denomination called the "Christian Church" along with many Baptist groups** propagate the "baptismal regeneration" doctrine. This means that you do not attain salvation as a free gift from God in the New Birth experience. They believe that a person must be immediately baptized to attain salvation. Certainly baptism is a required commitment to Christ, but it surely does not perform that operation that God performs in giving a new heart. Peter gives the Biblical definition of that which God intended for Baptism... *"The like figure whereunto even baptism doth also now save us {not the putting away of the flesh, but the answer of a good conscience toward God,} by the resurrection of Jesus Christ."* {*1Peter 3:21*} The answer to a good conscience is to be born again of the Spirit of God through believing in the resurrection of Jesus Christ. Paul continues to elaborate on this subject of baptism in Romans... *"Know ye not, that so many of us as were baptized into Jesus Christ were baptized into his death? Therefore we are buried with him by baptism into death: that like as Christ was raised up from the dead by the glory of God the Father, even so we also should walk in newness of life...For in that he died, he died unto sin once: but in that he liveth, he liveth unto God. Likewise reckon ye yourselves to be dead indeed unto sin, but alive unto God through Jesus Christ our Lord."* {*Romans 6:3-11*}

• **"Water"** does not perform a changed heart or a new life. It is the Spirit that giveth Life. If this is not clear enough, God has given one clarion scripture that should forever settle this question about baptism... *"Buried with him in baptism, wherein also ye are risen with him through the faith of the operation of God, who hath raised him from the dead."* {*Colossians 2:12*} The "operation" of God through giving a new heart by faith is that which SAVES! It is surely not the act of baptism that gives new Life! It is written!

223

• **Of all the mainline denominations, perhaps the Baptists** could be termed the most "diversionary" people. Their history is one of multitudes of splintered groups. Baptists were born out of the Radical Reformation, which began during the 16th Century. Their radical behavior has seemed to continue to this day, even among themselves.

Source: Baptist History html. "It was in Seventeenth Century England that Baptists began using the term for self-identification. Because of their differences on doctrinal issues, Baptists began to form associations of "like-minded" churches, which gave rise to the first Baptist denominations. Baptists grew in number, especially during the Great Awakening of the last half of the 18th Century. Soon, however, differences among Baptists began to divide the flock again. In 1845 the pro-slavery Baptists organized the Southern Baptist Convention. Later various Baptists agencies consolidated to form the Northern Baptist Convention in 1907. Twentieth Century Baptists have seen continued splits. From the Northern Baptist Convention came the General Association of regular Baptist Churches in 1932 and the Conservative Baptist Churches in 1940. From the Southern Baptist Convention came the Landmarkers in 1905 who formed the American Baptist Association and the Baptist Bible Fellowship in the 1950s. There are also the Baptist General Conference {which comes from the Swedish Baptists} and the North American Baptist Conference {which comes form the German Baptists} There are now more than 50 Baptist groups in the United States alone." End Quote

All these diversified opinions of men deny the scriptures which tell us... *"Now I beseech you, brethren, by the name of the Lord Jesus Christ, that ye all speak the same thing, and that there be no divisions among you; but that ye should be perfectly joined together in the same mind and in the same judgement." {1 Corinthians 1:10}*

All of this previous information concerning these various factions of religions only verifies that which I am writing about in this prophetic book. It is even the *"more sure word of prophecy."* It appears that the doctrine of "eternal security" is the only doctrine that all Baptists seem to be able to agree upon. The more common terminology for eternal security would be "once saved always saved." {OSAS} Baptists' teach that it is impossible to loose your salvation once you have been saved. Basically, their ideology is this...If you go back into sin after you have accepted Christ as Savior, you are only out of fellowship with God, but still saved. What does the Bible have to say about this vain philosophy?

Peter penned these stirring words as a warning to all true believers in Christ. *"But as there were false prophets also among the people, even as there shall be false teachers among you, who privily shall bring in damnable heresies, even denying the Lord that bought them, and bring upon themselves swift destruction. And many shall follow their pernicious ways, by reason of whom the way of truth shall be evil spoken of." {2 Peter 2:1-2}*

## A *"Damnable Heresy"*

is a lie that will ultimately damn your soul through out the ceaseless ages of eternity! Eternal security is that damnable Heresy! If your belief system will not take God at His Word, then you will die IN your sin and be eternally lost! NEVER to be in the presence of the God who made you for that eternal fellowship! Multitudes have followed this pernicious way!

God has given mankind His exceeding great and precious promises. Believers may now become partakers of His Divine nature having escaped the corruption that is in the world through lust. {2 Peter 1:4} This means that the carnal nature of man is eradicated! It is NOT just suppressed! The indwelling presence of the Spirit of God abides within and keeps the believer holy, as God is holy. The inspired writers of the Bible have made salvation very simple, but man's theology and traditional theories has confounded its simplicity! It is written: *"By grace are ye saved through faith; and that not of yourselves: it is a gift from God: Not of works, lest any man should boast." {Ephesians 2:8-9}*

Let us understand and accept the in depth truth of this scripture the way in which God intended it. "Grace" means God's unearned and undeserved favor to all mankind. This grace or favor comes to all mankind through Christ. Grace has been given through God's covenant with Christ. His grace has been given because of His Son's perfect sacrifice for mans' sin. When the Spirit of God brings conviction for sin, righteousness and judgement to come, He also brings the command to repent. To repent means to turn FROM sin unto righteousness, even unto Christ. We trust the reader understands the "grace" issue spoken of here.

Now, let us consider the word "saved." It is written that *"whosoever shall call upon the name of the Lord shall be saved."*

How are we saved? *"Believe on the Lord Jesus Christ and thou shalt be saved." {Acts 2:21 and Acts16:30}* To believe is an exercise of our faith. We choose to believe. What are we saved from? Being saved, means to be saved FROM sin, self {sinful nature} and Satan. According to Matthew 1:21, Jesus came to save His people FROM their sins, not IN them. Again this sure promise has been given to all believers...*"Wherefore he {Jesus} is able to save them to the uttermost that come unto God by him, seeing he ever liveth to make intercession for them." {Hebrews 7:25}* We trust that the reader understands the "saved" issue spoken of here.

There is a "faith" issue involved here in this scripture that has been overlooked by the multitudes who are propagating the damnable heresy of "eternal security." By grace are ye saved through what? By grace are ye saved through FAITH! Whose faith? It is your faith, my faith that saves us. Didn't Jesus say to everyone that He healed...*"Thy faith has made thee whole."* Baptist advocates of the eternal security doctrine place the emphasis on the wrong connotation in this scripture. They labor on emphasizing the "works" and leave the issue of "faith" out of it. They mistakenly think that it says the "gift" is "faith." NO! The scripture says that we are saved by OUR faith. The gift that we are receiving from God is His salvation. Being saved is the "gift" from God that Paul is writing about...not "faith."

We are saved by grace meaning God's unearned and undeserved favor through our faith. It is our faith in the finished work of the everlasting covenant, which God made through Christ. We begin with "faith" and we continue in faith until our faith becomes sight as we pass from this life to the next. It is written that the *"just shall live by faith."* We continue this justified relationship with God by faith. It is written...*"Therefore being justified by faith we have peace with God through our Lord Jesus Christ: By whom also we have access by faith into this grace wherein we stand, and rejoice in hope of the glory of God." {Romans 5:1-2}*

**This is a "standing grace" not a "falling grace."**
**However...it is maintained by OUR faith.**

We are admonished to give, *"diligence to make our calling and election sure: for if ye do these things ye shall never fail." {2 Peter 1:10}* Peter has written a "list" of things that believers are to do having become a partaker of God's Divine nature. He names them in the previous verses... *"Whereby are given unto us exceeding great and precious promises: that by these ye might be partakers of the divine nature, having escaped the corruption that is in the world through lust. And beside this, giving all diligence, add to your faith virtue; and to virtue knowledge; and to knowledge temperance; and to temperance patience; and to patience godliness; and to godliness brotherly kindness; and to brotherly kindness charity. For if these things be in you, and abound, they make you that ye shall neither be barren nor unfruitful in the knowledge of our Lord Jesus Christ. But he that lacketh these things is blind, and cannot see afar off, and hath forgotten that he was purged from his old sins." {1 Peter 1:4-9}*

Does this sound like God will accept OSAS? Do these scriptures teach the "eternal security" sin you will sin you must acceptance? Surely not! *"Now "Faith" is the substance of things hoped for, the evidence of things not seen." {Hebrews 11:1}* Without faith it is impossible to please God. God requires faith for everything that we receive from Him. Eternal security is a theory, which leaves the pathway of "faith" and gets sidetracked into the "works" issue. We repeat Ephesians 2:9 which said, *"Not of works, lest any man should boast."* Yet! James has written under the inspiration of God that "works" are surely accompanied by our faith. Hear the Word of the Lord...*"Yea, a man may say, Thou has faith, and I have works: shew me thy faith without thy works, and I will shew you my faith by my works. Thou believest that there is one God; and thou doest well: the devils also believe, and tremble. But wilt thou know, O vain man, that faith without works is dead?" {James 2:18-20}*

True! Salvation is not of ourselves, it is the gift of God. True! Salvation does not come by our works, lest any man should boast, it is the gift of God. However! We must receive salvation {being saved} through believing! It is through FAITH that we receive eternal Life. God has not taken away our freedom of choice in this matter. It is OUR choice to live by FAITH. There is a faith principle involved in our salvation experience. Faith is a lifetime principal in our probationary journey through this life. *"He that enndureth to the end, the same shall be saved." {Matthew 10:22}*

Christ is not a tyrannical King that makes us obey Him. He has given us this way of "faith" to respond to Him. Saving faith is a belief in the acceptance of God's favor to man through Christ by the intellect, affection and will. Faith is a condition on our part whereby we come to be partakers of the New Covenant. It is a *"faith that worketh by love."* It is not an idle, inactive faith, but shows itself by producing love and obedience to God. The Gospel is the "object" of faith. Faith produces a sincere obedience in the life at conversion. John wrote: *"For whatsoever is born of God overcometh the world: and this is the victory that overcometh the world, even our faith. Who is he that overcometh the world, but he that believeth that Jesus is the Son of God." {1 John 5:4-5}*

Hear the conclusion of the matter…*"Knowing that a man is not justified by the works of the law, but by the faith of Jesus Christ, even we have believed in Jesus Christ, that we might be justified by the faith of Christ, and not by the works of the law: for by the works of the law shall no flesh be justified. But if while we seek to be justified by Christ, we ourselves are found sinners, is therefore Christ the minister of sin? God forbid. …I am crucified with Christ: nevertheless I live; yet not I, but Christ liveth in me: and the life I now live in the flesh I live by the faith of the Son of God, who loved me and gave himself for me. I do not frustrate the grace of God: for if righteousness come by the law, then Christ is dead in vain." {Galatians 2:16-21}*

Eternal security advocates preach that a person can continue in sin that grace may abound and still be saved. They lift many scriptures from their original context to prove their point. They leave the FAITH and OBEDIENCE issue out of all their false theories! They frustrate the grace of God by doing this! The Apostle asks…Is Christ the minister of sin? No! Christ is not the minister of sin! IF we are crucified with Christ, we do not continue IN sin. What a contradiction and a reproach to Christ's sacrificial death and His resurrection power to preach a sin you will, sin you must religion! Or…once saved always saved heresy! Charles Stanley may have written a full-length book to persuade others of "Eternal Security," but when we ALL stand before God, we will be judged by God's Book, NOT Charles Stanley's book.

I would conclude with this clarion scripture concerning Christ's sojourn here on earth. *"Who in the days of his flesh, when he had offered up prayers and supplication with strong crying and tears unto him that was able to save him from death, and was heard in that he feared; Though he were a Son, yet learned he obedience by the things which he suffered; And being made perfect, he became the author of eternal salvation unto all them that obey him." {Hebrews 5:7-9}*

If God's own Son was commissioned and commanded to live by FAITH and OBEDIENCE though He was the only begotten Son of God, who do we think we are to speak such heresy! Who do we think we are that we may continue IN sin when Christ paid the ultimate price to redeem us FROM sin! The scriptures tell us that He was made perfect so that He could become the author of eternal salvation unto all that OBEY Him. ETERNAL SALVATION is for the OBEDIENT. Faith brings that obedience through the Spirit of Christ within. Eternal security rests on God's covenant through OUR FAITH.

## Please consider the seriousness of your decision.

- A Christian is born again...by FAITH {1 Peter 1:23}
- A Christian is justified......by FAITH{Romans 5:1}
- A Christian is made righteous ...by FAITH {James 5:16}
- A Christian is kept by the power of God through...FAITH {1 Peter 1:5}
- A Christian's righteousness comes through...FAITH {Philippians 3:9}
- A Christian has Christ dwelling in the heart by...FAITH {Ephesians 3:17}
- Christians' hold fast their profession in Christ through... FAITH {Hebrews 10:23}
- A Christian fights the good fight of...FAITH
- {1 Timothy 6:12}
- A Christian finishes his course by keeping the ...FAITH {2 Timothy 4:7}

It is the general consensus within the, *"Great City"* of religion that it is impossible to live a life free from sin in this present world. The unlimited efficacy of the blood of Jesus to eradicate sin is rejected by the majority of what we have come to call, "Christendom."

229

According to the Hebrew writer, the blood of bulls and goats could never take away sin. However, we read of the perfect sin remedy in Hebrews 9:11-12... *"But Christ being come an high priest of good things to come, by a greater and more perfect tabernacle, not made with hands, that is to say not of this building; Neither by the blood of goats and calves, but by his own blood he entered in once into the holy place, having obtained eternal redemption for us."*

**Redemption means to be "redeemed."**
**Redeemed means to be "saved."**

I would be remiss, if I did not mention another erroneous teaching that has done despite to the grace of God and has long hindered the Body of Christ. The great majority of Baptist denominations, the Churches of Christ and a variety of other sects do not accept the God given call of women into full ministry. It seems strange, but true that the "secular world" has addressed the situation of women's discrimination before the "church world." The secular world has termed this discrimination against women as, "male Chauvinism."

**I am sure that God uses the same terminology.**
**(*-*)**

# Women's place in Christ's Kingdom...

I have set myself in defense of the gospel, rather than in the defense of Jeanne Trovato, so I must relate what God's Word has to say on this most important subject... It is almost ludicrous to think that anyone who has done a simple unbiased study on the subject of the woman's place in the church would exclude the female gender! As we read the Word of God, common sense and reasoning tells us that the Author of the Book uses the word "man" to refer to humankind, whether they be male and or female. The word "man" has been used as a "neuter gender" and is applicable to ALL humanity. There are multitudes of scriptures that verify this stance. I have gleaned out but a few. I would direct our attention to several very elementary scriptures that should prompt our thinking into the truth...

- John 3:2-4 *"Jesus answered and said unto him, Verily, verily, I say unto you, except a MAN be born again, he cannot see the kingdom of God. Nicodemous saith unto him, How can a MAN be born again when he is old?"*

I pose this questions…Does this scripture exclude WOMEN? Can MEN only be born again? Why didn't the Lord make a distinction here? Why didn't he include the word WOMAN also as one that can be born again?

- 2 Corinthians 5:17 *"Therefore if any MAN be in Christ, HE is a new creature: old things are passed away; behold, all things are become new."*

I ask again…Can a WOMAN be in Christ? Are not WOMEN also made new creatures in Christ?

- Romans 6:6 *"Knowing that our old MAN is crucified with Him, that the body of sin might be destroyed, that henceforth we should not serve sin."*

Isn't a WOMAN crucified with Christ, that HER body of sin might also be destroyed? Do not WOMEN also share in this experience?

- *John 3:36 "HE that believeth on the Son of God hath everlasting life: and HE that* believeth *not the Son shall not see life: but the wrath of God abideth on HIM.*

Is a WOMAN denied everlasting life because the scriptures do not say SHE? Does the wrath of God abide on MEN only?

Are you getting my/God's point here? How ridiculous it is to make a distinction between a male and a female when the Word of God makes none! The traditional teachings of men have lifted out negative scriptures from their original context to build their case against a woman's place in the Body of Christ. This is their chosen one…1 Corinthians 14: 34-35. *"Let your women keep silence in the church; for it is not permitted unto them to speak; for they are commanded to be under obedience, as also saith the law. And if they will learn anything, let them ask their husbands at home: for it is a shame for a woman to speak in the church."*

## Let us hear the truth concerning this comment.

What command of obedience was Paul referring to and under what law? The Apostle Paul was stating a Jewish ordinance from the Jewish Talmud when he wrote, *"Let your women keep silence in the church."* The Scribes and the Pharisees had written the Jewish Talmud, which denied the WOMEN the privilege of participation in the synagogue worship. God did not inspire the Jewish Talmud! It was not ordained of God! It was not a part of the inspired Word of God. Men had usurped the position of honor in reading and studying the scriptures because of this Talmud ordinance. Before Christ came and elevated the woman on an equal plane with man, the Jews did not permit a women to teach, speak, or even ask questions in the synagogue. The women knew very little about God in that male dominated Jewish religion. They did not know the scriptures as the men did. This is why Paul wrote: *"If they will learn anything, let them ask their husbands at home."* It is true that the women were causing a disturbance in the assembly by asking questions.

**Adam Clark**, one of the most recognized historians and theologians of the Christian Judeo faith gives this understanding in his commentary…"It was permitted to any man to ask questions, to object, altercate, attempt to refute in the synagogue; but this liberty was not given to the women. Paul confirms this in reference to the Christian church. He orders them to keep silence; if they wish to learn anything, let them ask their husbands at home, because it was perfectly indecorous for women to be contending with men in the public assembly on points of doctrine, cases of conscience etc. but this by no means intimated that when a woman received any particular influence {calling} from God to enable her to teach that she was to obey that influence or calling; on the contrary, SHE WAS TO OBEY IT" All the Apostle Paul opposes here is the woman's questioning, finding fault, disputing in the Christian church, {because they knew not the scriptures} as the Jewish men were permitted to do in their synagogues; together with the attempts to usurp authority over the men by setting up their opposition to them, for the Apostle has in view especially acts of disobedience arrogance etc. Of which no woman would be guilty of, who was under the influence of the Spirit of God." End Quote

Why did Paul speak of this ordinance within the Christian assembly? It was for the same reason that had been prevalent in the Jewish synagogue. The women were still in ignorance of the scriptures, they were still causing a disturbance and acting out of order. They needed to learn what their husbands knew about God at home. The truth of this matter is very clear...IF...we all have an open heart to God's truth. The day of Pentecost should have settled all this continuing "questioning" concerning God's acceptance of both male and female genders as being equal in His Kingdom. The blessed Holy Spirit is the Giver of every gift and He gave some apostles, some prophets, and some teachers' etc. God made NO difference as to gender! Why do MEN {and even some women} not receive this assurance? Is their wisdom greater than God's wisdom? God is not the Author of confusion! His Word does not contradict itself! The clarion scripture to end all the controversy...*"And it shall come to pass in the last days' saith God, I will pour out my Spirit upon all flesh; and your sons and your DAUGHTERS shall prophecy."* {Acts 2:17}

**As believers...Let us just take God at His Word!**

*"For ye are all the children of God by faith in Christ Jesus. There is NETHER MALE NOR FEMALE; FOR YE ARE ALL ONE IN CHRIST JESUS."* {Galatians 3:26-28}

## Something to take note of...

I do not know whether the reader has been aware of one particular doctrinal issue that these various sects, cults and or denominations ALL agree upon! It is the MILLENIUM! Isn't that a coincidence! No! As a matter of fact, it is a well planned strategy of Satan! If there is that much agreement from one sect to another, it gives the Devil an edge on the deception. As we have reminded our readers through these messages, it is Satan's intent to present another time to be saved and some other way than Christ. This "agreement" within all the other erroneous teachings should not be surprising. A discernment for truth has been dimmed.

What a "potpourri" of traditional stances that Satan has set forth to deceive! I admonish all who are seeking God's unadulterated truth to examine these deceptions for yourselves in light of the Word of God. God has given each person this responsibility. God has in His infinite wisdom, Love and Grace made us free moral agents! We are each capable and able to *"prove all things whether they be of God or man."* The Bible is available for EVERY man, woman and child to investigate. This is a "personal" choice and a personal endeavor. God has ordained it this way. He is our loving and living Heavenly Father. He desires to communicate with each of us in a very personal way. This must be done through His Word, believing what He has spoken. It really isn't that difficult, for it is written that, *"the wayfaring men, though fools, shall not err therein."{Isaiah 35;8b}* When we stand in agreement with what God has said, we may rest assured that we will never be confounded, ashamed or deceived! Amen!

## We have exposed the deceitfulness that has emanated from...

### *"The Supper of the Great God"*

# *"Marriage Supper of the Lamb"*

*"Let us be glad and rejoice, and give honour to him: for the marriage of the Lamb is come, and his wife hath made herself ready. And to her were granted that she should be arrayed in fine linen, clean and white: for the fine linen is the righteousness of saints."* *{Rev. 19:7-8}*

We notice immediately that the Bride of Christ is already called His *"Wife."* This is "faith" speaking. The Bride is espoused to ONE husband. She does not have a plurality of husbands. She bears His name! The Lord Jesus Christ has only ONE Wife. He does not have a harem of concubines called wives! Multitudes of churches calling themselves by their various denominational names cannot be included in this marriage supper of the Lamb. The Harlot church and her daughters will not be included in this marriage. We will elaborate more upon this statement when we review the subject of *"Mystery Babylon, the Mother of Harlots"* in the seventieth chapter of Revelation.

Honour and rejoicing is given to the Lamb because the Wife has made Herself ready. The preparation of the Bride must precede the marriage of the Lamb. Let us look closely at what this preparation will be for this final wedding ceremony. John saw the Bride arrayed in, *"fine linen, clean and white."* What does this fine linen, clean and white symbolize? John tells us that, *"the fine linen is the*

234

*righteousness of saints."* The Bible has much to say about "righteousness." Righteousness incorporates being in right standing with God through Christ. The parable that Christ told will present this righteousness in its greatest understanding for this particular occasion... *"And Jesus answered and spake to them again in parables, and said, The Kingdom of heaven is like unto a certain king, which made a marriage for his son, And sent forth his servants to call them that were bidden to the wedding: and they would not come. Again, he sent forth other servants, saying, Tell them which are bidden, Behold, I have prepared my dinner: my oxen and fatlings are killed, and all things are made ready: come unto the marriage. But they made light of it, and went their ways, one to his farm, another to his merchandise: And the remnant took his servants, and entreated them spitefully, and slew them. But when the king heard thereof, he was wroth: and he sent for his armies, and destroyed those murderers, and burned their city. Then said he to his servants, The wedding is ready, but they which were bidden were not worthy. Go ye therefore into the highways, and as many as ye shall find, bid to the marriage. So those servants went out into the highways, and gathered all as many as they found, both bad and good: and the wedding was furnished with guests. And when the king came in to see the guests, he saw a man which had not on a wedding garment: And he said unto him, Friend, how camest thou in hither not having on a wedding garment? And he was speechless,. Then said the king to the servants, Bind him hand and foot, and take him away, and cast him into outer darkness; there shall be weeping and gnashing of teeth. For many are called, but few chosen."* {Matt. 22:1-14}

## The Wedding Garment

Consider this statement... *"He saw a man which had not on a wedding garment."* The parable surely speaks for itself, with this final explanation concerning the *"wedding garment."* Although the entire message is relative, this one sentence in the parable clarifies the truth concerning the garment of the Bride/Wife that we are considering in the prophetic word. The fine linen clean and white is referring to the wedding garment, which Christ places upon all who come by the designated Way. Throughout these progressive messages, we have defined the "designated way" to be accepted by God...IF... we would have our place at this pre-planned marriage supper of the Lamb. This is the miracle that God has granted to ALL who will hear His Word, respond in repentance with a broken and contrite heart, turn from sin and receive Christ as Saviour and Lord! They will be arrayed in fine linen clean and white. Yes! Even the *"garment of righteousness."* According to the scriptures, we are made the *"righteousness of God in Christ."* No wonder John was instructed to...*"Write, Blessed are they which are called unto the marriage supper of the Lamb. And he saith unto me, These are the true sayings of God." {Rev. 19:9}* May I have the liberty of explaining this Divine procedure of acceptance through the simplicity that is in Christ...

**First Step...God** in His great mercy must convict of sin, of righteousness and of judgement to come in the heart of every sinner. He does this out of His great Love for fallen mankind. The Bible says that we were all born in sin and in sin did our Mothers conceive us. The scriptures also tell us that we all go astray from the womb. We were born with Adam's sinful rebellious nature. This is called "original sin" or the "Adamic nature." Many deny this fact, others say it was an invention of the Catholic Church. They are both definitely in error! The Word of God has many references that verify the fact that we have all inherited the sinful fallen nature from our perpetual head called Adam. I would admonish the reader to do a good study on this subject. There is a wealth of information to prove this simple truth. First Corinthians, the fifteenth chapter would be an excellent beginning, then move on to the sixth chapter of Romans. These scriptures affirm the truth about man's fallen nature. However! There is even a more evident fact that ALL mankind has inherited this "Adamic nature" of rebellion. Just open your eyes and behold that very nature that is even seen in infants as they show forth that "me first" or "mine" and the many other expressions of selfishness, yea and even a little battle may develop over a toy. Yes! The original rebellion of sin is still seen clearly and unmistakably. Our first thought given was that God in His mercy convicts us of that rebellious sinful nature that is actually separating us from His Love and fellowship. It is God who actually seeks us in His great mercy and love!

**Second step...**IF we will hear His voice and heed His call which brings a broken and a contrite heart full of repentance, then He promises to do a miracle! The Bible calls this miracle being *"born-again."* To as many as received Him, to them gave he the power to become the children of God. At the moment of repentance and faith that the blood of Jesus Christ cleanses from all sin, we become new creatures in Christ. This is an operation done by the Spirit of God. It is not just a "change of mind" or a "decision" made by the individual. A definite change does come because of this NEW DIVINE nature that God imparts. *"Whereby are given unto us exceeding great and precious promises: that by these ye might be partakers of the divine nature, having escaped the corruption that is in the world through lust."* {2 Peter 1:4} The scriptures tell us that the old things {sinful acts} pass away and behold, all things become new. God has forgiven and forgotten all the past life of sin because He made an everlasting covenant through His Son's death on the cross. He promises us that the blood of Jesus Christ cleanses us from all sin. He keeps His Word and performs the miracle of a new heart to love and serve Him. This step of faith is termed "justification." *"Therefore being justified by faith, we have peace with God through our Lord Jesus Christ: By whom also we have access by faith into this grace wherein we stand, and rejoice in hope of the glory of God."* {Romans 5:1-2}

**The next step...**of faith comes by our obedience to that which God has provided for us to continue living this new life. Listen carefully to His plan for every believer...

*"I beseech you therefore, brethren, by the mercies of God, that ye present your bodies a living sacrifice, holy, acceptable unto God, which is your reasonable service. And be not conformed to this present world: but be ye transformed by the renewing of your mind, that ye may prove what is that good, and acceptable, and perfect, will of God."* {Romans 12:1-2}

When we present our bodies to God as His Temple, He indwells us with His Holy Spirit. Yes! This is another act of faith on our part to receive the fullness of God. He calls it *"sanctification."* We are released from the old Adamic nature through the indwelling Person of the Holy Spirit. The Holy Spirit enables us to continue to,*"walk in newness of Life in Christ."* This second work of grace is confirmed in the Galatian letter...5: 16-26. We shall quote the key verses from this passage... *"This I say then, Walk in the Spirit, and ye shall not fulfill the lust of the flesh...And they that are Christ's have crucified the flesh with its affections and lusts. If we live in the Spirit, let us also walk in the Spirit."* There is more to understand concerning this sanctified life..."*For this is the will of God, even your sanctification...And the very God of peace sanctify you wholly: and I pray God your whole spirit and soul and body be preserved blameless unto the coming of the Lord Jesus Christ." {1 Thessalonians 4:3 also 5:23}*

This is a continuing daily act of faith and discipline upon the part of every true believer until Christ calls us into His presence. Without holiness, no man shall see God. He has provided His very own Living Spirit for every true believer to KEEP US FROM SIN. This is the victory that overcomes the world of sin, the Devil, and the flesh, even our faith. God has promised to present the true believer faultless in that day of Christ's appearing. We are without excuse…IF…we deny that which He has promised. This book you have been reading called, "Mystery Babylon" is the testimony of Jesus! If you are a true child of God or are seeking to become a child of God, there will be a *"rejoicing"* for the truths that you have been hearing. It is the truth that sets men free! Jesus said, *"Ye shall know the truth and the truth shall make you free.*

## Christ's doctrines must of necessity be included in this "Supper of the Lamb."

**The Lord Jesus Christ stated emphatically**
*"I will build my church; and the gates of hell shall not prevail against it."*
*{Matthew 16:18b}*

A simple scriptural doctrinal pattern has been written that believers may use to permit Him to accomplish His purpose. May every member of the Body of Christ give heed to this pattern…

- **Christ is the Founder and foundation:** *"For other foundation can no man lay than is laid, which is in Christ Jesus." {1 Corinthians 3:11}*
- **Christ is the Head:** *"And he {Christ} is the head of the body, the church: who is the beginning, and the first born from the dead; that in all things he might have the preeminence." {Colossians 1:18}*
- **Christ named the Church of God:** *"And now I am no more in the world, but these are in the world, and I come to thee. Holy Father, keep through thine own name those whom thou hast given me, that they may be one, as we are." {John 17:12}* What is His name? "GOD" is His name. The name denotes His ownership of the redeemed church. Christ designated the name "God" to represent all three Persons of the Triune Godhead. The Church cannot be called, "The Church of Christ" because it would not be a complete representation of the Godhead.
- **The Church could not be called,** "The Church of the Holy Spirit" because this would not be a complete representation of the Godhead. The Church could not be called, "The Church of the Father" because this would not be a complete representation of the Godhead. The word "GOD" incorporates the fullness of the Godhead…God the Father, God the Son, and God the Holy Spirit. This is the "scriptural" name of the church, not a denominational name. The apostles honored and used this name as they wrote to the various churches…Paul wrote: *"Unto the church of God which is at Corinth, to them are sanctified in Christ Jesus, called to be saints, with all that that in every place call upon the name of Jesus Christ our Lord, both theirs and ours. {1 Corinthians 1:2}*
- **Being born again:** "Verily, Verily, I say unto thee, Except a man be born again, he cannot see the kingdom of God."
- **God admits the members:** *"For as the body is one, and hath many members, and all the members of that one body, being many, are one body: so also is Christ." {1 Corinthians 12:12}*

- **Only the "Saved" are members:** *"I am the door: by me if any man enter in, he shall be saved, and shall go in and out, and find pasture." {John 10: 9}*
- **There are no "sinners" in the church of God:** *"And ye know that he {Jesus} was manifested to take away our sins; and in him is no sin. Whosoever abideth in him sinneth not: whosoever sinneth hath not seen him, neither known him. Little children, let no man deceive you: he that doth righteousness is righteous, even as he is righteous. He that committeth sin is of the devil; for the devil sinneth from the beginning. For this purpose the Son of God was manifested, that he might destroy the works of the devil. Whosoever is born of God doth not commit sin; for his seed remaineth in him: and he cannot sin, because he is born of God. In this the children of God are manifest, and the children of the devil: whosoever doeth not righteousness is not of God, neither he that loveth not his brother." {1 John 3:5-10}*
- **A Holy Life is God's will for His children:** *"As obedient children, not fashioning yourselves according to the former lusts in your ignorance: But as he which has called you is holy, so be ye holy in all manner of conversation; Because it is written, Be ye holy; for I am holy." {1 Peter 1:14-16}* *"Follow peace with all men, and holiness, without which no man shall see the Lord." {Hebrews 12:14}*

## Christ's three ordinances...

**Baptism:** *"He that believeth and is baptized shall be saved; but he that believeth not shall be damned." {Mark 16:16}* Baptism by immersion was sanctioned by Christ as He presented Himself to John to be baptized...*"And Jesus, when he was baptized, went up straightway out of the water and, lo, the heavens were opened unto him, and he saw the Spirit of God descending like a dove, and lighting upon him: And lo a voice from heaven, saying, This is my beloved Son, in whom I am well pleased." {Matthew 3:16-17}*

**The Lord's Supper:** *"And when he had given thanks, he brake it, and said, Take, eat: this is my body, which is broken for you: this do in remembrance of me. After the same manner also he took the cup, when he had supped, saying, This cup is the new testament in my blood: this do ye, as oft as ye drink it, in remembrance of me." {1 Corinthians 11:24-25}*

**The Feet Washing:** *"If I then, your Lord and Master have washed your feet; ye also ought to wash one another's feet. For I have given you an example, that ye should do as I have done to you." {John 13:15-15}*

## God's Unity comes by obeying
## The
## "Word and the Spirit"

Jesus prayed to the Father for this Divine Unity…. *"That they all may be one; as thou, Father, art in me, and I in thee, that they all may be one in us: that the world may believe that thou hast sent me." {John 17:21}*

The world of unbelievers looks upon a divided Christendom! The world of unbelievers looks upon a potpourri of religion that baffles them! They stand in awe that everyone claims to read the same Bible and yet cannot be in agreement! What a reproach this confusion is to God! I have had many unbelievers make this statement to me…"When you Christians get it all together…then come and talk to me about the Bible being true!"

## This is one of the reasons why there is a great need for…
## God's
## FINAL RESTORATION

## *"The more sure word of prophecy"*

# Restoration Period
## *"Revival of the Two Witnesses"*

*"And after three days and a half the Spirit of life from God entered into them, and they stood upon their feet; and great fear fell upon them that saw them. And they heard a great voice from heaven saying unto them, Come up hither. And they ascended up to heaven in a cloud; and their enemies beheld them. And the same hour was there a great earthquake, and a tenth part of the city fell, and in the earthquake were slain of men seven thousand: and the remnant were affrighted, and gave glory to the God of heaven."*
*{Revelation 11:11-13}*

The continuing scriptures now present a marked change of events concerning these Two Witnesses. In the previous scriptures, we had seen the Two Horned Beast make war against them. We had seen their dead bodies in the street of that great city. We had seen them replaced by a *"form of religion denying the power thereof."{Revelation 11:7-10}* Now…the Two Witnesses are seen being filled with the Life of God and standing on their feet! The summons of God was heard saying, *"Come up hither."*

These symbols are declaring to us the reality of the promised revival of the Word and the Spirit. *"Great fear fell upon them which saw them."* The true child of God has an awesome fear of God and a desire to obey any further instruction that He may bring. God had found a people who evidently feared Him in the scriptural sense and obeyed His prophetic call. A remnant did come forth who again lifted up the Word and the Spirit to their ordained place in the Body of Christ. We were introduced to this remnant or the sixth seal ministry in our discourse of the Battle of Armageddon.

The sixth angel representing the *"kings of the east"* poured out his vial of judgement upon the Three Unclean Spirits. We see this same ministry in this present scene continuing to gain the victory. This *"voice from heaven"* represents the sixth seal ministry who came forth separated from the Great City of religion to lift up the Word and the Spirit. We remember Christ's own words as He said, *"If I be lifted up, I will draw all men to me."* In like manner, we see the Word and the Spirit being lifted up to draw all men to Christ.

## Theocracy...

is the totalitarian rule and reign of God over His people because they obey the Word and the Spirit. We notice as the Word and the Spirit were lifted up, *"their enemies beheld them."* Their enemies were the Apostate religions professing Christianity. Loyalty to any denominational system, structure or persuasion will make you an enemy of the Word and the Spirit of God. Why is that? It is because there is very little agreement between the Word of God and the traditions of false religions. Traditional people get offended because of the Word. Peter writes that the "Stone" {Christ} is a rock of offence to those who are disobedient to the Word. {1 Peter 2:8}

It is written also that in the hour of this *"earthquake"* {which means an earthshaking catastrophic change in the Spiritual realm} a tenth part of the city fell. They fell from their lofty positions meaning that their deceitfulness was exposed by the preaching of God's whole council. This tenth part of the city constitutes the hierarchies of Babylon that were slain by the Word of God. As we have previously stated, the Word of God will bring Spiritual Life to those who receive it. However! It will also bring Spiritual death to all who reject it! {2 Corinthians 2: 15-16}

The *"seven thousand"* symbolizes the completed work of God in separating the wheat from the chaff. Everyone who heard this *"earth-shaking message"* had the opportunity and choice to believe it and depart from Babylon's religions, or remain in Spiritual death. Many believed the, *"voice from heaven"* and departed from *"*Babylon the Great." These loyal followers of Christ constitute the *"remnant"* spoken of in this passage that, *"were affrighted and gave glory to God."* Through this sixth seal ministry, freedom returned to declare the whole council of God outside the *"Great City"* of religion. Let us consider the continuing details of this great Spiritual upheaval and change that God accomplished through the...

## Continuing Sixth Seal Ministry

These present events concerning the revival of the Two Witnesses have come to pass because of the faithful sixth seal ministry previously spoken of. The whole council of God including this vital Revelation prophecy will bring forth God's promised Restoration. The Pristine Glory of the first century church of the Living God will come forth in all its power once again! We would like to review this particular theme for a foundation and clarification at this time... *"And I beheld when he had opened the sixth seal, and, lo, there was a great earthquake; and the sun became black as sackcloth of hair, and the moon became as blood. And the stars of heaven fell unto the earth, even as a fig tree casteth her untimely figs, when she is shaken of a mighty wind. And the heaven departed as a scroll when it is rolled together; and every mountain and island were moved out of their places. And the kings of the earth, and the great men, and the rich men, and the chief captains, and the mighty men, and every bondman, and every free man, hid themselves in the dens and in the rocks of the mountains; And said to the mountains and rocks, Fall on us, and hide us from the face of him that sitteth on the throne, and from the wrath of the Lamb: For the great day of his wrath is come; and who shall be able to stand?" {Revelation 6:12-17}*

Extreme and unnatural upheavals in the realm of nature are seen through these symbols. We are being introduced to something that is *"earthshaking"* or a catastrophic change. The analogy as always will be found in the Spiritual realm. We will be presented with the events that came to pass historically and prophetically as the second stage of the apostasy was dealt with under the mighty power of the Word and the Spirit. We are viewing a catastrophic change in religious polity! This change will take place as the Word and the Spirit are given their proper authority again outside the denominational structures of traditional religion.

Let us first consider the symbolic language that is used. This style of language was used by Joel, then repeated in the book of Acts. Acts 2:16-21} In this passage of scripture from the book of Acts, God had used this same figurative language to present the drastic change that came as the Jewish polity was done away with. The New Testament worship that Christ instituted replaced the Old Testament ceremonial worship. The second chapter of Acts records the fulfillment of Joel's prophecy. This event did indeed usher in *"the coming of that great and notable day of the Lord."*

This event proved to be the completion of Christ's Atonement for ALL mankind. The Anointed One entered this world to bring salvation to ALL people. The entire third chapter of Galatians explains the blessing of Abraham through Christ. The Holy Spirit through the pen of Paul relates to us that, *"There is neither Jew nor Greek, there is neither bond nor free, there is neither male nor female: for ye are all one in Christ Jesus." {Galatians 3:28}*

The symbols in this present Revelation message under consideration are also referring to a catastrophic "Spiritual" change that is taking place. Let us summarize this Spiritual condition…The Word and the Spirit had been replaced by the development of denominational systems and sects since the 16th century Reformation. Now, God was bringing correction, reproof and instruction to ALL who would receive it. With this understanding, let us proceed in looking into that *"earthshaking"* Spiritual event which the Revelation is speaking of.

We notice the similar phraseology used in Joel's prophesy…*"the sun becoming black; the moon as blood; the stars of heaven departing etc."* The unnatural appearance of the sun and the moon depicts a revolutionary change in direction concerning religious polity or structuring once again. Various scriptures have often employed the natural elements in unusual phenomena to show forth God's intervention. We are viewing God's intervention now in this symbolic scene.

Let us once again employ the, *"line upon line, precept upon precept,"* method as we proceed in determining the meaning of these events. The symbols speak of, *"the stars of heaven falling unto the earth, even as a fig tree casteth her untimely figs, when she is shaken of a mighty wind."{Revelation 6:13}* These fallen stars symbolize the false ministry which had developed as Protestantism made her "Image." The Divine intervention came through the sixth seal ministry as they brought reproof, correction and instruction in righteousness to the *"kings of the earth."*

Protestantism's false ministry here is symbolized as, *"untimely figs when shaken by the wind…"* The mighty Wind of the Holy Spirit through the preaching of the Word by the sixth seal ministry caused these stars to fall from their exalted and lofty positions. Untimely figs are not ripe, they have not come to maturity, and they are unfit to eat.

These untimely figs represent the untimely or immature spiritual food that these apostate stars {Babylon's ministry} were feeding to their adherents.

The effects of God's preliminary judgement message are related in verses fourteen through sixteen...The symbols speak of, *"the heavens departing as a scroll."* This means that the scrolls of traditional beliefs were exposed, rolled away and departed or lost their power to deceive. John proceeds to explain that, *"every mountain and island were moved out of their places."* These mountains and islands represent the denominational systems of men, which were moved off of their false foundations as this preliminary judgement message came forth. Keeping in mind that these experiences relate to the Spiritual realm.

According to verse fifteen, people in every station of life are included in this upheaval. Everyone associated with the apostasy all, *"hid themselves in the dens and in the rocks of the mountains."* All these *"stars"* and their adherents within Protestantism were trying to *"hide themselves in the dens and in the rocks of the mountains."* They were trying to hide themselves in their profession of religion as they cried out for the hills and rocks to fall on them and to hide them from the wrath of the Lamb! They were void of a true relationship with Christ through the new birth experience! John concludes with a question...*"Who shall be able to stand?"* This question will be answered later as we see God's people gathered together STANDING with the Lamb on mount Zion. {Revelation14: 1}

## God's Preliminary Judgment

Many commentators have mistakenly projected this sixth seal message as the final judgement scene. Not so! This scene has presented the Spiritual reality of the fallen condition of Protestantism, which God has called "Babylon." The sixth seal message was and still continues to be the preliminary judgement from God! "Come out of her MY people that ye be not partakers of her sins, and that ye receive not her plagues."

The Apostate church continues on, each with their own individual religious stance under the umbrella of "Christianity." God is not mocked! He only honors His Word. He cannot work through the false ideologies of men's minds! He is calling the faithful back to His

Word and out of traditions of men! If God's people will not "heed" His call, they will receive these plagues. These plagues refer to the false traditions of this "earth born" religion. A "plague" is a transmittable disease! You can catch it! In other words, you will become LIKE those whom you associate with. You will accept what they accept! Amen? Amen!

This prophetically called sixth seal ministry had introduced the Revelation prophecy as God's Final message to His wondering, discouraged and searching people.This ministry was led of the Lord to search out the various types, shadows and visions that had been given through the Old Testament prophets. They found the anti-types to be a verification of that which would happen in this latter day Restoration. Yes...Types, shadows, and visions were given to many of the Old Testament prophets concerning this very time to confirm God's FINAL RESTORATION.

The Lord God gave insight to Jeremiah in this particular situation... *"Thus saith the Lord of hosts, Hearken not unto the words of the prophets that prophecy to unto you: they make you vain: they speak a vision of their own heart, and not of the mouth of the Lord. They say still to them that despise me, The Lord hath said, Ye shall have peace; and they say unto everyone that walketh after their own imagination of his own heart, No evil shall come upon you. For who hath stood in the counsel of the Lord, and hath perceived and heard his word? Who hath marked his word and heard it? Behold, a whirlwind of the Lord is gone forth in fury, even a grievous whirlwind: it shall fall grievously upon the head of the wicked. The anger of the Lord shall not return, until he hath executed, and till he hath performed the thoughts of his heart: in the latter days ye shall consider it perfectly. I have not sent these prophets, yet they ran: I have not spoken to them, yet they prophesied. But if they had stood in my counsel, and had caused my people to hear my words, then they should have turned them from their evil way, and from the evil of their doings."* {*Jeremiah 23: 16-22*}

It sounds like Jeremiah is describing the "sin you will sin you must" doctrine that has flooded the Christian community of today in his statement... *" They say still to them that despise me, The Lord hath said, Ye shall have peace: and they say unto every one that walketh after the imagination of his own heart, No evil shall come upon you."*

## The Lord says, "Harken not" unto the words of a ministry that is not speaking His Word, but speak a vision of their own!

*"Behold, a whirlwind of the Lord is gone forth in fury."* The religious world is reaping what it has sown...even a grievous whirlwind! God is grieved with the Spiritual indolence of a church society that professes faith in Him, yet does not bare the fruit of righteousness and holiness unto the Lord! We are now living in the *"latter days."* We are seeing this anti-type fulfillment in the Apostate church! It is a *"form of godliness denying the power thereof."*

Hear another anti-type fulfilled from Ezekiel's writings as he looked down through the ages of time. He describes the present condition of churchanity with accuracy..."*And they were scattered, because there is no shepherd...*{a hireling ministry has replaced the true shepherd} *My sheep wandered through all the mountains.* {meaning ecclesiastical churches} *For thus saith the Lord God; Behold, I, even, will both search my sheep, and seek them out. As a shepherd seeketh out his sheep that are scattered; so I will seek out my sheep, and will deliver them out of all places where they have been scattered in the cloudy and dark day."* {Ezekiel 34:5 through 12}

Yes! Today...God's people are wandering from one church congregation to another through the "Pale Horse" of Protestantism. Many of God's true children are seeking for more Light in this *"scattered"* condition! Ezekiel's ending message does give hope, for the Lord has promised that He will..."*seek out His sheep and will deliver them out of all places where they have been scattered in the cloudy and dark day."* This symbolic language of the *"cloudy and dark day"* is describing the Spiritual condition of the Apostate condition of our present church world. We have often stated the reason throughout this writing...Their traditions have made void the Word of God! The ecclesiastical churches have made Spiritual dwarfs and Bible illiterates out of their adherents. Their rituals and traditional forms have replaced the study of the Bible!

The reality of these anti-types and shadows of things to come are vividly portrayed within the Revelation prophecy and the promised Restoration. We know that Catholicism was that *"dark day"* and

Protestantism the *"cloudy day."* Is there any hope? Yes! I can assure the true child of God or the seeker of God's truth that He has made the "Way" clear! Christ's Revelation prophecy has presented ALL God's people with the, "Way, the Truth, the Light and the Life." It has exposed the counterfeit ways that Satan has tried to impose upon every generation since the Apostate church began!

Jeremiah's anti-type speaks of this present prophetic time period of Restoration... *"In those days, and in that time, saith the Lord, the children of Israel shall come, they and the children of Judah together, going and weeping: they shall go, and seek the Lord their God. They shall ask the way to Zion with their faces thitherward, saying, Come, let us join ourselves to the Lord in a perpetual covenant that shall not be forgotten. My people hath been lost sheep: their shepherds have caused them to go astray, they have turned them away on the mountains: they have gone from mountain to hill, they have forgotten their resting place.* {Then He admonishes them} *REMOVE OUT OF THE MIDST OF BABYLON."* {Jeremiah 50:4-8}

Since this is an anti-type prophecy, we know that the *"children of Israel"* refer to the New Testament Israel of God. These are the believers in Christ who compose His church. They are *"asking the way to Zion."* We have previously spoken of Zion as being the fulfillment of God's New Testament church. True believers are getting serious about asking just what is the church and where is it in the midst of all this confusion. True believers are desiring to have a personal relationship or an *"everlasting covenant"* with the Lord. Each believer MUST evaluate and compare their traditional stance with the Word of God. There is no other way that God can bring instruction, correction and reproof. As there was an expediency attached to *"fleeing from literal Babylon"* in the Old Testament time for God's Israel... So there is also expediency attached to this anti-type call to, *"Come out"* of Spiritual Babylon. Jeremiah continues in his discourse... *"Flee out of the midst of Babylon, and deliver every man his soul: be not cut off in her iniquity; for this is the time of the Lord's vengeance, he will render unto her a recompense."* {Jeremiah 51:6}

# The Anti-Types in Symbolism...

I trust that the reader recognizes that the anti-types are included in the symbolic language of the Lord. Many of the circumstances and events that happened to the Old Testament Israel of God have also come to pass in the New Testament Israel of God. This is why they are referred to as "types and shadows." As God delivered His ancient people from their physical and literal captivity and established them in a physical and literal place, so He is seen doing the same in the Spiritual reality of the anti-type.

The Lord gave this further message to Jeremiah..."*Babylon is suddenly fallen and destroyed: howl for her; take balm for her pain, if so be she may be healed, We would have healed Babylon, but she is not healed: forsake her, and let us go every one into his own country: for her judgements reacheth unto heaven, and is lifted up even to the skies; The Lord hath brought forth our righteousness: come, and let us declare in Zion the work of the Lord our God."*
*{Jeremiah 51:8-10}*

God can only bring forth our righteousness {right standing in Him} when we FORSAKE Babylon and enter into Zion's fair city. Only in Zion can we declare the work of full salvation! God can only establish Zion {The New Testament Church} as His people depart from ALL traditional religions. He MUST have a separated people who will permit Him to "*build His church*" through His Word and by His Spirit. Just listen to the lament of the ancient literal Israel of God when they were in their captivity....*By the rivers of Babylon, there we sat down, we wept, when we remembered Zion. We hanged our harps upon the willows in the midst thereof. For there they that carried us away captive required of us a song; and they that wasted us required of us a mirth, saying, Sing us one of the songs of Zion...*" And they answered, "*How shall we sing the Lord's song in a strange land?*"*{Psalms 137:1-4}*

Babylon is a strange land for the true child of God to be held captive in. It is my studied opinion that most of God's people do not even realize their plight. Most of God's people are ignorant concerning the prophetic truths of this Revelation message. They do not know about "Spiritual Babylon." The do not know that they have been taught by the "False Prophet." Most Christians within the institutionalized churches are not really aware of "why" things are not what they would like for them to be. Many report that they feel like something is amiss in the churchanity of today. They are seen wandering from church to church, trying to find a resting place and receive Spiritual food. They are not aware of the true Biblical pattern of worshiping God in Spirit and in truth and in the pure doctrines of Christ.

The Apostate church has mingled the "saved" with the "unsaved" together and made a church membership out of both. This is not God's design for His Church! Christ separates the "saved" from the "unsaved" as He builds His church. Thus the admonition written to the Corinthian church by the Apostle Paul. *"Be ye not unequally yoked together with unbelievers: for what fellowship hath righteousness with unrighteousness? And what part hath he that believeth with an infidel? And what agreement hath the temple of God with idols? For ye are the temple of the living God; as God hath said, I will dwell in them, and walk in them; and I will be their God, and they shall be my people. Wherefore come out from among them, and be ye separate, saith the Lord, and touch not the unclean thing; and I will receive you, And will be a Father unto you, and ye shall be my sons and daughters, thus saith the Lord Almighty."*
*{2 Corinthians 6:14-18}*

There will be more details to relate concerning this Sixth Seal Ministry as the White Horse reappears and we conclude our final message...We affirm through the *"more sure word of prophecy"* that the Seven Sealed Scrolls have been opened and we are now living out the fulfillment of the seventh and final scroll! No man knows the hour of this fulfillment but the Father. God is preparing the Bride for the Wedding Supper of the Lamb...

## He alone knows when the last guest will

## arrive and the marriage list is completed!

# *"Babylon The Great*
# *Is Fallen Is Fallen"*

*"And after these things I saw another angel come down from heaven, having great power; and the earth was lightened with his glory. And he cried with a loud voice, saying, Babylon the great is fallen, is fallen, and is become the habitation of devils, and the hold of every foul spirit, and a cage of every unclean and hateful bird. For all nations have drunk of the wine of the wrath of her fornication, and the kings of the earth have committed fornication with her, and the merchants of the earth are waxed rich through the abundance of her delicacies. And I heard another voice from heaven, saying, Come out of her, my people, that ye be not partakers of her sins, and that ye receive not her plagues. For her sins have reached unto heaven, and God hath remembered her iniquities. Reward her even as she rewarded you, and double unto her double according to her works: in the cup which she hath filled fill to her double." {Revelation 18:1-6}*

These were our opening foundational scriptures as we began our presentation of "Mystery Babylon." Now that we have traced the historical events back through the ages of time, we should be able to understand the overall picture of what John had seen when he wrote: *"After these things"* We have seen these "things" or the literal events all come to pass with exactness according to that which the prophecy has foretold.

This present announcement about the fall of Babylon and its condition came with great power; and the earth was lightened with glory. Why was that? It was because of the revival of the "Two Witnesses" through the sixth seal ministry. It was because many of God's people heard, believed, received and acted upon the, *"more sure word of prophecy."* This Revelation prophecy is God's FINAL message to awaken His true church! We have followed God's "Remnant" of true saints down through the ages that have always kept the testimony of Jesus and the Word of God. This Remnant is still heralding the message! This "angel" is symbolizing the earthly messengers sent by God to herald this continuing perpetual prophecy. John's previous announcement had told us...*"But in the days of the voice of the seventh angel, when he shall begin to sound, the mystery of God would be finished, as he hath declared to his servants the prophets."* The voice of the 7th angel has sounded! It has been sounding for over one hundred prophetic years since God gave it to a dedicated few at the close of the 18th century.

## Mystery Babylon is no Longer a MYSTERY

God has promised the *"power"* through faith for every one of His children to be delivered from the vast confusion of Babylon! This wonderful glory and power is fulfilled as God's obedient people flee or depart from this Great City of religion! There was a "Remnant" who heard, believed and received this Revelation prophecy and have dedicated themselves to BEING His separated church. This Remnant still remains as an active part of God's continuing plan to accomplish His purpose. Let me bring this reminder to all who are sincerely interested...The last book within the Big Book is called...*"The Revelation of Jesus Christ."* A "Revelation" means that which is "revealed." This is NOT a hidden or complicated message! It has been complicated and hidden by the false concept of another age to come! It has been complicated and hidden by devising a "literal" interpretation and relegating it to the Jewish nation. It has been complicated and hidden because the Divine "key" of symbolism has not been used! This is a message that can be understood, else why would John have written...*"Blessed is he that readeth, and they that hear the words of this prophecy, and keep those things which are written therein: for the time is at hand." {Revelation 1:3}*

This vital prophecy has been given to ALL mankind with the assurance that God will again RESTORE Mt. Zion or the Spiritual reality of Christ's original church. This visible church will be seen before the appearing of Christ. Even as Jesus said, *"I will build MY church and the gates of hell shall not prevail against it."* God has revealed all that His people need to know and understand in order to RESTORE His Church in the earth.

**He awaits the response of His people!**
**The need is to...**
*"Hear what the Spirit and the Word saith to the church."*

## Understanding Babylon's Confusion

We have found that God has used very graphic language throughout this prophecy in order to get His point across. In His infinite wisdom, He continues to use symbolic language based on analogy. We have previously mentioned the reason God has chosen this method. We reiterate…It is that symbolism based on analogy cannot be arbitrarily changed like men's languages from one generation to another. In our opening scriptures, Christ has chosen to use the name "Babylon" as an analogy to reveal the vast confusion of men's ideologies. This name or place is analogous to the ancient city of Babylon where the original tower of Babel was built.

## A brief history will be helpful for

## understanding…

Ancient Babylon was the first Kingdom to exist on the earth. Nimrod was the Pagan King who reigned supreme over the people of this Kingdom. The entire account of Nimrod and his intent to build a city and then a tower that would reach into the very heaven itself can be reviewed in Genesis11:1-9. Through this narrative, we find that the people's intent did not meet with the Lord God's approval! To express His disapproval, He sent a confusion of languages upon them so that they could not understand each other's speech. Why did He do this? Thus it is written: *"And the Lord said, Behold, the people is one, and they have one language; and this they begin to do: and now nothing will be restrained from them, which they have imagined to do. Go to, let us go down, and there confound their language, that they may not understand one another's speech.... Therefore is the name of it called Babel; because the lord did confound the language of all the earth and from thence did the lord scatter them abroad from the face of the earth."*

This insight from ancient times lets us know the reason why God has used the name of "Babylon" in the Revelation prophecy. He compares the modern "Babylon" of men's religion in this Great City of Protestantism with ancient Babylon. This analogy expresses His great displeasure as men "build their own towers" into heaven for their own desires. As God confounded their verbal language in Nimrod's time, so He has also confounded the Spiritual language of all the sects who are "building their towers" to reach heaven.

All these traditional religions within the denominational systems affirm that they are Christians reading the same Bible! Yet! Every denomination speaks a different spiritual language according to their particular wind of traditional doctrine! Catholicism and Protestantism both have built their own "Tower of Babel" by their own doctrines, dogmas and traditions. They all want to make a name for themselves so that they cannot be scattered. God calls this Great City of religious confusion "Babylon!"

### Jesus Christ is the ONLY Way, the ONLY Truth, and the ONLY Light and Life!

We again reiterate God's Divine admonition which has been written for ALL to obey... *"Now I beseech you, brethren, by the name of our Lord Jesus Christ, that ye all speak the same thing, and that there be no divisions among you: but that ye be perfectly joined together in the same mind and in the same judgement."*
*{1 Corinthians 1:10}*

# Sectarian Confusion

Confusion has always been Satan's best method of thwarting God's design and purpose! If Satan can confuse various issues in the minds of God's people, there will be dissention! Dissention causes divisions and division brings failure! The Body of Jesus Christ is to be unified through the Word and the Spirit. This is NOT accomplished by a set of selected rituals, rules or regulations through the various denominations. The pattern of division is evident in every sect and has been propagated by each. It would be impossible to enumerate the multitude of sects and their ideologies that have entered into this pattern.

**I would share just a few examples for understanding...**

**The 7th Day Adventist** base their ideology on the keeping of the Sabbath Day. They go to great length to "prove" that they are God's chosen to proclaim their message. They have to IGNORE the entire book of Hebrews in order to make this claim. God tells us that the Old Covenant with ALL its ordinances waxed old and passed away! This is only one of their false claims. They proclaim that all who do not worship on Saturday have the "Mark of the Beast." They overlook completely that the New Testament affirms the "FIRST DAY OF THE WEEK" commemorating the resurrection of Christ to be the "official" time of meeting together in the name of the Lord. This is called "The Lord's Day." They also do not accept the clear teaching of Christ concerning the place called "Hell" as to the eternal punishment of unbelievers. They also believe in a "soul" sleep, which is contrary to sound doctrine. It is clearly stated, *"To be absent from the body is to be present with the Lord."*

**Another example...**The various splits of Church of Christ sects affirm vehemently that their will be no music accompaniment in their worship services. "They" claim that musical instruments are not sanctioned in the scriptures. They surely must have overlooked the book of psalms completely on this issue. David, God's chosen servant played the harp to calm the evil spirits who possessed King Saul. This must be of some Spiritual value! The very last psalm even lists the musical instruments in which God's people praised Him through. *"Praise him with the sound of the trumpet: praise him with the psaltery and harp. Praise him with the timbrel and dance: praise him with stringed instruments and organs. Praise him upon loud sounding* *cymbals. " {Psalms 150}* Of course it is objectionably said by this sect that this was under the Old Testament and that the New Testament does not relate this. Wrong again! Harps, trumpets and other musical instruments are used fluently throughout the Revelation in many of the worship scenes. Perhaps these "narrow minded" people would not consider a *"reproof and correction"* from the Word of God since it has been spoken by a "woman." This sect has relegated women to a "subservient" level in their doctrine, as most Baptist persuasions have also done. They deny any women the privilege of being called of God to minister within the Body of Christ.

**The various Amish and Mennonites sects** distinguish themselves by their manner of dress and appearance. They have been schooled to believe that dressing in another age era of clothing is more pleasing to God than the customary clothing of the day. The scriptures do make mention of the wearing apparel of those who are people of faith. Peter mentions that our adorning should not be an outward adorning of wearing of gold or of putting on costly apparel, but let it be the hidden adorning of the heart of a meek and quiet spirit. As Christian men and women, we are admonished to be "modest" in all of our appearances and in all of our relationships as we walk though this world. Women having long hair is another controversial issue, which divides many to fellowship one with another. What a shame to sit in judgement on one another! How do these Christians answer this question... *"Who art thou that judgest another man's servant? To his own master he standeth or falleth. Yea, he shall be holden up: for God is able to make him stand." {Roman 14:4}*

Should a sect have the right to dictate a manner of dress for all their adherents to abide by? Does this mean that the hair should never be cut? Does this mean that men should all wear beards? Does this mean that the wedding ring should be considered as gold that should not be worn? Does this mean that no one should wear a gold watch?

### Think about this...

God has given each of His children the freedom to receive personal advice. Yes! Personal decisions can and should come directly from Him. I realize that this mind set is not always easy to follow. We all like to be among the "accepted." This is why many people are caught up in the "cloning" process of religious sectarianism. IF every Christian would only ask God in faith to release them from the bondage of men's dogmatic ideas, I am convinced that He could eliminate the "cloning" that appears to be in every sect! This can be done as Christ deals personally with each member of His Body as they, *"study to shew themselves approved unto God. {2 timothy 2:15}*

This is what is meant by coming under the "Theocracy" of God. He is able to take care of ALL the divisions...IF...men will cease to propagate traditional doctrines. The Pharisaical spirit still exists among the religious. As Jesus said in His dealings with them when He walked on earth...They bind heavy burdens and grievous to be borne, and lay them on men's shoulders. Let every child of God, especially those in leadership positions take an in depth and inside look at the motivations of their particular belief system. If there is a true Biblical foundation, God will deal directly with the true child of God, rather than making a set of rules and regulations.

Let us return again to our opening scriptures. This mighty strong voice from heaven declares that Babylon had not only fallen but had, *"become the habitation of devils, and the hold of every foul spirit, and the cage of every unclean and hateful bird." {Revelation 18:2}* What an indictment this is! What a disturbing message to herald! Remember! Through these symbols, God is describing Babylon's fallen SPIRITUAL condition. These *"foul spirits"* are enumerated in the Galatian letter... *"Now the works of the flesh are manifest, which are these; Adultery, fornication, uncleanness, lasciviousness, Idolatry, witchcraft, hatred, variance, emulations, wrath, strife, seditions, heresies, Envyings, murders, drunkenness, revelings, and such like: of which I have told you in time past, that they which do such things shall not inherit the kingdom of God." {Galatians 5:19-21}*

In chapters eighteen and nineteen of Revelation, the continuing description is given of Babylon's fallen condition and activities. Please redeem the time to study these symbolic expressions and you will be able to identify that which we are seeing come to pass before our very eyes today through...

## *"Mystery Babylon"*
## The Laodicean Church is the Fulfillment of
## "Fallen Babylon."

The Lord's full description of the fallen condition of Babylon is related through the Laodicean church. John wrote…*"And unto the angel of the church of the Laodiceans write: These things saith the Amen, the faithful and true witness, the beginning of the creation of God; I know thy works, that thou art neither cold nor hot: I would thou wert cold or hot. So then because thou art neither cold nor hot, So then because thou art lukewarm, and neither cold nor hot, I will spue thee out of my mouth. Because thou sayest, I am rich, and increased with goods, and have need of nothing; and knowest not that thou art wretched, and miserable, and poor, and blind, and naked; I counsel thee to buy of me gold tried in the fire, that thou mayest be rich; and white raiment, that thou mayest be clothed, and that the shame of thy nakedness do not appear; and anoint thine eyes with eyesalve, that thou mayest see. As many as I love, I rebuke and chasten: be zealous therefore, and repent." {Revelation 3: 14-19}*

Never has there been a time in the history of the "Christian Religion" that has so accurately reflected this description! Giant mega churches fill our world today! From the Crystal Cathedral to lavish Domes and Arenas with all the stage equipment and material to put on an MGM production.

It requires millions of dollars to keep everyone's great corporate ship afloat. TV ministries promote their "come on" gift package to help support their multi-billion dollar enterprises. All claim that they are promoting Christianity! Each have built their own "Religious Empire." The simplicity of the everlasting gospel has been buried beneath the worldly glitz of these Las Vegas productions! The "Jezebel fashions" and actions that accompany these productions are copies of the sinner's world!

The imbalance and distortion of worldly music has become accepted in most of the so-called Christian contemporary worship and songs of today's religious "in" crowd! The magnified disco-sound and disco-lighting draws thousands to embrace the sensual dancing and beat of this fleshly spirit of the world! The so-called Christian "rock, rap and hip hop" groups draw the same sensual crowds as the world's rock stars! "They" say these are ways that will attract the world to

Christ...Not so! Christ never packaged Himself in the world's customs to reach them. He depended completely upon the Holy Spirit and the Word of the Father as He journeyed upon this earth. In fact, the Holy Spirit reminds us to, *"Be not conformed to this present world: but be ye transformed by the renewing of your mind, that ye may prove what is that good and acceptable, and perfect, will of God." {Romans 12:2}*

You will not find the sanction of God upon anything the spirit of the world has to offer, even if it is offered in a so-called "Christian" setting. John has even written it more clearly for us to understand... *"Love not the world, neither the things that are in the world. If any man love the world, the love of the Father is not in him. For all that is in the world, the lust of the flesh, the lust of the eyes, and the pride of life, is not of the Father, but is of the world." {1 John2:15-16}*

These "fleshly innovations" have come from the false "Supper of the Great God" within Babylon! The scriptures identify true believers in these words..."*Now we have received, NOT the spirit of the world, but the Spirit which is of God; that we might know the things that are freely given to us of God."{1 Corinthians 2:12}*

The final verses of the eighteenth chapter of Revelation affirms that which is evident in this Laodicean church age. This is God's view of Babylon as He empties her of His people..."*And the light of a candle shall shine no more at all in thee; and the voice of the bridegroom and of the bride shall be heard no more at all in thee: for thy merchants were the great men of the earth; for by thy sorceries were all nations deceived. And in her was found the blood of the prophets, and of the saints, and of all that were slain upon the earth."{Revelation 18:23-24}*

John has portrayed the condition of Babylon AFTER the Lord's true believers had departed! They were the Light of the candle! They were the voice of the Bridegroom! NOW they are gone! How great will this darkness be as God's true saints depart from Babylon! Our Living Lord Jesus Christ has been building His church for more than two thousand years now. He has brought His church through their many persecutions throughout the past ages and now...to this final end time victory! It is called RESTORATION! The Revelation prophecy separates the "Redeemed" as being the church that Jesus said He would build! The blood of the Lamb has redeemed them

ALL! *"And in their mouth was found no guile: for they are without fault before the throne of God." {Revelation 13:5}*

## These "Children of God" are visibly seen in the next series...

# *"The 144,000 Standing on Mt. Zion"*

*"And I looked, and lo, a Lamb stood on mount Sion, and with him an hundred forty and four thousand, having his Father's name written in their foreheads. And I heard a voice from heaven, as the voice of many waters, and as a voice of great thunder: and I heard the voice of harpers harping with their harps: And they sung as it were a new song before the throne, and before the four creatures, and the elders: and no man could learn that song but the hundred and forty four thousand, which were redeemed from the earth. These are they which were not defiled with women; for they are virgins. These are they which follow the Lamb withersoever he goeth. These were redeemed from among men, being the first fruits unto God and to the Lamb. And in their mouth was found no guile: for they are without fault before the throne of God. And I saw another angel fly in the midst of heaven, having the everlasting gospel to preach unto them that dwell on the earth, and to every kindred, and tongue, and people, Saying with a loud voice, Fear God, and give glory to him; for the hour of his judgement is come: and worship him that made heaven and earth, and the sea, and the fountains of waters. And there followed another angel, saying. Babylon is fallen, is fallen, that great city, because she hath made all nations drink of the wine of the wrath of her fornication." {Revelation 14: 1-8}*

We have no question concerning the identity of the "Lamb." Jesus is consistently referred to as the "Lamb of God" which takes away the sin of the world throughout Holy Writ. We notice in particular where Jesus is standing…This mount Sion where Jesus is standing is mentioned in detail in the twelfth chapter of the Hebrew letter and refers to the city of the Living God. The scriptures affirm that this mount Sion is the Spiritual reality of the Kingdom of God, which Christ established though the New Covenant. Mount Sion constitutes the general assembly of the first born, or the born again children of God, whose names are written in heaven. This Mount Sion is the Biblical pattern of God's church given through Christ's unadulterated doctrines. God has also written them in the heart of every true believer. Christ is STANDING on His Word! The whole council of God! Mount Sion!

In this present scene, we are seeing the results that came from the preaching of the prophetically called sixth seal ministry. They brought a revival of the Word and the Spirit, and God in turn brought the results of this visible group of 144,000 people seen standing with Christ on Mt. Zion. This means that they have accepted the pure doctrines of Christ and the Spiritual pattern of God's church. Is this 144,000 referring to a "literal" number of people? No! If we depart from symbolic language, we loose the true message. The number of 144,000 then is used as an analogy. It is meant to represent something in the Spiritual realm. We find this analogy explained in the seventh chapter of Revelation, verses four through eight.

## The Twelve Tribes of Israel

ALL of the twelve tribes of Israel are listed there. In each tribe there were numbered 12,000 people. Twelve times twelve adds up to the 144,000 people. These twelve tribes were considered the complete representation of God's Old Testament kingdom of Israel. In this prophetic analogy then, the 144,000 standing with the Lamb are representing the complete representation of the NEW SPIRITUAL ISRAEL of God. The New Testament Church is now the Israel of God, or the Kingdom of God's dear Son. This 144,000 in this company of people represent ALL the redeemed of the earth. EVERY believer! This scene is referring to the completed Body of Christ.

The reason why Christ came into the world was to make a NEW Covenant with the house of Israel. We again affirm this truth... *"For this is the covenant that I will make with the house of Israel AFTER those days {after Christ came and established the new covenant through His perfect sacrifice at Calvary} saith the Lord; I will put my laws into their mind, and write them in their hearts: and I will be to them a God, and they shall be to me a people: and they shall not teach every man his neighbour and every man his brother, saying, Know the Lord: for ALL shall know me from the least to the greatest. For I will be merciful to their unrighteousness, and their sins and their iniquities will I remember no more. In that he saith, A NEW COVENANT, HE HATH MADE THE FIRST OLD. NOW THAT WHICH DECAYETH AND WAXETH OLD IS READY TO VANISH AWAY." {Hebrews 8:10-13}*

## THERE WILL NEVER BE ANOTHER
## JEWISH NATION FORMED BY GOD!

His chosen people are now ALL the redeemed by the blood of the Lamb under His NEW COVENANT! Here in this present scene, we see them standing with Christ on Mt. Zion. We should pay particular attention to the statement, *"having his Father's name written in their foreheads."* The "forehead" is a Biblical expression used to denote the "mind." When we are born again, God writes His laws upon our hearts and in our minds. We have just related this Spiritual experience through the scriptures from the book of Hebrews. If these analogies that I have been relating are not ample proof concerning the identity of these people, God just comes right out in plain language and says it like this in verse 3 b... *"and no man could learn that song but the hundred and forty and four thousand, which were redeemed from the earth."*

This gathering of people had heard and heeded the *"voice from heaven, and of great thunder and the voices of harpers."* They sang a *"new song"* before the throne. This is a worship scene of the people of God who had made their choice to "worship" God in Spirit and in Truth. These were those who had *"come out"* of Babylon's Great City of religion. John is given a further description of God's *"called out people,"* as he wrote...*"These are they which were not defiled with women; for they are virgins."* {Verse 4}

## The Harlot Daughters

True Christians are presented in the scriptural sense as being virgins espoused to their husband who is Christ. The *"defiled women"* spoken of in these scriptures represent the multitude of apostate churches professing to be a part of the Bride of Christ. These *"women"* are defiled because they have made all nations to drink of the wine of the wrath of their fornication. This means that they have fornicated the pure Word of God. They have adulterated the true doctrines of Christ. They have been unfaithful to Christ, as the true husband. The Apostate churches have always mixed their water with the Wine of God's Word.

We have previously related through the eye of prophecy how these heresies came to pass during the Great Apostasy of the Dark Age period. The Great Harlot Church changed the Word of God and

Mystery Babylon

replaced it with the intermingled Pagan ideologies and Idol worship. Protestantism then made an Image to Catholicism and continues in that Image to this present day. The Protestant bodies of all nations have been birthed by the "Mother Church." They are Her Harlot daughters. This is God's Word...NOT Jeanne Trovato's personal conclusion. This present scene verifies that God does have a visible "called out" Bride who will not be connected in any way to the "defiled" Harlot daughters of Babylon.

I should hasten to say that these people who have departed from ALL man-rule will be a most misunderstood people by the majority of "church goers." The "Way" will seem foreign to their thinking. However! God's ways are not man's ways and He will continue to bring His own into visibility to accomplish His purpose.

Let us return again to the fourteenth chapter of Revelation. In the *"midst of heaven"* or in the church realm on earth, Christ's called ministry and people had been given four distinctly different announcements to proclaim...

**1. Preaching the everlasting gospel** to all that dwell on the earth and to every nation, and kindred, and tongue, and people.{verse 6} The pure everlasting gospel had been perverted since the first falling away took place at the later part of the $2^{nd}$ Century. The Apostasy then obscured or eclipsed that Light even more. Protestantism only brought forth a "cloudy" or a "pale" representation of the gospel. Now, according to the prophecy, the purity of the everlasting gospel would again be heard.

**2. The message of the final judgement was also heard...** *"Fear God, and give glory to him; for the hour of his judgement is come. Worship him that made the heaven, and earth, and the sea, and the mountains of waters." {verse 7}* We have been engaged in a "preliminary" judgement during what the Revelation prophecy proclaims as the $7^{th}$ Seal Age. Now, we are informed that God's final judgement is at hand. We are living in a church age that has made a religion out of Christianity. They worship their particular "form" of religion and think that this makes them "Christian." As we have related through these messages, the Catholic adherents' worship through the virgin Mary and through dead people referred to as saints. They worship through a "Bloody Mass" and through their sacraments

265

etc. The Protestant denominations all have their "sacred cows" that they proclaim as "Biblical." It is as Jesus said to the woman at the well. *"Ye worship ye know not what. They that worship God must worship Him in Spirit and in truth."* There are "few" who have been born again of God that worship Him in Spirit and in Truth. I judge in righteous judgement as I make this statement. It is as Jesus said, *"Ye shall know them by their fruits."*

**3. Babylon is fallen, is fallen, the great city,** because she made all nations drink of the wine of the wrath of her fornication. {verse 8} The fall of Babylon is a "Spiritual" reality before God. Yes! The denominational systems do much humanitarian good. Yes! The denominational systems afford a support system for a moral environment for all age groups. Yes! The denominational systems are still visible, still functioning as pillars of the community. Still doing "good works." These "things" are not what God is referring to as he looks upon Babylon. He has specifically stated that Babylon is fallen because she has made all nations drink of the wine of the wrath of her fornication. We have learned what this means in our previous messages. The thirteenth chapter of first Corinthians has a list of many "things" that can be done and yet still be unprofitable in God's sight and acceptance. Here is what it says…You can speak with the tongues of men and of angels and if you have not "love" you are a sounding brass or a tinkling cymbal. You could have the gift of prophecy and understand all mysteries and have faith to remove mountains, yet, if you have not "love" you are nothing. If you would bestow all your goods to feed the poor and give your body to be burned and yet have not "love" it will profit you nothing. What is this word "love" referring to? It is surely not referring to a human love that is within man. It is referring to the Agape Love that comes from God's indwelling presence. None can receive this until one is born again of God's Spirit. Babylon has perverted this most imperative salvation message from God. This is why He sees Babylon as "fallen."

**4. The fate is told of all those who worship the beast and his image,** and receive his mark in his forehead, or in his hand. *"And the third angel followed them, saying with a loud voice. If any man worship the beast and his image, and receive his mark in his forehead or in his hand, The same shall drink of the wine of the wrath of God,* *which is poured out without mixture into the cup of indignation: and he shall be tormented with fire and brimstone in the presence of the holy angels, and in the presence of the Lamb. And the smoke of their torment ascendeth up forever and ever: and they have no rest day or night, who worship the beast and his image, and whosoever receiveth the mark of his name." {Revelation 14:9-11}*

This is a very serious message! It is expedient to give our full attention to this angel's message. In our day of "religious tolerance" when it appears that everyone's "religion" is counted to be acceptable with God, we are seeing an un-acceptance of it in the final judgement. God makes it clear that His indignation has been stirred and the wine of His wrath has been poured out without mixture. God uses specifics as He relates...*"If any man worship the beast and his image, and receive his mark in his forehead, or in his hand, the same shall drink of the wine of the wrath of God."*

## The message remains the same!

*"Come out of her my people"*
**is still available NOW to all who will**
*"Hear what the Spirit and the Word
saith to the churches."*

Through this present symbolic scene of the 144,000, we are viewing, the ongoing program of God's Final Restoration through His called out Remnant. Surely this final judgement scene should be a "wake-up" call for every true child of God to accept this present Revelation truth! Our Lord Jesus Christ Himself has revealed Babylon's fallen Spiritual condition through these prophetic messages. In reality...Yes! Today! We view the visible fallen condition of the institutionalized church professing to be "Christian.

## The Victorious Ones

A more detailed look is given to John of these victorious stalwart Christians, in Revelation 15:1-3...*"And I saw another sign in heaven, great and marvelous, seven angels having the seven last plagues; for in them is filled up the wrath of God. "And I saw as it were a sea of glass mingled with fire: and them that had gotten the victory over the beast, and over his image, and over his mark, and over the number of his name, stand upon the sea of glass, having the harps of God. And they sing the song of Mosses the servant of God and the song of the Lamb, saying, Great and marvelous are thy works, Lord God Almighty; just and true are thy ways, thou King of saints. "*

In the seventh seal message, these seven angels were given seven trumpets as they prepared to sound...{Revelation 8:6} Their messages were simply a recapping of all that John had seen through the previous six seal messages. We behold these seven angels as a sign in heaven. What does this sign mean? It simply means that these redeemed people had heard and believed ALL that the seven trumpets had proclaimed. It simply means that they obeyed God and permitted Him to again establish His Theocracy and preeminence over them.

These redeemed people are seen standing on the *"sea of glass."* The sea of glass mingled with fire is symbolic of the restored pure doctrines of Christ. References are given in James 21-24- 1 Corinthians 13:12 – 1 Corinthians 3:18. These scriptures verify the analogy of the sea of glass.

They were singing the song of Mosses. What was the song of Mosses? It was a song of deliverance! Just as Mosses had led God's people out of their captivity in Egypt, these redeemed people have been led out of their "Spiritual" captivity. It is stated that they had gotten the victory over the Beast {Catholicism} and over his Image. {Protestantism} They had NO "Mark of the Beast" attached to them! None in their foreheads or in their hands. They were marked with the Father's name ONLY as is related in Revelation fourteen. They had departed from ALL of Babylon's false traditional religions. They had obeyed God by "Coming out." This is confirmed because they were also singing the *"song of the Lamb."* What is the song of the Lamb? The song of the Lamb is knowing how to worship God through the Word and Spirit. They were born again of the Spirit of God. They had been redeemed by the blood of the Lamb and by the word of their testimony. They acknowledged God as their only means of salvation, saying, *"Great and marvelous are thy works, Lord God Almighty; just and true are thy ways, thou king of saints. Who shall fear thee, O Lord, and glorify thy name? For thou only art holy: for all nations shall come and worship before thee; for thy judgements are made manifest.*" (Revelation 15:3b-4)

God is long suffering and patient, not willing that one should perish but that all should hear and accept His gracious invitation to come under His authority alone. His judgements have been manifested through this Revelation prophecy.

**This author has done the very best I can in revealing God's final message**
**to**
**"whosoever will" hear and believe...**

# *"The Great Harlot is Judged"*

ROOTED IN PAGANISM

"*And there came one of the seven angels which had the seven vials, and talked with me, saying unto me, Come hither; I will shew unto thee the judgement of the great whore that sitteth upon many waters: With whom the kings of the earth have committed fornication, and the inhabitants of the earth have been made drunk with the wine of her fornication. So he carried me away in the spirit into the wilderness: and I saw a woman sit upon a scarlet coloured beast, full of names of blasphemy, having seven heads and ten horns. And the woman was arrayed in purple and scarlet colour, and decked with gold and precious stones and pearls, having a golden cup in her hand full of abominations and filthiness of her fornication: And upon her forehead was a name written, MYSTERY, BABYLON THE GREAT,THE MOTHER OF HARLOTS AND THE ABOMINATIONS OF THE EARTH. And I saw the woman drunken with the blood of the saints, and with the blood of the martyrs of Jesus and when I saw her, I wondered with great admiration. And the angel said to me, Wherefore didst thou marvel? I will tell thee the mystery of the woman, and of the beast that carried her, which hath the seven heads and ten horns." {Revelation 17:1-7}*

## Symbolism of the Harlot

The color "purple" has an express symbolic meaning and confirms the truths concerning this great Harlot church! The Roman Catholic Church has always chosen and reserved their purple garments for their Popes and Cardinals. Pope Paul II made it penal for anyone but the Cardinals to wear the hats of scarlet. In the book Roman Ceremonial chapter 3:5, which was complied several centuries ago by Marc, a Romish archbishop and dedicated to Leo X, it enumerated five different articles of dress of scarlet color, studded with pearls. The Popes miter is also of gold and precious stones. We notice through the description given in the previous scriptures that these are the same outward characteristics and garments that the Great Harlot is decked out with! The Harlot arrayed in purple and gold is without doubt the Church of Rome! The purple color is the badge of the Apostate Empire of the Roman Catholic Church. It mocks the very Christ it claims to represent, even as the purple robe was placed upon Him in derision before He was crucified.

The judgement of the "Great Whore" is the culmination of the subject matter of the entire Revelation Prophecy. She is called an "Harlot" because she has NO husband. Remember that we are speaking in the "Spiritual" realm. Christ has NEVER recognized the Apostate church as His Bride throughout this entire prophetic message, nor in the reality of history. The Apostate Church of Rome has NO husband! The reason being that this Great Harlot rejected Christ and His pure doctrine from the very beginning! Through the "more sure word of prophecy" God has verified that which history records. The Great Harlot has its roots in Paganism!

I have said with John, *"Come hither"* and I will show you... If you have read the contents of this book thus far, you have viewed prophetically, progressively, chronologically and historically the mystery of this Harlot and of the Beast, which carried her. In the beginning of my book, I stated that *"after"* we would investigate *"these things"* we would know about the mystery of this Great Harlot. The vast details within the various Revelation prophecies and the connecting themes of Daniel's prophecies have affirmed the events that are described in this present chapter of Revelation.

# After These Things...

• The first subtle falling away which Paul spoke of in the Thessalonian letter gave rise to this Apostate church and was indeed the beginning or birth of this Great Harlot. {2Thessalonians 2:1-12}

• We have viewed through the eye of prophecy, this Great Harlot that John describes as the one who has committed "Spiritual" fornication. Adulterating the Word of God and making the inhabitants of the earth drunk with the wine of her fornication. Her adherents have been intoxicated with her dogmas and superstitious ideologies.

• We have followed the gradual development of this voluptuously decked out Woman, as she became the Great Harlot who usurped the authority of Almighty God as the Papacy of Rome was formed.

• We have seen this Harlot as she deceitfully clothed herself in the robes of "Christianity" and made claim that she was the one true church throughout the past centuries. She makes the false claim that Peter was her first Pope.

• We have viewed the *"blasphemy"* of her courts as her potentates usurped the authority of God and changed His Word mingling it with Pagan worship and ideologies.

• We have also seen her sorceress and dastardly deeds during the Dark Age Period, as millions were branded heretics who would not bow down to her Popes!

• We have witnessed the tyranny and bloody persecution of humanity as this Great Harlot gained the civil support of the corrupted Emperors during the Dark Age period. She was *"drunk with the blood of the saints and with the blood of the martyrs of Jesus*

• We have comprehended the, *"golden cup in her hand full of abominations and filthiness of her fornication,"* as she lived in sensual pleasures under the guise of the Popedom. The history of her Popes is filled with corruption and abominations as they had their own concubines.

• We have seen this Harlot arrayed in her purple and scarlet, decked with gold and precious stones, as she confiscated houses and lands and became rich with her delicacies during the tyranny of the

Dark Ages. She still lays claim to vast wealth and riches to the present day.

- We have seen this woman as the Mother of Harlots, giving birth to the many daughters constituting the Protestant sects.
- The mystery was unfolded which explained the Beast with the seven heads and ten horns that was, and is not and yet is that carried this woman.
- John identifies the horns as the seven kings who made war against the Lamb.
- The Lamb did overcome this Great Harlots power, for He is Lord of Lords, and King of Kings!
- John concludes with... *"And the woman which thou sawest is that GREAT CITY, which reigneth over the kings of the earth." {Revelation 17:18}*
- We have seen this Great Harlot make her last final effort of revival through Second Unclean Spirit that has come forth in this very day we are now living in. {Revelation 16:13}

## The Mystery is Finished!

*"But in the days of the voice of the seventh angel, when he shall begin to sound, the mystery of God should be finished, as he hath declared to his servants the prophets. And the voice which I heard from heaven spake unto me again, and said, Go and take the little book which is open in the hand of the angel which standeth upon the sea and upon the earth. And I went unto the angel, and said unto him, Give me the little book. And he said unto me, Take it, and eat it up; and it shall make thy belly bitter, but it shall be in thy mouth sweet as honey: and as soon as I had eaten it, my belly was bitter.*

*"And he said unto me,
Thou must prophesy again
before many peoples, and nations,
and tongues, and kings."*

*Revelation 10:7-11*

273

# The "Little Book" is...

# The Revelation of Jesus Christ.

According to this Revelation prophecy, the seven sealed scrolls have all been opened to reveal the events that have come to pass during this Christian Dispensation. According to the scriptures, this dispensation is known as the "Gospel Age." There will be no other age to come! Eternity is eminent and next in God's timetable! God has taken the *"mystery"* out of the tangled speculations of men's wisdom concerning the history of Christianity, that is IF they will look at it through the eye of faith and symbolic prophecy. IF men will use God's key of symbolism based on analogy they will understand the message that Christ has revealed to His Church through this Revelation prophecy.

This *"little book"* and its content are very important for ALL of God's people to understand. I believe this *"little book"* symbolizes the book of the Revelation itself. I believe that it is symbolic of the entire prophetic message that is written therein. The voice from heaven said, *"Go and take the little book."*

A command is given...then a response. John is representing all those true and faithful servants who will receive this prophetic message. He responds by asking... *"Give me the little book."* This tells us that there must be a desire and willingness on the part of every true believer to submit to God's Voice concerning His final prophetic message. John was commanded to *"eat"* what was in the book. He was also told that what he ate would make his belly bitter, but be as sweet as honey in his mouth. Sure enough, according to the next verse John verified this is exactly what happened! What was in this book to eat? John's gospel assures us that this *"little book"* contains the "Bread of Life."

Listen to the Words of Jesus..."V*erily, verily, I say unto you, Mosses gave you not that bread from heaven; but my Father giveth you the true bread from heaven. For the bread of God is he which cometh down from heaven, and giveth life unto the world...I am the bread of life: he that cometh to me shall never hunger; and he that believeth on me shall never thirst."{John 6:32-35}*

Every true child of God must come to the place of faith that says to the Lord...*"Give me the little book,"* to rest secure in that hope of being accepted as a member of the Body of Christ. God will accept no less! He has commanded it! *"Come out of her, MY people, that ye be not partakers of her sins, and that ye receive not her plagues." {Revelation18:4b}*

## My Personal Note

As a servant of God who has heralded this Revelation prophecy during my lifetime of preaching, I can personally testify to the same experience that John speaks of! I make no apologies for speaking God's prophetic message. I have been true to my heavenly calling and continue unto this hour to proclaim the *"mystery of God"* that is finished! I have found that the bitterness of persecution always accompanies the message when those who hear it reject it. However! I have always found the *"honey"* sufficient enough to counteract the *"bitterness"* as the "Remnant" receives this glorious truth! Praise God! I have also received the final verse of this present scripture as a personal admonition from Christ and intend to obey it until my race is run...

*"And he said unto me,*
*Thou must prophesy again before many peoples, and*
*nations, and tongues, and kings."*
*{Revelation 10:11}*

275

This means that the Revelation prophecy will continue as a "perpetual" message. God will continue to call those who will herald this message until Christ splits the eastern sky and receives the Kingdom unto Himself!

**I intend to be among them...**
**by**
**His grace and strength!**

# *"The White Horse Re-appears"*

*"And I saw heaven opened, and behold a white horse; and he that sat upon him was called Faithful and True, and in righteousness he doth judge and make war. His eyes were as a flame of fire, and on his head were many crowns; and he had a name written, that no man knew, but himself. And he was clothed with a vesture dipped in blood: and his name is called the Word of God. And the armies which were in heaven followed him upon white horses, clothed in fine linen, white and clean. And out of his mouth goeth a sharp sword, that with it he should smite the nations: and he shall rule them with a rod of iron: and he treadeth the winepress of the fierceness and wrath of Almighty God. And he hath on his vesture and on his thigh a name written, KING OF KINGS AND LORD OF LORDS." {Rev. 19:11-16}*

As we enter into the finality of this Seventh Seal Age we view the return appearance of the "White Horse and Rider." This is that same White Horse and Rider that came forth as the First Sealed Scroll was opened in the Apostolic Period. That first symbolic scene of the Revelation proved to be Christ's victorious church, which was birthed into the first century. As each continuing sealed scroll was opened, we followed Christ's church into Her persecutions from Paganism; Her conflicts with the Roman Catholic Apostasy; Her prophetic time in the wilderness where She was nurtured by God; Her emerging through the 16ᵗʰ century Reformation; and Her battle against the "Image" apostasy of Protestantism.

## Christ and His army

In this present scene, which is the ending of the ages, we are seeing Christ and His army {the Church} as they continue in this Spiritual conflict of "Truth against Error." Through the opening verse, *"And I saw heaven opened,"* meaning the church realm on earth, John employs this symbolic phrase once again. What an awesome description John has been given of our victorious conquering Lord and King! As true believers, we rejoice with the understanding that has come forth from these unmistakable Revelation symbols! This dramatic scene now before us is portraying the Spiritual triumph of Christ and His victorious Church BEFORE His return! This is NOT a scene depicting the time of His Appearing. This is not a scene from another supposed age to come! The Despensational theory falsely presents this scene as a "literal" battle yet to come.

## Despensationalists...

project this scene as the Battle of Armageddon. They contend that it will be a grand scale all out "literal" war that is supposed to happen when Christ returns to this earth. They imagine that Christ will form a literal army, take up swords and slay all people who reject Him as King. They place this battlefield on the literal plan of Megiddo to be fought in Jerusalem. There is NO scriptural foundation for this false theory! This will never happen! Dispensationalists paint a gory scene of the mass destruction to all mankind! Swords clashing! A massacre so bloody that the hillsides will overflow with the blood of millions, even up to the horses' bridles. It is beyond my thinking how that such an insidious scenario came to be from those who profess faith in Christ!

Let us consider the scripture in its entirety that has been so misrepresented... *"And I looked, and behold a white cloud, and upon the cloud one sat like unto the Son of man, having on his head a golden crown, and in his hand a sharp sickle. And another angel came out of the temple, crying with a loud voice to him that sat on the cloud, Thrust in thy sickle, and reap; for the time is come for thee to reap; for the harvest of the earth is ripe. And he that sat on the cloud thrust in his sickle on the earth; and the earth was reaped. And another angel came out from the altar, which had power over fire; and cried with aloud cry to him that had the sharp sickle, saying, Thrust in thy sharp sickle, and gather the clusters of the vine of the earth; for her grapes are fully ripe. And the angel thrust in his sickle into the earth, and cast it into the great winepress of the wrath of God. And the winepress was trodden without the city, and blood came out of the winepress, even unto the horse bridles, by the space of a thousand and six hundred furlongs."* {Revelation 14:14-20}

Every competent commentary I have ever studied considers this expression concerning the *"blood out of the winepress, even unto the horses bridles,"* to be hyperbolical. This expression is not to be understood literally, but it is expressing a prodigious effusion of blood. Was this man's actual physical blood that came from the winepress? Of course not! This was alluding to the juice squeezed out of the grapes in the winepress. It is called *the "blood of the grapes"* in Genesis 49:11 This blood did not come forth by the sword of men fighting a literal battle! Let us consider what this scene is symbolizing... We have previously explained the 144,000 as the redeemed of the earth. This we found was a "preliminary" judgement concerning the fallen state of Babylon and her impending doom. {Revelation 14:1-11}

John concluded in verse twelve with these words... *"Here is the patience of the saints: here are they that keep the commandments of God and the faith of Jesus."* He is of course speaking about those true saints who have endured the persecutions of the False Prophet and the Beast during the Spiritual battle of Armageddon. As John begins in verse fourteen through twenty, he will be relating the harvesting and the vintage of this separation. Jesus spoke a parable, which explains what is going on here in this prophetic scene.

### Let us give heed to that which He has spoken...

*"And another parable put he forth unto them, saying, The kingdom of heaven is likened unto a man which sowed good seed in his field: But while men slept, his enemy came and sowed tares among the wheat, and went his way. But when the blade was sprung up, and brought forth fruit, then appeared the tares also. So the servants of the householder came and said to him, Sir, didst not thou sow good seed in thy field? From whence then came the tares? He said unto them, An enemy hath done this. The servants said unto him, Wilt thou that we go and gather them up? But he said, Nay; lest while ye gather up the tares, ye root up also the wheat with them. Let both grow together until the harvest: and in the time of harvest I will say unto the reapers, Gather ye together first the tares, and bind them in bundles and burn them: but gather the wheat into my barn."* {Matthew 13:4-30}

God is in NOW in the process of harvesting, of preparing a visible representation of the vintage of His true church. John wrote: *"Thrust in thy sickle, and reap; for the harvest of the earth is ripe."* He reiterates... *"Thrust in thy sharp sickle, and gather the clusters of the vine of the earth; for her grapes are fully ripe."* The vine was gathered and cast into the great winepress of the wrath of God. He had evidently gathered all the clusters and good grapes from this vine. What was left? It was the "wild grapes" spoken of in Isaiah 4:2. These were not acceptable unto God. This was not what He had planted from the good seed of His Word! All these scriptures verify this scene as a preliminary judgement. This is not the final separation, which will come at the Day of judgement.

What a DISHONOR to Christ to accuse Him of such a literal mass slaughter! What a horrendous accusation to make against the compassionate and loving Christ! He who said to Peter, *"put up again thy sword, into its place: for all they that take the sword shall perish with the sword. {Matthew 26:51-53}*

In every instance, the Revelation prophecy affirms that the battles fought by the church have all been "Spiritual" battles. They have NEVER been fought as physical battles!

## We reiterate through these scriptures just how their battles were fought...

• *"And I heard a loud voice saying in heaven, Now is come salvation, and strength, and the kingdom of our God, and the power of His Christ: for the accuser of our brethren is cast down, which accused them before our God day and night. And they overcame him by the blood of the Lamb, and by the word of their testimony; and they loved not their lives unto death."{Rev. 12:10-11}*

### *All the epistles of the New Testament affirm this SPIRITUAL WARFARE!*

• *"For though we walk in the flesh, we do not war after the flesh; For the weapons of our warfare are not carnal, but mighty through God to the pulling down of strongholds" {2 Corinthians 10:3-4}*

• *"For we wrestle not against flesh and blood, but against principalities, against powers, against the rulers of the darkness of this world, against SPIRITUAL wickedness in high places. Wherefore take unto you the whole armour of God, that ye may be able to withstand the evil day, and after having done all to stand. Stand therefore, having your loins girt about with truth, and having on the breastplate of righteousness; And your feet shod with the preparation of the gospel of peace. Above all, taking the shield of faith, wherewith ye shall be able to quench all the fiery darts of the wicked. And take the helmet of salvation, and the sword of the Spirit, which is the Word of God." {Ephesians 6:12-17}*

I must ask again…Do these scriptures describe the weapons of a LITERAL WARFARE? Of course not! All believers are engaged in a "Spiritual Warfare." Let us return again to this grand and glorious exhibition scene of Christ's gathering His armies. This scene makes clear to us the definite purpose of the One who is called, *"Faithful and True."* God has pronounced a preliminary judgement upon Babylon…This prophetic message is His final call to…

*"Come out of her, my people, that ye be not partakers of her sins, and that ye receive not her plagues. For her sins have reached heaven, and God has remembered her iniquities." {Rev. 18:4-5}*

## Preliminary Judgement

The Lord is judging in righteousness during this End Time Spiritual war. Christ is granting a "preliminary judgement" as He gathers the army of the redeemed into a visible Body of believers. Theologians have always admitted to a visible and an invisible church. They have always maintained that the visible bodies of people constituting the full membership of denominational structures do not represent the count of every true believer. They maintain that the "saved" or "redeemed" are invisible or rather only known unto God. There is certainly a strain of truth here. This is that which the Revelation prophecy foretells. I hope this will not sound like "double-talk" but what is happening is this…God is calling His "invisible, redeemed, saved believers" out of the "visible" mixture of the denominational systems of religion. In faithfulness God has promised a "Final Restoration" to all who will accept His prophetic truth.

God has also given this warning to all who do not obey His final preliminary call before the FINAL judgement … *And the beast was taken, and with him the false prophet that wrought miracles before him, with which he had deceived them that had received the mark of the beast, and them that worshipped his image. These both were cast alive into a lake of fire burning with brimstone." {Rev. 19:20}* Take careful notice of who the *"deceived"* were that were cast into the lake of fire. It was those that had *"received the mark of the Beast and those who worshipped the image."* The deceived were NOT God's true believers. They had obeyed God and departed from... "Mystery Babylon The Great, The Mother of Harlots and The Abominations of the Earth"

## Let us review John's glorious description of the Mighty Conqueror...

- John saw that Christ's *"eyes were as a flame of fire."* This represents Him as the Omniscient One, {the all seeing One} affirming the all-penetrating nature of His wisdom.
- The many crowns that He wears denote His many conquests throughout the past ages.
- His vesture dipped in blood surely signifying the everlasting "Blood Covenant" for the salvation of all mankind. It is the "Blood" of Jesus that cleanses us from all sin. Without the shedding of Blood there is no remission for sin.
- The Rider is called, *"The Word of God."* Jesus is the Living Word! It is written that we shall all be judged by THE WORD OF GOD. This is extremely important for every believer to grasp! We will all stand before God and give an account of our probationary time that we have spent on this earth.
- The armies that followed Christ were the separated redeemed church of the earth, for they were clothed in fine linen clean and white. {Revelation 19:8}
- According to Revelation 19:15, we have heard this declaration...*"Out of His mouth goeth a sharp sword, that with it he should smite the nations: and he shall rule them with a rod of iron:"* We are admonished to *"live by every word that proceedeth from the mouth of God.* The "sharp sword" is the Word of God! These scriptures declare that the unadulterated Word of God will come forth again through Christ's separated redeemed Remnant! The Word of God will either smite {bring spiritual death} or rule with the Rod, depending on the rejection or acceptance on the hearers part.
- The harvest time has arrived for it is written that... *"He treadeth the winepress of the fierceness and the wrath of Almighty*

*God."* All the redeemed bow before Him and acknowledge Him as *"KING OF KINGS AND LORD OF LORDS."*

**Yes!** Through this magnificent symbolic scene, we are viewing the gathering together of ALL the redeemed in this last age into the visible separated Body of Christ!

**Yes!** Christ's Bride will be made visible BEFORE He catches Her away. She will have come back to the Theocracy of God's design.

**Yes!** The WAR is on! This is a battle of God's TRUTH against Satan's EVIL deceptive LIES!

## War Against Christ
## Remember who the war is with...

John verifies all these events that will come to pass at the re-appearing of the White Horse and Rider. *"And I saw the beast, and the kings of the earth, and their armies, gathered together to make war against him that sat on the horse, and against his army." {Revelation 19:19}*

The "Beast" and the "Kings of the earth" have already been identified as the Apostate churches called, "Babylon." We have previously related the full details about this final battle which the prophecy calls, "The Battle of that great day of God Almighty" or "The Battle of Armageddon." The scriptures have affirmed that this battle is one and the same, only referred to by the two names...

### *"The Battle of that Great Day of God Almighty,"*
### *or "The Battle of Armageddon"*

As we have related through the messages of the "Three Unclean Spirits," this is an ongoing and intensified conflict! God's truth against Satan's errors! The Apostate church traditions against the TRUE church of the Living God and His Word! This battle will intensify and continue until Christ splits the Eastern sky to receive the Kingdom of God unto Himself. It is evident that only a minority of Christians are aware of the true message of this vital Revelation prophecy! I have claimed God's promise that, *"He has set before me an open door and no man shall shut it."* I am believing that this book,

"Mystery Babylon" will be the Spiritual breakthrough that God will use to awaken many of His true believers.

# Christians!
## There is a SPIRITUAL WAR going on!
## This is the battle that will end ALL battles!

We affirm then the identity of these armies that have gathered together to make war against the White Horse and His army. Through the more sure word of prophesy, we have previously identified the "Beast" and the "Kings of the earth" as the amalgamation of ALL branches of the Apostate church! They represent the ecclesiastical systems of men which God has called, "BABYLON." They have now gathered for the express purpose of, *"making war against Him that sat on the horse, and against His army."* This actually means that these three forces will be supportive and cooperative with one an other in order to accomplish their ultimate purpose. They will be united in fighting against the *"Remnant"* which will be holding true to God's Word! Their ultimate purpose is to uphold and maintain their elaborate systems of religion and their corporate structures at any cost! Their ultimate purpose is to prevent people from hearing and believing the unadulterated Word of God! Their ultimate purpose is to undermine and persecute those believers who have departed from their ranks.

## Silence in the Church
The ultimate purpose of the Apostate church world is to *"silence"* God's prophetic message of truth that reveals their deception! In fact this *"silence"* is mentioned as the Seventh Sealed Scroll is opened. Since this is an important aspect of our understanding in this closing message. let us consider this silence now... *"And when he had opened the seventh seal, there was silence in heaven about the space of half an hour. And I saw the seven angels which stood before God; and to them were given seven trumpets. And another angel came and stood at the altar, having a golden censer; and there was given unto him much incense, that he should offer it with the prayers of all saints upon the golden altar which was before the throne. And the smoke of the incense, which came with the prayers of the saints, ascended up*

284

*before God out of the angel's hand. And the angel took the censer, and filled it with fire off the altar, and cast it into the earth: and there were voices, and thunderings, and lightenings, and an earthquake."* {Revelation 8:1-5}

John wrote that there was *"silence in heaven."* We keep in mind our guidelines concerning symbolism. As we have learned, *"heaven"* always refers to the events that are taking place in the religious realm or the church activities on earth. Now, as the seventh sealed message opens, John writes… *"there was silence in heaven."* Let us rehearse and pursue the continuing events that came to pass through the sixth seal ministry. This will help us to understand the meaning of the silence. In our previous discourse on the Sixth Seal Scroll, we had learned that this ministry and the people based their reason for coming into existence upon a Divine prophetic call from God. According to their church history, this would have been in the late eighteen hundreds.

A man by the name of Daniel Sidney Warner could be called the founder of what came to be a movement of God during this period of time. It is my studied opinion that this man was used as mightily as Luther was to accomplish God's purpose in the scheme of prophetic events. This new movement grew rapidly as many other denominational ministers "saw the church" outside of the sectarian walls. Many departed from what they now saw as "Babylon" and began as itinerate preachers to herald the prophetic message of Revelation… "Come out of Her My People."

Multitudes of God's people believed their prophetic message and did indeed follow and "Come out" of Babylon's religious institutions. These sixth seal ministers called themselves "Reformers." As God's scattered people within the denominational systems heard and responded to the prophetic preaching of this ministry, small congregations began to form. Although their prophetic message was slow to be received at first and not very popular, it has been estimated that there were thousands who had "forsaken Babylon" in a period of about fifteen years! F.G Smith who was a strong advocate of this Revelation prophecy did much to promote the message through his writings. I would share a portion of F. G. Smith's vision from his book called…

285

## "The Last Reformation."

"This reformation is the movement of God. It is not a humanly organized movement depending for its success on the ability of men to persuade people to leave their churches and join them. God himself is breaking down the barriers that divide, and in response to His call the redeemed are forsaking human sects and creeds., and their hearts are flowing together. The center of this movement is not a particular geographical location, nor is its nucleus a particular set of infallible men: the center of and the nucleus of this world wide movement is our Lord Jesus Christ, and the operating force of the Spirit of the living God, which draws the faithful together in bonds of holy love and fellowship. Multitudes already recognize no other bonds of union than the moral and spiritual affinity which is the common heritage of all the disciples of Jesus that know the blessed experience of the heavenly birth. Multitudes more are beginning to see the light of this glorious truth, and in due time Christ, the Light, will illuminate the hearts of all the saved ones. All hail that day." End quote

The original printing of this book was done in 1919. Evidently there were many other Christians who shared his scriptural viewpoint, because the movement continued to grow rapidly. F.G.Smith also completed a full commentary called, "The Revelation Explained." This book was so widely read that it was in its twelfth edition only three years later. This gathering of people ultimately became known as, "The Reformation Movement of the Church of God."

{Their General Headquarters are in Anderson, Indiana yet today} In their first beginnings, the leadership of this movement was very careful and prayerful in keeping God's prophetic truth as the focus and the foundation of their preaching. They were careful and prayerful about the Biblical restoration of Christ's doctrines as the only foundation for His church. They lifted up the scriptural preeminence of Christ as the ONLY Head of the church. Yes! These early reformers believed that they were Divinely chosen to restore the doctrines, teachings and pattern of the first Century Church of God. They believed that there would be a visible "FINAL RESTORATION" of God's church separated from "Babylon." They believed in the scriptural pattern of the "Theocracy" of God. They believed that the church was meant to function under Christ as autonomous congregations through the restoration of the Word and the Spirit of God.

286

They believed this because it was a scriptural revelation that Christ had honored them to hold true.

## The following chart will be of value in seeing the simplicity of God's plan...

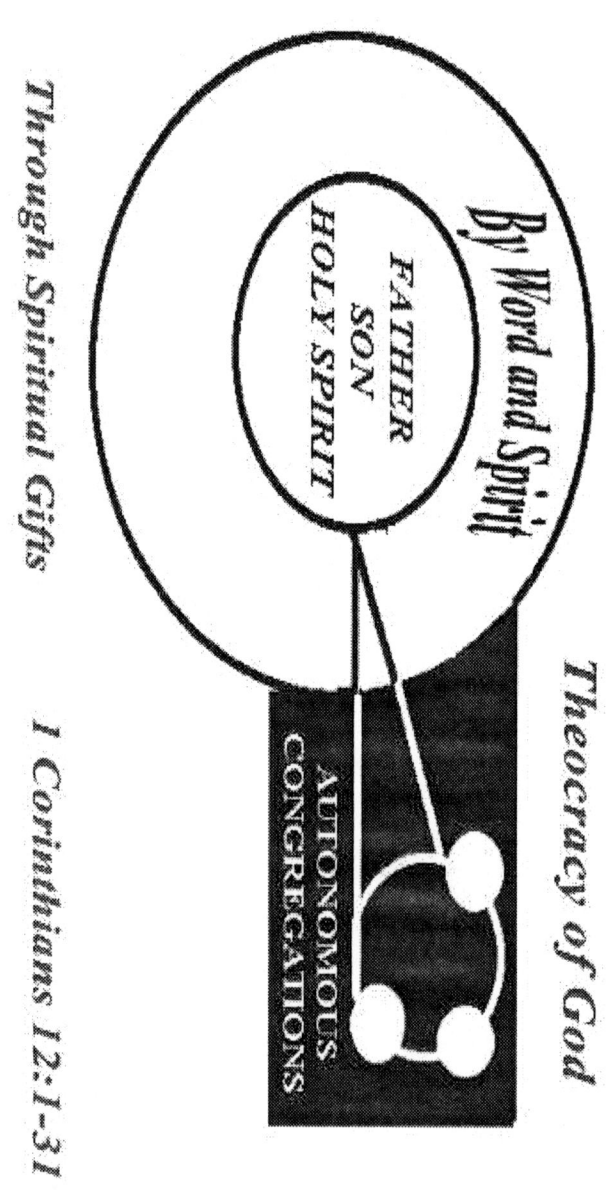

By Word and Spirit

FATHER
SON
HOLY SPIRIT

AUTONOMOUS
CONGREGATIONS

Theocracy of God

Through Spiritual Gifts

1 Corinthians 12:1-31

# The
## *"gifts of the Spirit"*
## were the accepted scriptural pattern
## of each local fellowship.

Each local congregation adopted the Biblical name of the "Church of God." It was not used in a "denominational" sense, but as it is in truth the only name given throughout the New Testament to denote the ownership of God's church. According to the history of this movement, these stalwart saints committed themselves to God in a desire to become that *"glorious church without spot or wrinkle."* Some among them were gifted songwriters who began to write prophetic songs that sang their message. Soon, a Church of God hymnal was printed and became a unifying tool for all the local congregations. What glorious truths came forth in these anointed songs. I would share several verses and the chorus of one of their many foundational songs...

### The Churches Jubilee

The Light of eventide now shines the darkness to dispel,
The glories of fair Zions state ten-thousand voices tell;
For out of Babel God doth call His scattered saints in one,
Together all one church compose, the Body of His Son.

The Bible is our rule of faith, And Christ alone is Lord,
All we are equal in His sight when we obey His Word;
No earthly master do we know, to man rule will not bow,
But to each other and to God eternal trueness vow.

O Church of God, the Day of jubilee...
Has dawned so bright and glorious for thee...
Rejoice be glad! Thy Shepherd has begun...
His long divided flock again together into one.

This movement of Christians referred to themselves as "saints of God" and were zealous to become a leavening agency for God in the vast maze and confusion of Babylon's religion. Anointed preachers came forth to proclaim God's promise of "Restoration" through many Old Testament types and anti-types. According to Zechariah's prophecy... *"But it shall come to pass, that in the evening time it shall be light."{14:7b}* This movement of people perceived themselves to be heralds of that restored Light which would prepare the Bride of Christ for His return. They perceived that the ending of the gospel day was near for it was the *"evening time."* They believed that the *"more sure word of prophecy"* declared this truth through the opening of the Seven Sealed Scrolls.

As we have previously stated...Something unusual seems to have happened between the opening of the Sixth Sealed Scroll and the Seventh Sealed Scroll. Let us compare the circumstances. As the Sixth Seal was opened there was a great *"earthquake"* and unusual calamities in the heavens took place. We learned that these unnatural celestial happenings symbolized a catastrophic change in religious polity. Now...according to John's Seventh Seal message there is a strange change that has taken place! As this Seventh Seal Scroll is opened there is a *"silence"* that has taken place in the church. What church? What was this silence that had taken place?

As we pursue the historical account within the archives of The Reformation Movement of the Church of God, we will see what this *"silence"* was about. The prophetic confirmation that this *"silence"* emanated from this particular church will be seen through the events that came to pass within this very movement of people. Remember...we are speaking about the people who originally believed that God had called them to herald this Revelation prophecy in the eighteen hundreds.

The details of the decline of this Movement are varied and lengthy, for they now cover over a one hundred-year span of time. Perhaps the word "departure" would be a more explanatory word than "decline." I will strive to give a brief, honest and concise account of the causes and events that brought about this *"silence in the church."* The *"space of half an hour"* that John mentions is in keeping with the very short span of time that this Revelation prophecy was preached within this movement.

As time progressed, a subtle but gradual *"silence"* of the message, *"Come out of her my people"* and *"Babylon is fallen"* began to fall upon the leadership of this Church of God movement. Yes! Sad to say, a *"silence"* came over the very people that God had *"called out"* to herald this prophetic message! I am able to speak first hand, because of my past affiliation within this movement for many years. I will endeavor to build a bridge of understanding as to how and why this glorious prophetic ideal began to diminish.

In the infancy of this movement, there was no centralized earthly headquarters or ecclesiastical government. There were no boards or committees to govern the people. As we have previously stated, each local congregation was "autonomous" and practiced the "Theocracy" of God. They proclaimed their doctrines to be from God the Father, because they adhered to the scriptures alone for their rule of faith. They believed in the Great Commission to... *"Go ye therefore, and teach all nations, baptizing them in the name of the Father, and of the Son, and of the Holy Spirit: Teaching them to observe all things whatsoever I have commanded you: and, lo, I am with you always, even unto the end of the world. Amen." {Matthew 28:19-20}*

Great emphasis was placed upon the preeminence of the Word and the Spirit, which had been "slain" by the Apostate religions. This Church of God ministry guarded against the mixture of truth with traditional errors that were commonly accepted within Protestantism. Their emphasis was to teach and to observe all that Christ taught and observed. Their desire was to permit Jesus to "build His church" through His doctrine working within their lives.

This stance brought with it much misunderstanding and persecution. After about fifty years into the Sixth Seal Age, compromises concerning sound doctrine began to surface. This came as a natural result when other sectarian Christians became a part of their fellowship. Christians who had come from other sectarian churches began to vie for some of their Babylon practices. Some brought with them their many diversified traditional teachings from Babylon. The leadership began to wane in reproving, correcting and instructing in the doctrines of Christ ONLY. Every wind of doctrine began to be accepted, tolerated or overlooked.

The Revelation prophecy became "offensive" to many, and was blamed for lack of growth in the congregations where it was still believed and preached. To others, the Revelation message became an embarrassment. Chart teaching of the Revelation message, which had been much in demand throughout the past, now began to wane. Many people within their ranks now desired to be just another "church among churches" and be socially accepted. The leadership began to look on the Revelation prophecy as too controversial. There was now a "mixed" multitude of various sectarians within this movement. They introduced "boards and committees" in order to "oversee" the work of the church. State districts began to form with credential committees' overseeing these districts. Soon ministerial assemblies' arose to "govern" various functions. Man-made ordinations became necessary for acceptance in order to preach within this man-made structure. A yearbook was then formulated to present the structural functioning of this another "earth born" religion.

Soon a Liberal Arts College became a part of this movement...other colleges soon followed. There was little or no foundational teachings in the college curriculums concerning the original prophetic calling and purpose for the Church of God. Their publishing house, which originally was called "Warner Press," ceased to print many of the early Reformers books, especially those having to do with the Revelation prophecy. Popular sectarian books now filled their bookshelves for earthly gain. It was evident that many within this movement had lost their first prophetic love that birthed them. The long-standing name of their periodical called, "The Gospel trumpet" was changed to sound more acceptable. It was now called "Vital Christianity." The problem was that the "Trumpet" ceased to sound as a certain sound!

### Another added factor...

Most congregations had built church edifices and now had financial obligations to consider. Because of all these extenuating circumstances, it became more and more difficult for the ministry to lift up the Word and the Spirit. It became more and more difficult for them to stand on the *"more sure word of prophecy."* FEAR rather than FAITH took over in the majority of congregations. Numbers and growth began to be more important than the admonition of the Lord to to, *"preach the more sure word of prophecy, lift up the Word and the Spirit* and to, *"rebuke with all authority"* anything that was contrary to sound doctrine. As the years passed, the conditions only grew worse! According to the history of this movement, many schisms developed and much dissension accompanied this particular "Church of God" people.

A conservative leadership developed within this movement some years ago called the…

## "Reformation Witness."

Their position is stated in their present periodical and I quote…"May 1973 Pastor's Fellowship was conceived in the hearts and minds of a number of concerned Pastors who were burdened for the faithful and ongoing preaching, re-preaching, declaration and dissemination of those doctrines and teachings that brought this Reformation Movement of The Church of God into existence. It is our purpose and mission to continue, by every means available, to carry this same vision to our generation and those who follow." End Quote.

At the present time, this more conservative group has a publishing house that continues to reprint the old reformer's books. They maintain their dedication in striving to keep alive the former prophetic truths and doctrines of the Church of God. Those who have come to be known as the "liberal" faction of Church of God people have recently identified themselves with a caption on their church marquee. "Headquarters at Anderson Indiana."

Most of the separated conservative branches of Church of God people have continued to preach the Revelation prophecy {although divided on some issues} while the majority of the Anderson Church of God has become *"silent"* on the prophecy. I am in agreement with many others who believe that this is a direct fulfillment of John's prophecy…*"And when he had opened the seventh seal, there was silence in the heaven about the space of half an hour."*
*{Revelation 8:1}*

As we return to the scriptures in Revelation 8:1-6, there is a scene of another angel, with the prayers of the saints that ascended before God. As these continuing scriptures relate, this *"silence"* on the part of some did not stop the prophetic message from being heralded. Praise God! This scene symbolizes the faithful saints whose prayers rose like incense before the throne of God asking that this prophetic message of freedom would persevere! We know that God heard and answered their prayers, for we read of the same catastrophic symbolic circumstances related. The censer was filled with fire off the altar and cast into the earth; there were voices, and thunderings, and lightenings, and an earthquake. God again sent the fire of the Holy Spirit as the faithful sounded their trumpets

God continues to bless in this same power today within the "Remnant" wherever they are gathered together. It is God's business to place the members in the Body as it pleases Him! He is more than able to bring visible fellowships together to carry out His purpose. Christ does not need a structure or an organization of men connected to one another to prove that He has a visible Bride. The Body of Christ, the Church of the Living God, is a Living organism not fleshly organizations looking to men to hold it together. It is written that where two or three are gathered together, Christ is present in their midst.

Why is it that man always considers BIG or MORE as representing the church of God? Why is it that man thinks he has to be "connected" to one group or another to proclaim "WE" are the church? Perhaps the sin of pride is involved? Let the church BE the church as God brought it together in its Pristine glory through the Word and by His Spirit! God will continue to send the fire of the Holy Spirit today upon all who will stand true to this precious and vital prophetic truth!

The ecclesiastical Churches of God {Headquarters in Anderson Indiana} may close their hearts and their pulpits to this once loved and accepted prophetic message; other denominations and sectarians may be troubled and offended by its truth; other factions may be divided on the issues of prophecy; but truth crushed to the ground will re-seed itself and multitudes of God's people will hear and heed His call to... *"Come out of her MY people."* They will be under the "Theocracy" of God once again!

### IT IS WRITTEN!

I must hasten to say that God has always had a people and He always will! He will never be without a Voice to proclaim His Truth! There has always been a "Remnant" who have kept the commandments of God and the testimony of Jesus. There are many who comprise this "Remnant" today who are diligently striving to present, live, keep and propagate the testimony of the, *"more sure word of prophecy."* I am only one among multitudes who claim to be a part of this "Remnant" over the length and breadth of this earth.

# I would be pleased to share my personal stance from my heart through the
# Love of Christ...

Forty-five years ago I was born again into the Kingdom of God. The blood of Jesus Christ has cleansed me from all sin and unrighteousness. I have been translated from the kingdom of darkness into the Kingdom of God's dear Son. I belong to the Biblical church of God! I am a member of the Body of Christ. My name is in the Lamb's Book of Life. I am a Christian. I am now standing on the *"sea of glass"* {Revelation 15:2} which is God's eternal Word! I am standing on His Holy ground. I have come to Mount Zion, and unto the city of the Living God. {Hebrews 12:22-24}

I do not belong to any man-made schism, sect or denomination. I have removed out of the midst of Babylon. I am an itinerate minister just like our Lord claimed to be! Christ did not join up with the Sadducees, the Pharisees or the Samaritans of His day to promote His Kingdom. He just simply proclaimed the everlasting gospel! I have vowed to do the same. I have obeyed God's command to, "Come out of her MY people." I do not have any "Mark of the Beast" upon me! I am a part of the Bride of Christ, making myself ready for His glorious appearing. I meet with and teach the Word of God in a home Discipleship Fellowship. I continue in my Prophetic Ministry as God leads me. I am still trusting in Jesus Christ to save me to the uttermost and present me faultless before His throne. I live by faith! This is all God requires!

### I stand upon these scriptures for fellowship
### with all my brothers and sisters in Christ...

*"This is the message which we have heard from him, and declare unto you, that God is light and in him is no darkness at all. If we say that we have fellowship with him, and walk in darkness, we lie, and do not the truth: But if we walk in the light, as he is in the light, we have fellowship one with another, and the blood of Jesus Christ his son cleanseth us from all sin." {1 John 1:7}*

**It is essential to keep in mind that the armies which followed Christ are called the**

# "REMNANT"

Let us re-examine the key scriptures concerning this REMNANT throughout the entire Revelation prophecy...

- We first viewed this REMNANT in the Apostolic period. *"And the dragon was wroth with the woman, and went to make war with the REMNANT of her seed, which keep the commandments of God, and have the testimony of Jesus Christ."{Revelation 12:17}* The full explanation of this event has previously been given.

- This REMNANT re-appears as the Word and the Spirit were again lifted up through the, *"earthshaking message"* brought forth by the sixth seal ministry. It is written: *"And the same hour was there a great earthquake, and the tenth part of the city fell, and in the earthquake were slain of men seven thousand: and the REMNANT were affrighted, and gave glory to the God of heaven."* {Revelation 11:11-13}

## This same REMNANT Is NOW Christ's Army

Many movements have come forth in every age to proclaim that "THEY" are the chosen ones that God will use to show the world the true church, but all have failed! Each has fallen prey to the same paradigm. They simply make an image of their own traditions and try to prove everyone else is wrong. God has another plan! His plan is Christ! It may sound a bit simplistic to realize that God is able to bring His church into existence without the availability of men's governing, structural or ecclesiastical powers that be.

God birthed His church into existence in the first century. He has held it together through His Word and by His Spirit every since! As we have proven through this prophecy, God has ALWAYS had a true people on the earth to *"testify of Jesus and keep His commandments."* Although they have been persecuted, branded as heretics, spent time the wilderness and many still scattered within Babylon's systems...Yet...God has promised that He will again restore the Pristine Glory of His church. Their visibility will be seen as they exit from Spiritual Babylon one by one! The scriptures affirm this and history has verified it. This will come to pass as true believers take seriously the admonishment of the Lord to, *"Search the scriptures; for in them ye think ye have eternal life: and they are they which testify of me."*

• God will restore the church...when true believers obey the scriptural pattern that is clearly given through His Word.

• God will restore the Pristine Glory again...when every Christian takes time to, *"prove all things whether they be of God or man."*

• God will accomplish this seemingly insurmountable objective because the *"more sure word of prophecy"* has proclaimed it!

All Seven Sealed Scrolls have been opened! All the events have come to pass, just as they were prophesied. The message has been completed! John wrote of this completion... *"But in the days of the voice of the seventh angel, when he shall begin to sound, the mystery of God should be finished, as he hath declared to his servants the prophets." {Revelation 10:7}*

## The "mystery of God" has been
## revealed or finished!

## *"MYSTERY, BABYLON THE GREAT,*
## *THE MOTHER OF HARLOTS*
## *AND*
## *ABOMINATIONS OF THE EARTH"*

John's message was clear! He wrote, *"but in the days of the voice of the seventh angel, when he shall begin to sound..."* John speaks more specifically of just when... *"he shall begin to sound."* According to Revelation 8:6, it was after the worship scene of the prayers of the saints ascending to the throne. John wrote, *"And the seven angels which had the seven trumpets prepared themselves to sound."* When the seven angels which had the seven trumpets began to sound, they were simply resounding all the events that had already taken place! These are not new trumpet judgements. They have already been sounded. The events of each of these trumpets can be retraced back through the history that we have just come through. You will find that the remainder of this present chapter along with chapters nine and ten are a recapping of all the previous events that have taken place.

The voice of this seventh angel is symbolizing the continuing lineage of God's prophetically chosen ministry that came forth to expose this mystery about Babylon. For more than a hundred years now this prophetic message has encompassed the sea and the earth! According to John's statement, this Revelation prophecy is to be a perpetual message until the Lord's return. Although in the minority of mainline Christianity; although only spoken of as a Remnant; this truth has been kept alive! It will never die out! I believe that the apostle John himself is a symbolic representation of ALL God's servants who will continue to herald this prophecy. Though misunderstood and rejected by the masses, this Revelation prophecy still remains the only message through which God can again restore Unity to the Body of Christ.

We recall the continuing message given to John from the angel…*"And he said unto me, thou must prophesy AGAIN before many peoples, and nations, and tongues, and kings."*
*{Revelation 10:11}*

# Prophesy Again!
## And Again! And Again!
### Until Christ's Bride is prepared for His return!

I would share this timely message from a prophetic voice of the past. This book written by T.R. Gates in the year of 1812 called Truth Advocated. He comments on the Beast and the Image in Chapter 13: 11-18… "Concerning the Beast and his Image, as it exists in Protestant countries, seems in this place particularly meant; and our own land is full of the number of his name. That such a testimony will one day go forth we must believe, or else John saw that which will never be: and…the testimony will certainly be received; for a company in the next chapter are to be seen that had gotten the victory over the beast, his image his mark and his number. {Revelation 15:2}

It is at this very time, no doubt, that the three unclean spirits, like frogs, come out of the mouth of the dragon, the beast and the false prophet; spirits of devils working miracles, which go forth to the kings of the earth and the whole world to gather them together to the great battle of God Almighty. The greatest possible efforts indeed will now be made by all sectarians to keep up their existence…nor is it any wonder that the hireling ministers and systems of worshippers {Demetrous like} should be stirred up and raise no small stir about "The Way" for it is evident, not only that their craft {sect} is in danger at being set at naught by this testimony, but also the Great Diana of the systems and forms of religion would be despised and their magnificence destroyed, whom now almost the whole Christian world worshippeth through. The same round of things will continue until this evil is remedied...when this will take place, time only can determine with certainty. It will probably commence slowly, and not come with any great observation...few will at first see and embrace "The Way" being strange to them because of their prejudices and the way they have been taught by the false prophet to be wrong and improper. Those who will depart from sectarianism will be few in number, despised and hated...yet the Lord will confirm with signs and wonders the true Word and the Spirit's revival. A true and living testimony will go forth before this last period of awful judgement of God comes to a close.

I am but one crying in the wilderness of error and sin, of wickedness and delusion, testifying according to the best light given me; and any light that I can possibly communicate will in a little time become feeble light of the sun, by reason of the greatness of the light that shall shine hereafter. The authors of this testimony...unlike to all who have gone before them, will attack the evil at its roots, expose its deceit, hypocrisy and wickedness of the various sects in such a way that has never been done. You may look on these things as reveries of my own fancies; but someday other people will witness the truth I now write. Whenever any body of people come into notice, establish their rules and institutions of learning and become a "respectable sect" they are the people of God in name only., and they cease to have the nature of the true Biblical church of God and whosoever unites himself to the same institution constitutes himself as one of the beast's party, and so far as his influence extends, he helps to establish the kingdom of anti-Christ in the earth." End Quote

What a Divine prophetic utterance was given through the Spirit of God to this studied man of prophecy as far back as 1812! What an insight into this end time Restoration that he had received! We, who stand on the *"more sure word of prophecy"*, are in perfect agreement with this saint of the past. Thus it is written: *"And the seventh angel* {God's human ministry through the church on earth} *poured out his vial* {judgement on Babylon} *into the air; and there came a great voice out of the temple of heaven from the throne, saying, It is done."* *{Revelation 16:17}*

It may seem a strange action to pour out a vial of something into the air! What does this symbolize? We know that this vial represents the judgement preaching upon this religious kingdom of "Babylon." This judgement comes from the "Word" of God. We know that the Word of God is "seed." What happens to seed if you throw it into the air? It goes anywhere and everywhere. Some falls on stony ground; some falls among thorns; some falls by the wayside and some falls on good ground! This is God's intent! God will plant it in the ground as He sees fit. His Word does not return unto Him void. His purpose will be completed through *"pouring out this vial into the air."* This Revelation Prophecy is not just another denominational message! It is God's invitation to, *"whosoever will hear what the Spirit and the Word saith to the church."*

God has led me into an Internet ministry, which I believe is a fulfillment of this scripture in my own life. I am throwing the prophetic seed into the vast Universe of air through the World Wide Web. God has set before me an open door and no man can shut it! I have created two Web Sites and have had about 30,000 people thus far check them out. People from all over the world have contacted me! The majority of people who have contacted me have been in agreement with the message and the majority also have told me that they have NEVER heard this concept before!

I invite you to review my Web Sites at:
**www.RevelationScrolls.com**
**www.ChristianityRestored.com**

I have received numerous requests for my previous book, "The 7 Sealed Scrolls" from many interested people over the length and breadth of the earth. Some seed has fallen on "GOOD" ground! Praise God! I am expecting even greater acceptance of this more detailed follow up book that you are now reading called...

## "Mystery Babylon"

God desires to speak individually with us as His children to accomplish His purpose. We can understand Him...IF we will clear our minds of our traditions, ideologies and fleshly innovations from our various brands of religion. Amen? Listen to this wonderful promise from God... *"But ye have an unction from the Holy One, and ye know all things."* {1 John 2:20}

What wonderful promises God offers to ALL His children who are willing to lay aside "their concepts" and accept only His infallible Word. Every true believer has received an anointing from God to hear and understand His Word...IF...they clear their minds of ALL traditional concepts!

*"But the anointing which ye have received of him abideth in you, and ye need not that any man teach you: but as the same anointing teacheth you all things, and is truth, and is no lie, and even as it hath taught you, ye shall abide in him." {1 John 2:27}*

Many sincere Christians are seeking and asking...Where is this visible church today? Where can I go to find an autonomous body of believers that are under the Theocratic rule of God? God's answer...YOU take the first step of faith by departing. He will place the members in the Body as it pleases Him. Christ said, *"I will build my church."* He did not ask you or I to build it. He asks us to BE the church. He will bring it together and maintain it. It is all done by faith! The book of Acts tells us this about the church of the first century..."*And they {believers} continuing daily with one accord in the temple, and the breaking of bread from house to house, did eat their meat with gladness and singleness of heart. Praising God, and having favour with all the people. And the Lord added to the church daily such as should be saved." {Acts 2:46-47}*

The First Century church met from house to house and existed for one soul PURPOSE. This was to bring others into a saving knowledge of Jesus Christ and make TRUE believers of them. Their purpose was not to begin a denomination! Their purpose was not to build up "their" church membership, or "their" game plan for fellowship, or to play a numbers game in church attendance. In today's church world, it appears that everyone wants to GO to church, when all God desires is that Christians BE the church. What a MIRACULOUS church that first church was! Never! Have we known a time when such glory has been manifested since! Why was that? It is because they had nothing other than the Word of God! They had NO denominational traditions! ONLY the Word and the Spirit to guide them into all truth!

It is a natural inclination of the flesh to want to "belong" to something that is ready made. It is a natural inclination of the flesh to want to "go" where something has been all prepared. It is a desire of the flesh to be in a "comfort zone." It is a natural desire of the flesh to

301

be "entertained" or programmed in a structural church setting. But...What of the "Spirit" man? It is evident that the Spirit man becomes indolent through the vain repetitious Sunday morning format! It has made him Spiritually lazy! Eventually, he looses his ability to activate his own personal faith. *"He whist not that the Spirit left him."* He will ultimately become religious...but lost!

You will not find the "pre-planned" so-called liturgical worship services recorded in the book of Acts or in any of the continuing epistles. However! There was plenty of "action" going on through the Holy Spirit's Presence when the church met together! The first century church was blest of the Lord with thousands of people being saved at one time through the simple message of Christ's resurrection! {Acts 2:41} The Holy Spirit was present to convict of sin of righteousness and of judgement to come. The Holy Spirit was present in great power because the simplicity of Christ's gospel was preached...nothing added and nothing taken away!

Today's church statistics tell us that it takes approximately six hundred people about a year to win one soul to Christ. In that first century church, there were no congregations filled with spectators sitting in a padded pew waiting for the "show to go on." In that first century church, it was a "spontaneous combustion" of the Holy Spirit coming upon the people and they ALL participated! According to the scriptures, one had a psalm, one had a testimony, and one had a word of praise as they expressed the joy of their salvation together. The Lord confirmed His Word with signs, wonders and miracles of healing. Christ continued to manifest His healing through believers AFTER He returned to Heaven. His Presence and power was with them, as they became His witnesses to an unbelieving Pagan society!

**It is written:** Stephen full of faith and power did great wonders and miracles among the people. {Acts 6:8}

**It is written:** Paul and Barnabas performed miracles and wonders through the power of God. {Acts 15:12}

**It is written:** God wrought special miracles by the hands of Paul, so that from his body were brought unto the sick handkerchiefs or aprons, and the diseases departed from them, and evil spirits went out of them. {Acts 19: 11-12}

**It is written:** Peter took hold of a man's hand and said, *"Silver and gold have I none; but such as I have give I unto thee: In the name* *of Jesus Christ of Nazareth rise up and walk.... and immediately his feet and ankle bones received strength."* {Acts 3:6-11}

## Did Christ leave the church powerless?

No! The entire twelfth chapter of first Corinthians speaks of the spiritual gifts for the church as being perpetual. Paul begins with these words of exhortation... *"Now concerning spiritual gifts, brethren, I would not have you to be ignorant."* Verse nine of this chapter mentions emphatically the gift of healing. In the "Great City" of apostate religion today, they are "ignorant" concerning the Spiritual gifts. Some denominations even teach that the miracles passed away after the gospel had been preached in the earth. They falsely teach that there was no more need for miracles since we now have the written Word. Yet, Jesus said, *"These signs shall follow them that believe,* He also included that, *"They shall lay hands on the sick, and they shall recover."* {Mark 16:17-18}

I do not read anywhere in the scriptures that Jesus placed a time limitation on this promise to His believers. The very last scriptures that Mark penned tells us that Christ followed through with His promise. *"So then after the Lord had spoken unto them, he was received up into heaven, and sat on the right hand of God. And they went forth, and preached every where, the Lord working with them, and confirming the word with signs following. Amen."*
*{Mark 16:19-20}*

## The Word is forever settled in heaven!

**Preachers often quote** the familiar scripture found in Hebrews 13:8... *"Jesus Christ the same yesterday, and today, and forever."* Yet! Few really experience the miraculous change that Bible salvation and Divine healing bring!

**The nominal church world talks** about the miracles Jesus did when He walked on earth, however, few expect or believe in Him to perform miracles in their midst today!

**The nominal church world sings songs** that have been written about the blind seeing, the lame walking, and the deaf hearing, but should we ask the question that the prophet of old ask... *"Where be the miracles of our fathers...Judges 6:13.*

**The ministers preach about** all of the miraculous things Jesus did when He walked among men…He walked on the water; He commanded the sea to be still; He blest the crowd with 5,000 fish and the bread; He raised the dead; He cast out demon spirits…We ask, Where are these manifestations of Christ in the church world today? The prophetic truths of this Revelation message that we have just concluded have shown us the reason why God is not pleased to bless with *"signs and wonders and miracles of healing."* It is His Word that He will confirm! He will not confirm the adulterated word of an Apostate church! The Apostate churches present an "apologetic" Christianity rather than a victorious Christianity! Christ presents Himself as a full redeemer for His redeemed children. He has promised that…*"We are more than a conquer through him that loved us."* According to our Lord, the greatest miracle of all is the experience of salvation! *"Wherefore, he is able also to save them to the uttermost that come unto God by him, seeing he ever liveth to make intercession for them."* {Hebrews 7:25} God's salvation was the express purpose for bringing the church into existence. Salvation from sin was the GLORY of the Pristine Church, even as John wrote…*"Now is come salvation, and strength, and the kingdom of our God, and the power of his Christ…"* {Revelation12:10}

God is NOW in the process of RESTORING that GLORY to any and all who will but believe and walk in this prophetic truth! One Christian at a time! This is His ultimate purpose and promise… *"That he might sanctify and cleanse it {church} with the washing of the water by the word. That he might present to himself a glorious church, not having spot, or wrinkle, or any such thing; but that it should be holy and without blemish."* {Ephesians 5:26-27}

This Revelation prophecy has revealed the full scope of God's operation from the opening of the First Sealed Scroll to the present opening of the Seventh Sealed Scroll. There are no more scrolls to be opened! We have followed the events of God's people through this Revelation prophecy chronologically. All these events did come to pass which validates the prophecy as being from the Lord.

## God has given His final
## Ultimatum of Love…

It is written: *"God honors His Word even above His name."* He will not honor "MAN'S TRADITIONAL" beliefs! As it is written: *"Judgement should begin with the house of God,"* God's true believers must execute judgement upon this GREAT HARLOT which God has identified as Catholicism along with Her daughters which He has identified as Protestantism. The deception must be exposed! God has pronounced this preliminary judgement. He has done His part, but it must be delivered through His TRUE Church to bring forth God's "Final Restoration."

**Will YOU obey His final call to.......**

Come Out of Her
My People

## The "Exodus"

There is a great "Exodus" now taking place over the world! Multitudes of God's people are departing from the Institutionalized churches. They are calling themselves "Home or House churches." Most of these people have little if any knowledge of the promised "Restoration" through Christ's Revelation prophecy…yet…they are hearing the Spirit of God and obeying His call. I personally believe this to be that "striking at the root" which Theodore Gates spoke of prophetically in his writings in the centuries past. I also believe that God will reveal *this "more sure word of prophecy"* to these people that have been wondering from mountain to mountain seeking Zion. The Lord spoke these words to Jeremiah describing this end time condition…*"My people hath been lost sheep: their shepherds have caused them to go astray, they have turned them away on the mountains: they have gone from mountain to hill, they have forgotten their resting place." {Jeremiah 50:6}*

Thousands of God's people have been going from one congregation to another, {symbolized by mountains and hills} trying to find a resting place for their souls that they might be fed the Word of God. They have been and are as lost sheep without true Shepherds. They have only experienced the hireling ministry within the institutionalized church. God has begun to call His people out of this Spiritual bondage. He will be calling true shepherds to feed these flocks which He is leading out of Babylon. These true shepherds will lead these flocks into the knowledge of Spiritual Zion, which is the true pattern of the church of the Living God.

On the negative side, the message of "Mystery Babylon" has been focused upon apostasy, which is a departing from the written Word of God. On the positive side, the message of this book has presented the design of the Theocracy God. It is essential that God's departing people gain knowledge of and accept His pattern and foundation, else they will be building with "wood, hay and stubble" The apostle Paul gives this warning for the church of all ages. *"According to the grace of God which is given unto me, as a wise masterbuilder, I have laid the foundation, and another buildeth thereon. For other foundation can no man lay than that is laid, which is in Jesus Christ. Now if any man build upon this foundation gold, silver, precious stones, wood, hay stubble; Every man's work shall be made manifest: for the day shall declare it, because it shall be revealed by fire; and the fire shall try every man's work of what sort it is. If any man's work abide which he hath built thereupon, he shall receive a reward. If any man's work shall be burned, he shall suffer loss; but he himself shall be saved; yet so as by fire." {1 Corinthians 3:10-15}*

There is a vital message here given for those who are departing or removing themselves from Babylon's religious institutions. We, who have departed are not free to do as we please in this calling. We must come under the reign and rule of the preeminence of Christ...IF...we are to fulfill His purpose in calling us out. We must *"take heed"* how we build upon this foundation of Christ. We must be diligent to follow His instruction in building upon this foundation. We must use the *"gold, silver and precious stones."* This figurative language represents the scriptures. If God begins a "Home fellowship" He will use His pattern to begin it and follow through in its development. He has specified this plan in the letters to the early church. This plan MUST be followed, if we are to BE His final restoration and Bride. Ephesians 4:3-16 should be the first message to be understood and acted upon.

If this portion of scripture is obeyed, God will place the members in the local Body as it pleases Him. This is not a structure of man, but the plan of God for His church. Verse eleven tells us that, *"He gave some, apostles; and some, prophets; and some evangelists; and some pastors and teachers; For the perfecting of the saints, for the work of the ministry, for the edifying of the body of Christ."*

These are not "appointed" offices programmed by the methods of men. These are callings from God. If a group of people desire to become a part of the church that Christ said He would be building through this called out *"Remnant,"* they MUST build with the *"gold, silver and precious stones"* of the doctrine from Christ. They must be diligent in prayer seeking the mind of God as to their individual gifts of the Spirit. This is an individual responsibility. As Christ's redeemed people we are instructed to, *"covet earnestly the best gifts."* A Group of people meeting without someone at the helm of the ship will be only drifting without purpose. I will agree that the Denominational churches have abused and misused these callings which are stated in the scriptures. However, as God's *"called out"* we cannot make void the scriptures because of man's traditional views. As those who have been enlightened, we can now see the many pitfalls that Satan has deceived man by throughout the history of Christianity.

God's calling of His people out of Babylon's confusion is only the beginning of this Spiritual journey. As His *"called out"* people, we must continue to press on to the ultimate purpose of God. As Paul continues... *"Till we all come in the unity of the faith, and the knowledge of the Son of God, unto the perfect man, unto the measure of the stature of the fullness of Christ: That we henceforth be no more children, tossed to and fro, and carried about with every wind of doctrine, by the sleight of men, and cunning craftiness, whereby they lie in wait to deceive; But speaking the truth in love, may grow up into him in all things, which is the head, even Christ."*

**May God bring this to pass is our prayer...**

# I present my final summary through this illustrated prophetic Chart...

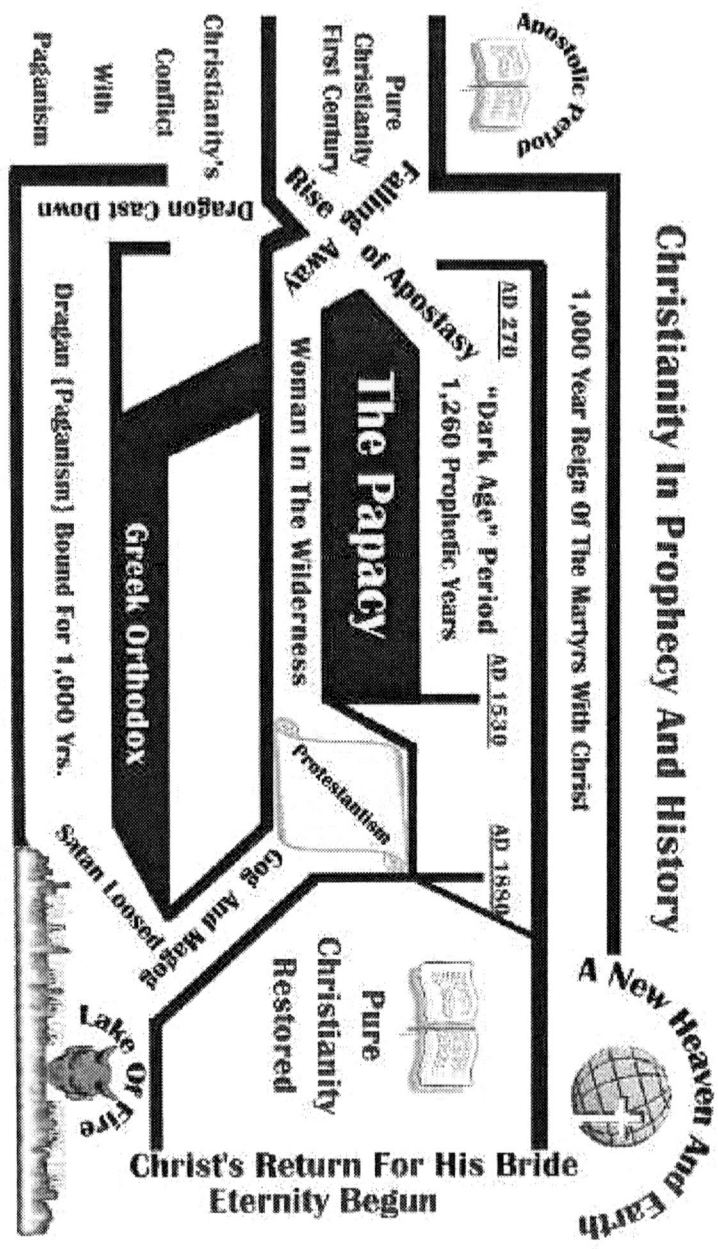

It was God's predestined plan before the foundation of the world to provide humankind with His salvation through Jesus the Anointed Christ. Based upon the Old Testament and New Testament prophecies, He has accomplished this plan. From the beginning, we have traced the fruition of His plan through this Revelation prophecy. We have examined the events and circumstances throughout history that have been connected with God's people. Through the Apostolic; Medieval; Sectarian; and the Restoration Periods...We have first viewed the birth of Christianity and beheld Her Pristine Glory; we have understood Her first conflict with the "Dragon" representing Paganism; we then saw Her triumph over Paganism only to be persecuted again by the rise of the great Apostate church of Rome; we have viewed Her in the wilderness protected of God for the 1,260 years; we have seen Her again as She immerged through the 16th Century Reformation called Protestantism; we saw through the eye of prophecy that an "Image" was made by Protestantism also styled the False Prophet; we then beheld the Three Unclean Spirits as they united in their effort to deceive, distort, persecute and undermine God's true separated Bride of Christ; We found this to be that "Spiritual" battle identified as Armageddon, or The Battle of that Great Day of God Almighty; Satan was loosed or permitted for a season to deceive once again through Pagan ideologies using Gog and Magog. {Symbolic of Catholicism and Protestantism}

Continuing on our present chart, we also view the "Lake of Fire" where we see the end result of all those who have rejected God's truth concerning "Mystery Babylon." It is thus written: *"The beast was taken, and with him the false prophet that wrought miracles before him, and which deceived them that had received the mark of the beast, and them that worshipped his image. These both were cast alive into the lake of fire burning with brimstone." {Revelation 19:20}*

Notice on the chart that there is no opening from the Papacy and Protestantism as an entrance into this final Restoration of "Pure Christianity Restored." Why is that? Because it must be an "act of faith." Yes! A step of faith must lift each believer out of Babylon's religions into this Remnant or army of Christ. This will bring the visible Body of separated redeemed people together who will constitute the Bride that has prepared Herself for the Bridegroom.

*"Let us be glad and rejoice, and give honour to him:*
*for the marriage of the Lamb is come,*
*and his wife hath made herself ready.*
*And to her was granted that she should be arrayed in fine linen,*
*clean and white:*
*for the fine linen is the righteousness of saints.*
*And he saith unto me, Write, Blessed are they which are called unto*
*the marriage supper of the Lamb.*
*And he saith unto me,*
*These are the true sayings of God"*
*{Revelation 19:7-9}*

Christ's return for His Bride is that next great, notable and final event to come! At His appearing, He will deliver up the Kingdom to the Heavenly Father. As it is written... *"Then cometh the end, when he shall have delivered up the kingdom to God, even the father; when he shall have put down all rule, and all authority and power."*
*{1 Corinthians 15:24}*

There will be no age or events to follow! This will be the culmination of all things! Christ is returning to *"judge the living and the dead."* He is returning to judge the *"good and the evil doers,"* simultaneously. Peter declares this event in graphic terms... *"But the day of the Lord will come as a thief in the night; in which the heavens shall pass away with a great noise, and the elements melt with a fervent heat, the earth also and the works that are therein shall be burned up. {NOT OVER} Seeing then that all these things shall be dissolved, what manner of persons ought ye to be in all holy conversation and godliness. Looking for and hastening unto the coming {singular} of the day of God, wherein the heavens being on fire shall be dissolved, and the elements shall melt with a fervent heat? Nevertheless we, according to his promise, look for new heavens and a new earth, wherein dwelleth righteousness. Wherefore, beloved, seeing that ye look for such things, be diligent that ye may be found in him in peace without spot and blameless." {2 Peter 3:10-14}*

Many theologians and clouded traditional beliefs have complicated the simplicity of Christ's activities at His return. They theorize about a so-called great white throne judgement; they theorize about two judgements in a supposed millennial age; they theorize about the good being judged first and then the evil doers. They

312

theorize about some being "Left Behind." I can state emphatically and unequivocally that the Bible presents none of these complicated, suppositions or theories! Pure and simple…We shall ALL stand together before God and give, *"an account of the deeds that we have done in the flesh."*

## Jesus spoke these words of confirmation as He walked among us…

• *"Marvel not at this: for the hour is coming, in which all that are in the graves shall hear his voice, And shall come forth; they that have done good, unto the resurrection of life; and they that have done evil, unto the resurrection of damnation." {John 5:28-29}*

• *"When the son of man shall come in all his glory, and all the holy angels with him, then shall he sit upon the throne of his glory: And before him shall be gathered together all nations: and he shall separate them one from another, as a shepherd divideth his sheep from the goats: And he shall set the sheep on the right hand, but the goats on the left. Then shall the King say unto them on his right hand, Come ye blessed of my Father, inherit the kingdom prepared for you from the foundation of the world." Matthew 25:31-34}*

## God is not the author of confusion!

These scriptures are plain and simple to understand…if…we eliminate the traditional errors and philosophies of men.

• John wrote… *"And I saw a great white throne, and him that sat on it, from whose face the earth and the heaven fled away; and there was found no place for them. And I saw the dead, small and great, stand before God; and the books were opened: and another book was opened, which was the book of life: and the dead were judged out of those things which were written in the books, according to their works. And the sea gave up the dead which were in it; and death and hell delivered up the dead which were in them: and they were judged every man according to their works. And death and hell were cast into the lake of fire. This is the second death. And whosoever was not found written in the book of life was cast into the lake of fire." {Revelation 20:11-15}*

The second death spoken of in this scripture confirms that this will be an eternal separation from a loving and Living God. Many people brazenly say that, "God would not send anyone to Hell." This is true! God sends no one into Hell. If people enter into Hell, it is because they have rejected the proffered mercy, grace and provision of God in their probationary period of life on this earth. God cannot violate His own decree. He cannot violate people's will to choose! God has graciously created humankind with a free will. We are all free moral agents! We have the power to resist God or we have the power and choice to receive God as our Father.

**Thus it is written:**
*"Today is the day of salvation."*
**IT MUST BE DONE IN THIS LIFE.**

## The Place Christ is Preparing...

When Christ walked upon this earth and talked with His disciples, He gave them and all who will believe this wonderful hope...*Let not your heart be troubled: ye believe in God, believe also in me. In my Father's house are many mansions: if it were not so, I would have told you. I go to prepare a place for you. And if I go and prepare a place for you, I will come again, and receive you unto myself that where I am there ye may be also." {John 14:1-3}*

We are given a pictorial symbolic view of this *"new heaven and new earth"* by the same apostle in the Revelation prophecy as he wrote: *"And I saw a new heaven and a new earth: for the first heaven and the first earth were passed away: and there was no more sea. And I john saw the holy city, new Jerusalem, coming down from God out of heaven, prepared as a bride adorned for her husband. And I heard a great voice out of heaven saying, Behold, the tabernacle of God is with men, and he will dwell with them, and they shall be his people and God himself shall be with them, and be their God. And God shall wipe away all tears from their eyes; and there shall be no more death, neither sorrow, nor crying, neither shall there be any more pain: for the former things are passed away. And he that sat upon the throne said, BEHOLD I MAKE ALL THINGS NEW. And he said unto me, Write: for these words are true and faithful. And he said unto me,*

***IT IS DONE.***

314

*I am Alpha and Omega, the beginning and the end. I will give unto him that is athirst of the fountain of water freely. He that overcometh shall inherit all things; and I will be his God, and he shall be my son." {Revelation 21:1-7}*

The mystery has NOW been revealed through the Revelation prophecy that you have just finished reading!

**It should no longer be a "mystery" to you!**
**It has been proven to be the**

***"More sure word of prophecy."***
**Let ALL who have believed**

## *The "Revelation of Jesus Christ"*

**And**

**All who have obeyed His message**

**Now ...**

**Rejoice in this final hour of victory!**

# *"Maranatha"*

**THE 7**

**SEALED**

**SCROLLS**

*By: Jeanne Trovato*

**A full-length paperback book presenting**
**The**
**Revelation Prophecy**

**The 7 sealed scrolls are opened in chronological**
**succession to reveal the symbolic message of the events**
**throughout the past Christian dispensation**

# Study Booklets
## By: Jeanne Trovato

Come Out of Her My People
The Mark of the Beast 666
Key to Symbols
The Revelation, Blessing or Curse?
The Question? TV and Thee
Are Women Called of God to Preach?
200 Reasons Why I Use the KJV
Are You a Christian? Embezzler?
Sinning Christians???
Membership in the Lodges, Is it a Sin?
Was the Devil Ever an Angel in Heaven?
Christianity Restored
Restoration of the church of God
It's the Little Foxes That Spoil the Vine
Speaking in Other Tongues


**Available From**
**The Prophetic Ministry of Jeanne Trovato**
**2922 Satsuma Dr. Sarasota, Florida 34239**
email jeanjesus@aol.com

www.RevelationScrolls.com
www.ChristianityRestored.com

## About the Author

Jeanne Trovato has written her book *Mystery Babylon* as the fulfillment of her forty-five years of study and of preaching the Revelation prophecy. Jeanne was in the Pastoral ministry in the midwest for twenty years, then accepted the calling of Christ to begin a full time prophetic ministry. This ministry has led her into various congregations to relate the vital message of The Revelation. Jeanne has also written a previous full-length paperback study book called *The 7 Sealed Scrolls* along with fifteen other short-study booklets on various Christian doctrinal subjects. She has created her own two web sites, www.RevelationScrolls.com and www.ChristianityRestored.com as a means of communicating God's "End Time" prophetic message.

Printed in the United States
55929LVS00002B/292-300

9 781420 844207